LINDEN'S
LAST LIFE

ALSO BY ALAN COHEN

Are You as Happy as Your Dog?
A Daily Dose of Sanity (available February 2010)*
Dare to Be Yourself
*A Deep Breath of Life**
Don't Get Lucky, Get Smart
The Dragon Doesn't Live Here Anymore
*Handle with Prayer**
*Happily Even After**
Have You Hugged a Monster Today?
I Had It All the Time
*Joy Is My Compass**
*Lifestyles of the Rich in Spirit**
Looking In for Number One
Mr. Everit's Secret
My Father's Voice
The Peace That You Seek
Relax into Wealth
*Rising in Love**
Setting the Seen
Why Your Life Sucks and What You Can Do about It
*Wisdom of the Heart**

*Available from Hay House

Please visit Hay House USA: **www.hayhouse.com**®
Hay House Australia: **www.hayhouse.com.au**
Hay House UK: **www.hayhouse.co.uk**
Hay House South Africa: **www.hayhouse.co.za**
Hay House India: **www.hayhouse.co.in**

LINDEN'S LAST LIFE

The Point of No Return
Is Just the Beginning

ALAN COHEN

HAY HOUSE, INC.
Carlsbad, California • New York City
London • Sydney • Johannesburg
Vancouver • Hong Kong • New Delhi

Published and distributed in the United States by: Hay House, Inc.: www.hayhouse
.com • *Published and distributed in Australia by:* Hay House Australia Pty. Ltd.:
www.hayhouse.com.au • *Published and distributed in the United Kingdom by:*
Hay House UK, Ltd.: www.hayhouse.co.uk • *Published and distributed in the
Republic of South Africa by:* Hay House SA (Pty), Ltd.: www.hayhouse.co.za •
Distributed in Canada by: Raincoast: www.raincoast.com • *Published in India
by:* Hay House Publishers India: www.hayhouse.co.in

Design: Tricia Breidenthal

Library of Congress Cataloging-in-Publication Data

Cohen, Alan.
  Linden's last life : the point of no return is just the beginning / Alan Cohen. --
1st ed.
    p. cm.
  ISBN 978-1-4019-2415-7 (tradepaper : alk. paper) 1. Spiritual life--Fiction. I.
Title.
  PS3603.O328L56 2009
  813'.6--dc22

                                                              2009008400

ISBN: 978-1-4019-2415-7

12 11 10 09   4 3 2 1
1st edition, October 2009

Printed in the United States of America

For Dee,
who teaches me daily
how worthwhile is life
and how present is love.

I

1

For as many times as I wondered how I would die, I never imagined it would be at my own hand.

I stood on the burnt-orange railing of the Golden Gate Bridge, my knees shaking violently, staring into the icy water 200 feet below. The full moon cast an eerie glow over the angry black churning swells, about to swallow me whole. Fear clutched my naked throat like an icy hand, and my body stiffened. A voice in my head screamed: *Get down and save yourself while you can!* But I had made up my mind. Even a painful death could be no worse than the agony that had ravaged me for so long.

The night I found them still tortured me. Through the fogged window of a dark green Mercedes I saw my girlfriend straddling her boss. Vicky's dress was up around her waist, and she was riding him like an animal. Jesus . . . *they couldn't even wait until they got into her apartment, just steps from the car.*

Crimson fury exploded through my brain. "What the hell do you think you're doing, Vicky?!" I yelled as I pounded on the window.

Jarred, Vicky straightened her dress and rubbed the fog off the inside of the window. When she saw that it was me, she made a pained face and lowered the window. "I'm sorry, Linden," she called through the darkness. "I didn't plan on this—it just sort of happened."

"Take a hint, man," Ian muttered from the shadow. "This woman deserves to be with a man who can take her places."

Vicky caught my eyes for a brief moment, and then the electric window silently rolled closed, shutting me out like a stray dog. I slammed on the roof and stumbled away, crazy with humiliation and outrage.

The next six months were pure hell. The following day *Time Out* laid me off, and on my way home, my car's transmission died on the 101. By the time I gathered the money to have it fixed, the city had towed and junked it. Within two months I couldn't make my rent; my landlord locked me out and left my stuff on the sidewalk; when I returned, it was pillaged and gone. I tried desperately to find another job, but nobody was hiring. Finally I called my mom, hoping she would send me a little cash. But before I could even ask her, she told me that my best friend from high school had hung himself in his living room three days earlier. When I heard that, the bottom dropped out of my gut. I started walking the streets for I don't know how long. Eventually a blister grew on my foot, and it got infected; when I went to the emergency room, they wouldn't treat me without insurance.

I made my way to the bridge.

Vicky wasn't the only girlfriend I'd ever had—just the only one I loved. Her stunning looks and coquettish smile melted every guy who came into the *Time Out* office, and I was no exception. When I dropped off my movie reviews, her velvet voice disarmed me and our conversations turned into hypnotic interludes. I would walk out of the office all aflutter and find excuses to come back just to see her. When she agreed to go out with me, I thought my heart would leap out of my chest. Our dates evolved into marathon lovemaking sessions seasoned with metaphysical discussions and childlike laughter. Yet when Vicky practically drooled over dresses she saw in the Macy's window and she seemed overly impressed by her ego-bloated boss's new C350, I should have seen the bomb coming. But my hope for what could be blinded me to what was, and I had to learn the hard way that betrayal lurks behind even the sunniest moments.

But none of that mattered now—in a few moments it would all be over. I steadied myself for a moment against a thick upright cable, took a breath, and held it. *This is your last chance to turn back*, that voice pleaded with me. But there was no turning back. I had to stop the pain in my heart. *Just one little step and it will all be over.*

Suddenly I felt something touching my foot. I looked down to see a hand wrapped around my ankle. It wasn't grabbing or forcing—just firm, yet gentle.

"Don't try to stop me!" I shouted as I broke free and scampered up to the roof of a small maintenance shed to my left, my fingers in hole-ridden gloves stinging against the windswept steel. I strained to see down into the foggy night, but all I could make out was a silhouette against the stream of passing headlights.

"Next time it will be worse," a voice called from the darkness.

It was a man's voice—youngish, slightly nasal.

I looked harder. Still just a dim form. "There won't *be* any next time!" I shouted back. "I'm outta here!"

"That's what you say now, but you'll be back—and your pain will be deeper, much deeper."

I kneeled to peer over the edge of the shed, where I could see Cheshire cat–like teeth and large almond-shaped eyes.

"Who do you think you are—God?" I asked.

"Of course!" He chuckled. "Just like you!"

As if by some unseen hand, the mist swirled and evaporated enough for me to make out a black overcoat with a maroon skirt flowing beneath it. *Just what I need—a cross-dressing messiah.*

"Get the hell out of here and leave me to do what I came to do!" I yelled, feeling the cold sore on my lip crack.

Silence. *Maybe he got the message.* I turned back to face the bay.

"There's no place to die *to*," he called out, his voice carrying through the wet night like a ghost. "You can get rid of your body, but your fear will haunt you through the corridors of time. This is just a taste of worse things to come."

Angry now, I stepped back down to the railing. His eyes were sparkling, even in the dark.

"You made your own hell, and you will just take it with you over and over again," he went on, "unless you learn how to find your way out."

I jumped down to the sidewalk and faced him squarely. To my surprise, he was quite short. His skin was dark, and his thick eyebrows butted up against the bottom lip of a maroon knit cap that covered most of his forehead.

"If you're going to leave, do it like a master, not a coward," he told me.

Livid, I grabbed him by the collar and lifted him to his tiptoes. I could have easily tossed him into the bay, yet he didn't seem afraid.

"You are very strong-willed," he said. "That's good. Now just point your will in the direction of what you really want."

I let him go. "And what do *you* think I want?" *I can't believe I'm taking this jerk seriously.*

"What everyone wants," he answered. "To be free."

I couldn't argue with that. "And you know how I can be free? . . . Without jumping?"

The gnomish man moved back a bit and sized me up. I thought he might step into the roadway and get creamed. Part of me hoped he would, so I could get on with it. But part of me was curious now.

"Give me a week and I'll show you how to finish with style," he told me. "How to live and how to die. Then you will really be free."

"You're trying to con me," I argued, and started up toward the rail again.

"Then go ahead and jump," he came back. "Shall we meet here again in, say, a hundred years?"

I froze. The thought of going through a life like this again was horrifying. Deeper despair was unthinkable.

"Hurry up," he called after a minute. "It's getting cold out here."

I took a long breath. "And if you don't convince me?"

"Then I will bring you back here myself, help you up to the rail, and pray for you all your way down into the bay."

I looked into those strange eyes and felt an odd sense of relief. Something inside me told me to pay attention.

"Who are you?"

"My name is Tashi," he answered, pulling up his collar to shield his neck from the harsh wind.

"Tashi?"

"It means 'good luck,'" he explained. "You just had some."

"What are you doing here? Were you just walking by, or are you some kind of angel?"

"Both," he answered as he turned and headed for the city.

2

The morning before I went to the bridge, I went to see my mom and stepfather. My real father left when I was eight. One day he told me, "Linden, nothing in life is what it appears to be. Everything is what you make it." Then he closed the door behind him, and I never saw him again. To this day I'm not sure if he was a sage or a bastard.

A year later my mom met Bill at a political fund-raiser. She was a hotel banquet manager, and he was running for reelection to the state legislature. She was lost and alone without a man to take care of her, and he was lost and alone in a dysfunctional world of wealth and power. Six months later they married, and when Bill lost the election, they moved to ritzy Nob Hill, largely on the booty my stepfather collected from side deals he'd made while in office. They were in their glory in that neighborhood, but to me it felt like a big competition for luxury cars, sculpted gardens, and million-dollar views. Was it really heaven, or a slice of hell disguised as heaven?

My mother was always the one who answered the door.

"Linden!" She greeted me with a mixture of surprise and disappointment. With the exception of her marriage to my father, I was her biggest letdown in life. But she tried not to turn me away.

I don't know if she just loved me and hoped I would turn into something, or if she just couldn't bear the sorrow of her failure as a mother.

"Who's there?" Bill called over his shoulder from his brown leather La-Z-Boy. "Better not be someone selling something."

"It's Linden," Mom called back, with a tone that was welcoming to me and apologetic to him.

No response from the La-Z-Boy.

"Come on in, dear," she said, holding the door open.

Bill turned up the volume on CNN, and a voice droned on about the ailing economy. Mom motioned for me to sit on the couch next to her, trying to disguise her fear that I would dirty the expensive settee. Bill mumbled a gruff hello—the best greeting he was capable of offering. CNN's volume went up one more notch.

"So, how are you doing, dear?" Mom asked in her sweet-as-sugar voice.

"What is it now?" Bill grunted over his shoulder, astounding me that he could hear over the market-downturn report. "You broke? Need a lawyer? Got some girl pregnant?"

Mom made a face. "Lay off, Bill," she told him. "We're just glad to see Linden, aren't we? He hardly ever comes around."

CNN's volume went up yet another notch. End of "conversation" with Bill.

I looked my mom in the eye and dove headlong into a generous portion of humble pie. "I sort of hit a streak of bad luck, Mom," I told her. "This girl I was seeing dumped me hard."

Mom pursed her lips compassionately and shook her head. I could read her mind: *Poor kid. How did he get to be such a loser? Must have inherited his father's defective genes.*

"Then *Time Out* gave me a pink slip."

She sighed.

"Then I found this eviction notice on my door." I produced the paper, mostly for dramatic effect. I admit I was on a sympathy mission.

She sighed again. Bill's bald head shook just over the horizon of the La-Z-Boy. Man, he had to have superhearing.

"I was wondering if I could stay here . . . just for a while . . . till I get back on my feet." Read between the lines: *Not that I want to. I need to.*

Mom, God bless her, looked truly torn. I didn't want to rock her world. I just wanted a bed to sleep in.

Suddenly CNN went mute. Bill stood and faced me, his belly hanging unceremoniously through his Izod golf shirt over khaki Banana Republic shorts. If he had been a bird, he would have puffed his feathers; or if a bear, stood on his hind feet.

"The answer is no," he barked. "*N-O.* The last time we let you stay here, we came home from a trip and the place reeked from pot for a week! We had to have all the drapes dry-cleaned. I didn't spend three decades in politics to live in an opium den. You're thirty-three years old. Get a decent job, you lazy ass."

Without waiting for a response, Bill returned to his chair, and within moments we were hearing (at maximum volume) about the new (and possibly incurable) flu on its way from Africa.

Mom looked even more pained. "I'm sorry, dear," she offered wistfully. "If it were up to me . . ."

3

"Where are we going?" I asked Tashi as we stepped off the bridge ramp and made our way toward Lincoln Boulevard. I felt silly talking to his back.

He looked over his shoulder and saw me limping, trailing him at a distance. "What happened to your foot?"

"Blister got infected."

He offered a kind nod. "We'll get you taken care of at the dharma center," he told me and slowed his pace enough for me to catch up.

As we turned onto McDowell Avenue, I was tempted to turn around, but just then I caught sight of the abandoned stables where I'd slept for a couple of nights until I was chased out by the cops. The buildings reminded me of the long nightmare my life had become: Dirty, itchy clothes. Finding rank public toilets if you could. Standing in bone-chilling weather next to freeway ramps, breathing ghastly exhaust fumes, hoping some merciful soul would roll down a window and toss you a buck. Compromising human dignity a hundred times a day. Blaming myself for trashing a life that could have been something, but was not and never would be.

There was no way I would go back now to my life as a goddamn bum. If this joker didn't come through, I would find my way back to the bridge, and this time I wouldn't stop.

"Why are you wearing that dress?" I asked him as we worked our way over a four-foot rock wall to cut through the big military cemetery.

Tashi extended his hand to me. His eyes were extraordinarily clear, like a little child's. "This is the robe worn by the monks in my order."

"Your order?"

"I am a Tibetan Buddhist monk."

"You mean like the Dalai Lama and all that?"

"Yes, 'like the Dalai Lama and all that.'" Tashi seemed pleased that I knew that much.

"I saw him speak at Berkeley once," I reported proudly. "A very cool dude."

"Yes, an extremely cool dude," Tashi agreed, divulging a half smile. Then he turned and continued into the graveyard. The image of him stepping into a sea of headstones seemed like a statement of life walking past death.

I decided to shut up out of respect for the dead. To be honest, the place didn't seem that peaceful. Maybe some spirits were still writhing in their personal hells.

"So are you, like, planning to teach me Buddhism?" I asked as we approached the other side of the cemetery.

"I'm planning to teach you how to put sorrow behind you—call it what you'd like."

As we stepped onto the sidewalk, a guy and his girlfriend walking hand in hand stared at us. Quite the odd couple: a robed monk and a distraught vagrant emerging from a burial ground. At nearly six feet, I practically towered over my companion's mid-five frame—not to mention the contrast of his impeccably clean-shaven cheeks against my scraggly brown beard; and his neat coat and robe against my torn, dirty jeans and faded green Army jacket I'd picked up for a quarter at the Salvation Army thrift shop.

"Come on, man, what are you going to do—screw with my mind for a week?" I asked him in a belligerent voice.

Tashi stopped and faced me. "Maybe your mind could use a few screws," he answered authoritatively. "It doesn't seem to be helping you very much the way it's been working."

✹

Half an hour later we arrived at a large, well-kept Victorian mansion with a big red door. Tashi lifted the oversized steel knocker and rapped three times, the sound spilling down West Pacific Avenue. Moments later another monk answered the door. He, too, wore a maroon and yellow outfit; he was taller than Tashi, but just as thin. *Don't these people eat?*

After a few brief pleasantries, I followed my mysterious guide up a stuffy staircase with a mahogany banister. At the second-floor landing, Tashi opened a door to a large dark room. As the light from the hallway cast a beam into the chamber, I spied four futons arranged symmetrically on the floor, with maroon blankets neatly tucked around them. "This is where you sleep," he instructed, pointing to a futon in the far corner near the window.

It wasn't much, but it sure was an improvement over the cold sidewalk alongside a tree stump reeking of dog pee and crap.

"Your training begins in the morning," Tashi told me.

"Training?" I cringed.

"You said you would give me a week. If you expect to be free, you must do as I say."

"Hey, is this some kind of cult?"

Tashi smiled. "You are free to leave anytime you wish." Then his smile morphed into an intense glare. "You are also free to kill yourself and be reborn a million times into a suffering world."

The monk placed his hands together in a prayer position and bowed to me. Then he turned and made his exit so gracefully that I could swear he was floating.

I turned and checked out the room; it was stark and clean. A half dozen small, colorful flaglike cloths with Tibetan designs hung neatly against an eggshell-colored wall. In one corner I noticed a small altar bearing a photo of an old toothless monk, a stick of incense in an ornate wooden holder, and an ivory candle. Other students' meager possessions were stacked neatly at the feet of their beds. No closets.

I slipped off my jeans and dropped them on the floor. Then I let my body collapse onto the futon and expelled a deep sigh. *I should have been dead by now.*

4

The damn bell wouldn't stop ringing. I pulled the pillow over my head, but it was too late—I was up. I looked out the window. It was still dark, with faint fingers of light starting to creep over the building next door.

I squinted and sat up on my elbows. Sniffling, I watched my roommates rise from their futons. One was a tall, thin, fair-skinned guy with sandy hair, about college age. Another was middle-aged, with salt-and-pepper hair, and balding. I noticed that the skin on his arms hung flabbily, as if he'd lost a lot of weight. The other guy looked Japanese, small, wiry, maybe thirty-five; he reached down next to his bed and picked up little round spectacles, reminding me of a World War II Japanese army interrogator in some old movie. The three students bowed their heads to each other and dressed in silence. The young guy saw me first and nodded to me slightly. I didn't respond.

At the foot of my bed I found a simple purple robe, obviously placed there overnight by Tashi or someone he dispatched. I didn't want to put it on, but it was a vast improvement over my stinky jeans and sweatshirt, so I complied. I must have looked odd in it, being taller than most of the Tibetans it was designed for. I made my way to a bathroom across the hall, looked in the mirror for the first time in weeks, and nearly gagged. My hair was a long mess, and my beard had grown matted and scraggly. I remembered how clean-cut I'd looked just a half year earlier, and shuddered to think how far a man could sink in such a short time.

I followed the others downstairs to a large meeting room where a group of monks and students were sitting cross-legged on thick, round black cushions. The room wasn't heated, and the early-morning cold penetrated me unmercifully. I sat down on a vacant cushion and tried to get settled. Soon I felt a hand on my shoulder and looked up to see Tashi. "So, I see you decided to stay," he said softly.

Of course I decided to stay, you dork—I'm obviously sitting here, I answered in my head, my thoughts almost loud enough for him to hear.

"Your meditation practice begins now," Tashi told me in a voice barely above a whisper. "Just keep watching your breath. The more you stay with it, the less your thoughts will distract you."

Tashi drifted away and lowered himself onto a nearby cushion without using his hands. I tried to get comfortable, wiggling and squirming until I accidentally let out a loud fart. I looked around to see if I had disturbed the other meditators, but they paid no attention. *Maybe I was sent here to test their concentration.*

The meditation went on for hours—at least that's how it felt. After a short time I started to feel fidgety. My legs ached, and my thoughts rampaged like a swarm of angry bees. A couple of times my mind started to settle down, but then Vicky's face showed up as if on a huge plasma screen inside my forehead. Immediately the heartache and anger that had shredded my soul for those long, dreadful months started to return. I wanted to rage, bawl, and lash out like I had in the parks and bus-stop shelters that had become my home. Half a dozen times during the silence I was tempted to bolt, but I forced myself to stay. I hated the meditation and decided I would blow off this ridiculous place as soon as I could.

Finally I heard a bell ring, and I opened my eyes. I looked around to see the other students starting to stretch; I couldn't have been more relieved to unfold my aching legs. *If only Vicky could see me now.* But I was sure I was the last person on her mind at the moment; she was in some Ritz-Carlton screwing her brains out with her upwardly mobile boyfriend.

❀

The muted bell gave way to a louder gong that echoed through the meditation hall. An elderly monk entered the temple and slowly edged his way forward. He had a shaved head and a wide, flat nose, and he walked with a hunch that reminded me of Yoda. Finally he took his place at the front of the room on a cushion obviously saved for him. All the monks and students bowed reverently.

The old man, who I later learned was the revered Lama Sherap, closed his eyes, and an expectant hush fell over the assembly. After a long silence, he opened his eyes as slowly as a hundred-year-old turtle, and spoke with soft power: "Life is suffering," the lama began with a deep, resonant voice. "Suffering springs from desire. If you do not get what you want, you become unhappy. If you get what you want, you are happy for a moment, but then when you lose it, you become unhappy."

Ah, the ballad of Linden and Vicky.

"Nothing in this world will bring you peace. No one can make you happy or take happiness from you. Uproot desire for anything outside yourself, and you are free. Buddha achieved liberation in his lifetime, and so can you."

The lama paused again and took a long moment to formulate his next teaching. I started to feel antsy, but everyone else seemed to be eagerly awaiting his transmission. "For many years I sat in meditation practice like you," he finally said. "I struggled with my passions, my fears, my self-absorption, my wandering mind, and my sore legs. I was sure I would never find peace. Then one day when I least expected it, my resistance fell away like a marionette whose strings had been cut. Suddenly my legs did not hurt, I wanted nothing, and I was free. That was the day I died to the life that billions of other human beings struggle to maintain. Now

17

I live only to complete the karma I set in motion long ago. I have no desire to live or to die, and when this body falls away, I shall dwell in spirit and meet Lord Buddha face-to-face."

The lama closed his eyes and fell silent. When it was obvious he was done with his lecture, a student began to chant: *"Om mani padme hum. . . . Om mani padme hum. . . . Om mani padme hum."* Immediately the others fell into cadence. I simply listened; I wasn't about to get sucked into this regimen. I would stay for one more night and leave in the morning.

5

My eyes couldn't have been closed for more than a few minutes that night when I heard the creaking of footsteps on the stairs leading to the bedroom. Groggy, I lifted my head and saw the doorknob turning. The door opened a crack, just enough to let in a sliver of light.

"Linden? Are you in there?" I heard a woman's voice whisper.

I recognized the voice. But it was impossible. . . .

"Linden, it's me."

I sat up and watched the door open to reveal a silhouette against the yellow hall light. It was the silhouette I had dreamed about for six months.

How could she know I'm here? Did she follow me to the bridge and then back to the dharma center? Is this all some kind of test to see if I really love her?

Stealthy as a cheetah, Vicky slipped into the room and quietly closed the door behind her. I looked around to see if there was any motion from my roommates. None.

As she approached my bed, I recognized the perfume that used to turn me to mush. "Vicky?" I called out. "What are you—?"

"Shh . . ." She pressed her index finger over my mouth. A moment later her lips were against mine, more luscious than ever.

She cupped my cheeks with her hands and began to slip under the covers. *Tashi and the lama were all wrong about this suffering thing. This is heaven.*

Seconds later her body was undulating against mine. A gentle rocking motion at first, then more intense. Our hips began to get into the rhythm until a minute later I feared I might climax too soon. *Slow, boy, take your time.*

Yet Vicky's body didn't feel as soft as I remembered it. Her kisses started to trail away. *Did she come to tease and torture me?* I reached out to pull her closer to me, but I couldn't. It was as if her body was slipping away from me. I started to feel terrified and broke into a sweat.

"Vicky!" I called out, but she didn't respond. I called again, louder. Then she began to shake my shoulder. Softly at first, then harder.

"You okay, man?" she asked. But it wasn't her voice. It was deeper and gruffer.

"Are you okay?" the voice came again, more forcefully.

I tried to find Vicky's eyes, but couldn't. Instead, I found those of my roommate, the guy with the flabby arms. He was leaning over my futon, shaking my shoulders.

"You okay?" he repeated one more time.

"Uh . . . yeah," I answered in a fog.

"Try to get some sleep," he told me. "The morning bell will be going off before you know it."

6

Tashi stopped me just as I grasped the knob of the great red door. "A week," he issued sternly from behind me. "You promised me a week." The voices of chanting students drifted from the meditation hall behind him.

I removed my hand from the doorknob and faced him. "Look, Tashi, this place isn't for me," I told him point-blank.

He just stared at me, as if he knew what I was going to say.

"This temple is like a torture chamber, and the woman who blew me off is haunting me. I doubt that even Buddha himself could cure me."

The monk remained steadfast. "I've seen worse cases. Usually it gets harder before it gets easier."

I gazed down at the floor for a long moment, shaking my head.

"You are fighting the only battle you must ever win, Linden," he went on. "The battle for your mind."

His spiritual talk was starting to irritate me. "And what makes you such a master, Tashi? If you're so smart, why are you still in the world and not off in some blissful Nirvana?"

Tashi said nothing, but turned around and lowered the top of his robe. He lifted his yellow shirt, revealing his bare back. I was stunned to see a half dozen thick scars running across his entire back. "Do you see these welts, Linden?" he asked.

Speechless, I simply nodded.

"One night last year I saw a drunken man on the street take off his belt and whip his dog. I was enraged and tried to stop him. His buddy emerged from a car and held me over the hood while the guy whipped me with the belt. Finally someone came by and the men fled, but my back still tells the story. My self-righteousness cost me that beating.

"No, Linden, I'm not perfect. I have sexual fantasies about women I see on the street, and I get depressed when I look in the mirror and see more wrinkles and gray hairs. I'm a man in a human body, just like you. I'm just trying to keep my misery to a minimum and save you more trouble."

Tashi turned and walked back to the meditation hall, leaving me to decide for myself. I peered in at all of the monks meditating. They looked like stone statues. If that was all there was to life, it didn't seem much better than death. I opened the door and walked out.

7

The neon sign in the shop window glared at me: MISS ROSA— READER AND ADVISOR. I looked down at the crumpled card in my hand that a server at the Glide Church soup kitchen had given me. It matched the sign. I pursed my lips and went in.

To my surprise, the place wasn't spooky woo-woo. No crystals, voodoo masks, or granola girls in fairy-princess costumes. Instead, the place looked like someone's living room, with a small couch against the wall, a couple of tables, and two plush armchairs facing each other. The walls were painted light violet; the drapes were a shade of indigo.

When she heard me enter, Miss Rosa emerged from the back room. She looked like someone's grandma: portly, dyed black hair, with a long green flowered muumuu and lots of jewelry. (Okay, we wouldn't get away without *any* crystals.)

"What can I do for you?" she asked in a professional voice.

"I'd like to ask you some questions," I told her, almost arrogantly.

Miss Rosa wasn't shaken by my attitude. "Please, have a seat." She pointed to one of the chairs; I acceded, and she sat down opposite me.

"What would you like to know?"

I looked around the studio. "Don't you use cards or a crystal ball or tea leaves?"

Miss Rosa laughed. "No, honey, I'm just psychic. I don't need any props."

Fair enough.

"Do you believe in reincarnation?" I asked her.

She rolled her eyes. "I don't just *believe* in reincarnation . . . Larry? . . . Lindsay?"

Whoa, she almost guessed my name. "Linden," I told her.

"Reincarnation is as real to me as yesterday is to you, Linden," she explained. "I've seen more people's past lives than Google has seen Web pages."

I scrunched my brow. "Then why doesn't everyone remember?"

Miss Rosa nodded as if she'd been asked this at least a thousand times, but didn't mind explaining it once more. "For the same reason you don't remember a lot of stuff that happened in *this* life. You have to focus on what's in front of you. If you kept all of those memories in your awareness, your mind would be too cluttered, and it would drive you crazy. But if you need to access information, it's there."

"And *you* can access it?"

She placed a hand on my forearm. "It's a gift I've had since I was a child. I thought everyone could read other people's thoughts and know what was going to happen. But when I started to tell people, they thought I was crazy. So I shut up for years. When I grew up, I realized people want to know what I know, so I tell them. It pays my rent."

Miss Rosa stood up, walked to a small refrigerator, and pulled out a soda. "Would you like a Diet Pepsi?" she asked.

I shook my head as she returned and took her seat. "You're at a crossroads in your life," she told me.

Duh . . . but that would be true for just about anyone.

"I'm seeing a woman around you . . . pretty and smart . . . but unhappy."

Okay, we're onto something.

"Did you just have a breakup, or did someone die?" she asked.

"I'm seeing a photograph of you and this woman, and it's torn between your faces . . . like she's on one path and you're on another."

"Yes! Yes!" I blurted out.

Miss Rosa took a sip of her soda. "You've been with this woman many times in previous lives," she told me. "Married to her often, and several times as brother and sister." She furrowed her brow. "But there's always been some kind of conflict or hitch. This woman has a very restless soul, always searching, looking, reaching out. She's terrified of love and can't accept it where she is, so she's always trying to find it elsewhere. This has been the story of your relationship with her more times than I can count. It always ends in heartbreak for you."

Her story made sense. "Do you see any hope for me to be with her?"

The psychic shook her head. "I would steer clear of this woman and anyone like her. She's not a bad person, but she has to learn to love herself before she can love someone else."

Suddenly Miss Rosa looked very sad, almost disappointed. "I see terrific pain in your past incarnations, Linden. Tragedy and loss. You haven't had it easy. It seems that every time you start to get somewhere, something backfires and you plunge into a pit. I feel your sorrow. It's almost as if you are—well, I hate to say it—cursed."

I knew it.

"What do you see about my future?" I asked, hoping for some better news.

Miss Rosa closed her eyes and looked frustrated. "This is really weird," she told me. "I don't see anything. When I see people's futures, it's like I walk into a theater and watch a play. When I step into your future room, it's empty. Not good, not bad. Just blank."

Finally I just asked her outright: "Do you see any hope for me, Miss Rosa? Is there any way I can find love or happiness in this world?"

The woman looked down as if avoiding my glance. "It's hard to say, Linden. Sometimes people with troubled pasts have a shift, and their lives improve. Sometimes they just keep getting worse. If you're going to change your luck, you may have to do something pretty radical."

"Yeah, that's pretty much what I've come to." I stood up, reached into my pocket, and fished out a crumpled $20 bill I'd borrowed from one of my roommates at the dharma center. "How much do I owe you?"

Miss Rosa just shook her head. "Nothing, young man. I'm sorry I haven't given you very good news."

That makes two of us.

8

I found Tashi in the temple garden. "I'll stay," I told him. A simple nod was his silent welcome. "But I can't sit through all the meditations," I added. "They'll drive me crazy."

Tashi went to a small shed, pulled out a rake, and handed it to me. "Then you can work in the garden," he told me. "Touching living things is healing, and using your hands will be a moving meditation. You'll feel better doing this."

I took the rake and considered that he might be right. I'd been living in my head for so long that sweating a bit would probably do me some good. I began to work the soil.

❀

My time in the garden amid growing things became a tiny window of salvation. The patch, in an empty lot beside the temple, faced West Pacific Avenue, directly across the street from Julius Kahn Park. In the morning young mothers brought their little children to the playground; older kids came after school. As I weeded and dug and planted, the children's voices carried across the street and soothed my tattered soul. Voltaire said that God is a comedian playing to an audience too afraid to laugh. I was that audience, and on those early-spring mornings, the children were God.

By Thursday, my fifth day at the dharma center, the battle between my ears had escalated to a frenzy, the voices of fear and hope vying for the upper hand a thousand times a day. It could take lifetimes, I figured, to offset my insanity. My only relief was to get outside and move my body in the garden. The more I focused, breathed, and perspired, the more the voices shut up. I began to have some moments of respite from my inner tyrant.

"Linden!" I heard a voice call as I was shoveling some compost into a bed of lettuce. "Can I see you for a moment?" It was Tashi.

I set my shovel across the wheelbarrow and strode toward the door where Tashi stood wearing his long dark overcoat.

"I have good news, Linden," the monk reported when I reached him. "Lama Sherap has invited you for an interview."

"Interview?" I shot him a quizzical look. "Like for a job?"

Tashi smiled and shook his head. "No, it's a private talk with the master—a real honor. You can ask him whatever you want."

I shrugged my shoulders. "I don't know, Tashi," I replied. "My world is such a mess that I don't know what I would say to someone like the lama."

"All the more reason to see him. He can help you make some sense of your life."

I shook my head. "Right now I'm not sure I'll *have* a life after Saturday."

Tashi took a step closer to me, and his eyes grew serious, almost zealous. "Many people travel great distances to have even a few minutes with Lama Sherap. He is a very wise man. I suggest you not miss this opportunity."

As I thought about Tashi's invitation, I considered that he might be sincere. I craned my head back and gazed at the sun reaching over the house bordering the garden. I took a breath and answered, "Sure, why not?"

※

The lama's quarters bore the heady aroma of incense prayer-fully offered over many years. Like the rest of the dharma center, the space was austere and impeccably clean. On a small altar I surveyed pictures of several lamas in his lineage, overshadowed by a large color photo of the Dalai Lama. As always, the spiritual master was smiling as if he knew the punch line to a big joke he was just waiting for everyone else to get.

Tashi ushered me to a *zafu,* what they called the cushions the monks meditated on. As I sat down, I grew fearful that I would have to meditate. Instead, Tashi leaned over and whispered, "Drop your act, Linden. When the lama comes, tell him the whole truth. That's the only way he can help you." Dead serious, he bowed and floated out of the room on his signature cloud.

Drop my act? I bristled. I've always prided myself on being a straight shooter. If I have something to say, I say it. I liked some of what I saw and heard at the temple, but there was a lot I'd kept my mouth shut about—like the wild reincarnation stories. Many of the monks and students seemed more fascinated with who they had been than who they were now. They either attributed their good luck to positive karma from previous lives or they resolutely accepted their troubles as the result of foolish acts from the seventeenth century. It was all a bit too out-there for me. *If you fall in love with someone,* I thought, *you should just go for it; you don't need to make up a story that you were soul mates in Egypt. And why is it that everyone was John the Baptist or Cleopatra in a past life, and no one was a maidservant?*

My musings were interrupted when the door opened and in strode Lama Sherap, followed by his assistant, Choden. I greeted the two with a nod, and Choden backed away respectfully to leave me alone with the master.

The lama bowed and deftly lowered himself onto a zafu, facing me. Up close he looked even older than he did from a distance; he had many liver spots on his hands, and his arms seemed frail. Yet his youthful, vital spirit belied his age.

Lama Sherap took a long, slow breath, looked me squarely in the eyes, and told me, "I've been watching you."

"Watching me?" I started to get nervous.

The elder nodded. "These eyes are old, but they see clearly. . . . I have observed you struggling to persevere."

He has that right. (I didn't dare tell him all the names I had mentally called him during long chants while my knees felt like they were pinned under a truck.)

"Would you like some tea, Linden?" he asked.

I must admit, I felt honored to be on a first-name basis with the big kahuna. "All right, thank you."

I watched, fascinated, as Lama Sherap set a teacup before me, leaving the handle in the perfect position for me to lift it. Then he poured the tea with impeccable focus, as if the well-being of the world depended on it. Maybe it did.

"Tashi tells me you want to leave," he said.

"The dharma center? . . . Sure, I think about leaving every night, and every morning I decide to stay."

"No," he replied. "I mean for good. He tells me you want to leave your body . . . you know—kick the frame?"

Okay, Tashi said to shoot from the hip. "That's right, Lama. I've about had it with this world. Everyone I've ever known has let me down. My father deserted me, my mother married an emotional Nazi and lives in the mall, my friends have turned their backs on me, and the only woman I ever loved blew me off for a guy with a fat wallet. Everything I dreamed of has gone down the toilet. Yes, I'm ready to leave."

The guru listened carefully and nodded. "Me, too," he told me in a forthright voice.

"You, too?" I was shocked.

"I'm pretty much done here."

I thought he might be kidding, but he wasn't. "What's wrong with your life?" I asked. "You seem to have your bases covered."

Lama Sherap sat with his arms crossed, nodding his head slightly. "I haven't always been a monk, Linden," he divulged. "I once had a family and a business."

"No way!" I practically shouted.

"Yes way," he came back, surprising me with his vernacular. Then he folded his hands behind his head and leaned back—

a position very uncharacteristic of a lama. "I repaired motorcycle engines, smoked cigarettes, drank tequila, and had a wife and daughter."

Now you're playing with my head. "So what made you become a monk?"

Lama Sherap sighed. "One day I came home from work early and found my wife with another man."

"Holy . . ." I exclaimed, flabbergasted.

"Not just another man," the lama added, shaking his head. "My best friend."

Whoa. "Dude, that is harsh!" I blurted out.

"Yes, Linden, it was very harsh. And it got even more harsh. The next day when I came home from work, my wife was gone—along with my daughter and furniture. She didn't even leave me a note."

I didn't know what to say. All I could mouth was: "I'm sorry to hear that."

The lama nodded as if he appreciated my sympathy, but he'd obviously traveled far beyond that sorry moment.

"So did you, like, take off and join a monastery?"

The old man shook his head. "Actually, I became severely depressed and contemplated suicide. I locked myself in my empty house, pulled down the shades, and slipped into a black hole I was sure I would never escape."

I just sat staring at him, like a kindergartner waiting for the teacher to turn the next page of the storybook.

"Then one day I went to the corner grocery store. There I ran into a friend who knew my wife. He told me she'd gone to live with the man she left me for. This news made me even more depressed. I decided I would go back to the house and end it all with booze and pills. I left my groceries on the counter and walked out the door. . . . Then I saw him."

"Him?"

Just then we were interrupted by a soft knock on the door. Choden tiptoed in with a bowl of fruit and a plate of homemade cookies. He set them beside us on a low table, neatly laid out some napkins, and exited quietly. As soon as the door was closed, the lama continued.

"Outside the grocery store I saw a homeless man sitting on the sidewalk begging for a handout. His clothes were torn, his hair disheveled, and he smelled terrible. Usually I passed by people like that, but since I was going to depart this world within the hour, I reached into my pocket, took out all the cash and change I had, and dropped it into his hand. I started to walk away, but he grabbed my arm and pulled me toward him. For a moment I got scared, but I sensed he meant no harm. He held me firmly until his eyes found mine. He told me, 'Thank you, my brother, thank you. You are a good person—very, very good. God bless you.'"

"And that got to you?"

The High Lama's eyes took on a glow. "It wasn't what he said. It was the look in his eyes, as if some invisible power was speaking to me through him."

I reached for a cookie and began to munch it quickly. This was getting better by the minute.

"When I arrived at my house, I couldn't get the beggar's eyes or his words out of my head. Someone or something wanted me to know that my life was valuable, and running away would not resolve my pain. I decided to hang in there until I could learn how to live and die like a master."

I felt ashamed and started to squirm. This old man had the courage I lacked.

Lama Sherap leaned forward as if he were about to tell me a secret. "The only way out is to graduate, Linden," he said.

"Graduate?"

"Suicide means you still believe the world has authority over you. But it doesn't. If you're going to leave, do it on *your* terms, not because life has defeated you."

"Easier said than done," I came back quickly. "My girlfriend dumped me for some executive asshole." Aw, shit, now I'd gone and insulted the lama with bad language. I watched to see if he'd get upset, but I saw no sign of it. The elder held my gaze steadily.

"You gave your girlfriend power over your life, Linden. That's a bad trade."

I'll say . . .

"So how do I get it back? Am I supposed to become a monk? I can hardly take the meditation here, let alone practice it for a lifetime."

"No, that is not your path." He shook his head. "You must break the chain of karma."

"The chain of karma?"

"Every thought you think, word you speak, and deed you do sends ripples into the universe, like the wake a motorboat creates on a lake. The waves hit the shore and bounce back to affect you long after they were created. The more you pursue desire, the more it rules you. The wheel of karma cranks on for many cycles of reincarnation over millions of years. But since the nature of life is suffering, every time you come back, you keep repeating and intensifying the cycle."

Hey, that's what the psychic said. If the lama wants to prove that life is suffering, I would make a great poster boy. "So why not just end it all instead of waiting around?" I asked. "Wouldn't an overdose be quicker and easier than struggling until life does you in?" I sat back and folded my arms, feeling a bit smug that I'd challenged the High Lama.

"That's just the point," he came back, not ruffled in the least. "You must recognize that the spirit within you is more real and powerful than the world that seems to threaten you. You can't end illusions by feeding them, fighting them, or running away. You end the dream only by waking up."

"And how do you wake up?"

The lama's eyes grew fierce. He took a final sip of his tea, lifted the cup, and smashed it on the floor. Shocked, I pulled back.

"That's all your body is, Linden—a cup," he told me in a rumbling voice that echoed off the walls. "One day it will be broken into little pieces, and worms will feast on it. But the invisible force that fills the cup will go on. Wake up to your true self . . . and no body, no woman, and no thing in this world will defeat you ever again. You can make this your last life, Linden. Awaken from your nightmare and escape the wheel of karma now and forever!"

9

I quit going to church long ago because the Christians tried to scare me into obedience with the threat of eternal hell after death. Now the Buddhists were intimidating me with the threat of eternal hell on Earth. So I decided to put up with the meditations, the chanting, the bland rice and vegetables, and the wild reincarnation stories. Meanwhile, I wondered if Lama Sherap was a master teacher or a snake-oil salesman; if Tashi was truly concerned with my well-being, or simply brainwashed; if Buddhists were enlightened, or just living their own private illusion.

One night while I was getting my jeans ready to put in the dharma-center laundry, I found a small wrinkled photo that had gotten wedged in a secondary pocket. It was a picture my mom had given me, showing her, my stepfather, and me when I was younger, at some relative's wedding. Just looking at my mom's phony smile and the way Bill flaunted the cigar in his mouth reminded me how much I hated being with them. Eager to put them and that dark time behind me, I tossed the photo in the wastebasket in the corner of the dorm room.

The next afternoon I was resting on my futon when one of the monks, Yongten, came in to perform his cleaning chores. As he emptied the wastebasket, he noticed the discarded photo.

Surprised to find it in the trash, he turned to me and asked, "Are you sure you want to throw this away?"

"Definitely," I told him.

"Why, Linden?"

Seems like a no-brainer to me. "Because I'm ready to finish my karma with my parents. I intend to leave them and everything behind so I can graduate."

Yongten set down the wastebasket and took a step closer to me. "You can't really finish your karma until you make peace with your relatives," he told me.

Aw, c'mon . . .

"If you resent your family, you'll have to be reborn and live out a drama with them again," Yongten continued. "You might even be married to the one you hate the most."

My church pastor's hellfire-and-damnation sermons were love stories compared to the horror scenarios these Buddhists cooked up! At a loss for words, I just stared at the monk.

"If you really want to end your karma, do what you can to heal your personal conflicts with kindness." Yongten smiled and went back to his cleaning.

With kindness? Nearly everyone in my family had a degree in backbiting, gossip, competition, and guilt-laying. If there was one thing my family did not own, it was kindness.

Much as I hated to admit it, what Yongten said made sense. I'd heard the same message in some of the talks by the lamas, but I'd shoved it under the rug. Yet if I was going to graduate without leaving karmic ties that would snap me back to the world like a big cosmic bungee cord, I'd feel better saying good-bye to my relatives than having them receive a call from the coroner's office. So after the monks and students retired for the night, I slipped into the office to phone my mom and stepdad. As I pressed their number on the keypad, I noticed that my hand was shaking.

Bill answered, and as usual, the minute he heard my voice, he called out: "Madeline, it's your son." No "Hello," "How are you?" "What is your life about?" "Would you like to come over for dinner?" (not that I would), or even a cordial "Go to hell." Even on the phone I felt like little more than an unwelcome appendage to him, a kind of wart you'd go to a doctor to have burned off. But I'd gotten used to that by now and expected no more.

"Linden, is it you?" my mother asked after she took the receiver. I could practically see the crease between her eyebrows, evidence of years of worry about my nonproductive existence.

"Yeah, Mom, it's me." *Bill already said it was me.*

"We haven't heard from you in a while, dear. Are you all right?" (Insinuating that if I *were* all right, I surely would have called sooner. They say that the Jews invented guilt and the Catholics perfected it. My mother raised the bar on them both.)

"Yeah, pretty good. I'm staying at a sort of spiritual center." I peered out the office door at the Buddha statue in the hallway. This place was light-years away from any reality she recognized.

"A church?" mom asked, excited but anxious. "Are you getting . . . born again?"

"No, it's not like that. This is a Buddhist place."

Heavy silence. Then: "You're not becoming a Hare Krishna, are you?"

"No, no, nothing like that." I laughed. "It's a pretty mellow scene."

"Well, all right," she answered, relieved. "Just stay away from the Kool-Aid."

Okay, spit it out. "The reason I'm calling, Mom, is . . . well, I just wanted to tell you I love you."

"Oh, I love you, too," she came back precisely on the heels of my statement. I wished she'd taken even a moment to absorb what I was trying to communicate. The words rolled off her tongue like some corporate "Please listen to the following options" recording.

I decided to try anyway: "I've been thinking a lot about my life. I just want things to be right between me and the people I know . . . I don't want to leave stuff hanging. I want to feel good about us."

"Well, that's just lovely, dear. . . . Are you dating anyone?"
Did she hear a word I said?

"Not really." I started to play with some paper clips in a cup on the desktop.

"Well, don't give up. If you keep trying, you can find a good woman, not like . . . what was her name?"

"Mom, I just—"

From the background, I heard: "I didn't get where I am by sitting on my ass and smoking pot all day."

Mom quickly covered her handpiece, almost hurting my ear. I could hear snatches of a muffled argument. A minute later she was back on the line and reported, "Bill says he knows you have what it takes."

I know he didn't say that.

"Mom, I—"

"Okay, darling, drop in and see us next time you're in the neighborhood." Click.

The worst thing about our conversation was not that it was demeaning and demoralizing. The worst thing was that it was typical.

10

One afternoon while I was propping up some tomato starts, Tashi showed up at the patch with a short fellow, maybe five-foot-four, in his early twenties. He was a white guy, head shaved, wearing the traditional robe of a Tibetan monk. Fair skin, green eyes, and wide lips made him an anomaly among the predominantly Asian lamas and students at the center. He looked a bit distraught, and the way he carried himself signaled that he might be gay.

"Linden, this is Alex Leister." Tashi motioned toward the fellow. "He has just arrived from the Ojai center. He will be working in the garden with you."

"What's up?" I greeted the new guy as I extended my hand. But he didn't reach out to shake it. Instead, he placed his hands in a prayer position, bowed slightly, and said nothing.

"What's the matter?" I asked the kid. "Cat got your tongue?"

"Alex is on *mona*," Tashi informed me.

"*Mona?* Is that his girlfriend?"

Tashi just shook his head; apparently my joke went over (or under) his head. "Mona is a vow of silence. It helps keep one's mind focused on inner meditation." Alex just stared at the ground.

"How am I supposed to have a conversation with him?"

"You may be surprised by how much you can say without words," Tashi explained.

"Whatever." I shrugged my shoulders and handed Alex a hoe. Still not making eye contact, he took it and obediently started to ruffle the soil.

"Try to make Alex feel welcome," Tashi told me.

"Sure," I answered politely.

Great. Now I have to manage a possibly gay mute—as if my other problems aren't enough.

❀

When Alex was assigned to sleep in my dorm room a few days later, I grew edgy. By then I was pretty sure he was gay, and he trailed me like a shadow. In my street days, a number of gay guys had come on to me, and I wasn't about to go there.

The next afternoon I called Tashi aside in the garden. "This kid, Alex . . . he's nice enough, but he gives me the creeps," I told him in a half whisper. "He follows me around and looks at me funny. I think he's gay. I'm afraid that he might, you know, try and put some moves on me. . . ."

Tashi nodded as if he understood my apprehension. "I wouldn't worry about that, Linden," he told me. "Alex has taken a vow of celibacy. It's required for monks in our order."

"Well, that's a relief." My shoulders dropped. "But if he tries to pull anything, I won't put up with it. I'm a pitcher, not a catcher."

Tashi smiled. "Just stick with your meditation and let me umpire the game."

Okay, I can live with that.

Sexual preferences aside, Alex turned out to be more of a chore than an assistant. He tried to help in the garden, but he wasn't very strong and couldn't do much more than hoe and weed. When I asked him to tote a bag of compost to the broccoli bed, he had a hard time lifting it, so I had to do it. When I told him to empty a wheelbarrow full of rocks we'd gathered, he couldn't maneuver it. The damn thing tipped over, and I spent more time helping him pick up the rocks than I would have if I'd done the whole job myself. *Graduate, Linden, graduate.*

❀

The next morning I was planting some pepper starts with Alex when a mother and her little boy, maybe five years old, were passing by on their way home from the park. Suddenly the kid bolted toward me.

"Jeremy, get back here!" his mom called. But Jeremy was intent on seeing what I was up to. I signaled to her that he was okay, and she let him stay and watch me. Sensing he wanted to participate, I handed him the trowel and guided his hand to transplant a tiny seedling.

I'll never forget the sheer joy in the boy's eyes as he lifted the tool and together we set the little plant into the earth. You'd have thought he'd climbed Mount Everest! When the operation was done, Jeremy giggled, dropped the trowel, and sprinted back to his mom. She nodded in thanks, and the two continued on their way.

I turned to see Alex standing beside me, with a stunned look on his face. He had silently watched the whole encounter. I couldn't understand why he was staring at me. "What's the matter?" I asked him, a bit irritated. "Did I do something wrong?"

But rather than displaying disdain, Alex simply smiled for the first time since he'd been there. Then he went back to planting. *A strange bird, this one.*

❀

Exhausted after a long morning's work outside, I headed to my room for a nap after lunch. I still wasn't sleeping well at night.

As I dropped onto my futon to stretch out, I noticed a book resting on it—a very old hardback with a scuffed maroon leather cover and faded gold lettering. The pages were yellow with age and looked like they'd crumble if handled carelessly. Curious, I picked the book up and read the title: *Secret Meetings with Mystic Masters.*

Stumped as to the identity of its donor, I scanned the room and noticed that one of the four futons was stripped, the one that had been occupied by the guy with flabby arms who woke me from my nightmare. His clothes, usually at the foot of the bed, were gone. Carl was a burned-out high school teacher who'd abandoned his old life and set off on a spiritual quest to Bhutan, a tiny country north of India, where he'd meditated in remote monasteries. That was all I knew. Now he was gone, and this book on my bed was his legacy.

A small pink sheet of paper, the kind they use in offices to leave phone messages, was inserted between two pages. I opened the book and pulled the sheet out. On it Carl had inscribed a note in thick, black Sharpie letters:

I KNOW WHY YOU'RE HERE

Intrigued, I glanced at the open page and noticed a section titled "Off the Wheel." I drew the book closer and read this passage:

> *Chensum was intent on making this his last life, so he went to the master Rinpoche and asked him how he could escape the suffering of further incarnations.*

Whoa . . .

> *"You can appeal to the Lords of Karma," Rinpoche told the disciple.*

"'The Lords of Karma'?" I said out loud, furrowing my brow. "Who the hell are they?"

> *"Go to the secret temple in the Cave of Khadroma atop Mount Lasya and fast and meditate for a full day. When your mind and heart are purified, the Lords of Karma will come to you. Ask them to release you from the effects of all thoughts, words, and deeds that would impel you to return to a human life on Earth. Tell the Lords with absolute certainty that you wish for this to be your last incarnation. . . ."*

"Holy guacamole," I whispered under my breath. *Pay dirt.*

"If your intention is strong," Rinpoche explained, "the Lords of Karma will grant your request and your soul will be liberated."

Rinpoche took Chensum by the shoulders and looked him piercingly in the eye. "I must warn you, Chensum, that once you utter this prayer and it is granted, there is no turning back. The decision of the Lords of Karma is final and cannot be reversed. If you succeed in getting off the wheel, you will be so for eternity, and you will never be allowed to come back to Earth, even if you want to."

Chensum returned the master's stare with equal gravity. "This is my decision, master. I want liberation for eternity."

"Then so be it," Rinpoche answered.

I slammed the book shut. "I'm outta here," I said aloud.

Sensing movement behind me, I turned with a start. There was Alex standing behind me. He'd been looking over my shoulder the whole time, reading with me. He'd heard my vow.

I stood up abruptly and grabbed Alex by the shoulders. I was scaring him, but I didn't care. "Don't you dare tell anyone about this—not a soul," I demanded, shaking him. His eyes bulged and he began to quiver. "If you do, I'll beat the shit out of you—do you understand?"

Breathing rapidly, his face blanched, Alex nodded vigorously. I believed him.

"Now leave me alone and quit following me around."

11

"What do you mean I can't go through Tibet on my own?" I yelled into the phone, hoping none of the monks heard me.

"The Chinese rule Tibet with an iron fist now," the travel agent explained. "They invaded in 1950, later drove out the Dalai Lama and his monks, and clamped down on tourism. I can get you on a guided tour with a group, but you'll only be allowed to visit certain places. The Chinese government is aware of the legends and mysticism surrounding the area you're asking about, and they protect it fiercely. You'll be arrested, imprisoned, or shot if you try to go there."

I slammed the phone down. "Tashi!" I called out.

Tashi hustled in from the adjoining room. "What's the matter?" he asked anxiously.

"Is it true nobody can explore Tibet without a group and a guide?"

Tashi appeared relieved that there was no immediate emergency, but he still looked a bit pained, like a parent whose child was asking a distressing question. "Come with me." He motioned for me to follow him.

My mentor led me to another room, where he perused several oversized books lying flat on a shelf. He removed a large hardcover volume with a jacket photo of staggering Himalayan peaks: *SACRED TIBET: WHEN THE SNOW LION ROARED*.

Tashi opened the cover and thumbed through the pages, which were filled with many pictures.

"This is the glory that Tibet once was," he explained, pointing to a photo of a huge ornate edifice wedged artfully into the side of a rugged mountain, bathed in sunrise colors of gold and mauve. The structure was massive but graceful, with pointed towers and scores of long, thin, colorful flags flapping in the wind.

"Behold the Drepung Loseling Monastery," Tashi pointed out. "At its height it housed over 10,000 monks who spent their lives meditating and praying for peace."

As I studied the photo, I could practically hear the gongs at the temple entrance echoing through the deep valleys on all sides. Other pictures showed monks lighting candles and incense and spinning long rows of tall prayer wheels.

"The Himalayas of Tibet are considered the crown chakra of the world," Tashi told me, resting his open hand on the photo as if he were absorbing its energy simply by touching it.

Crown chakra? I shot him a puzzled look.

"The human body has numerous chakras, or energy centers," he explained. "Each one is a door to express a different aspect of your life. The heart center, for example, is where you experience love." Tashi placed his hand on his heart as reverently as he'd touched the monastery photo. I did the same, but I couldn't feel anything.

"The crown chakra at the top of the head is the opening at which a human being makes contact with divine wisdom," Tashi went on. "You know how kings and queens wear crowns with pointy sides and an opening in the middle?" he asked. I nodded. "That crown derives from an ancient time when the leader of a nation was spiritual, not political. The person most connected to the divine was in the ideal position to receive wisdom and guidance for the nation, and the physical crown represented that his or her crown chakra was open and receptive."

I touched my head; I still felt nothing. "So why are the Himalayas the crown chakra?"

"They reach to heaven higher than any other mountain range on Earth; and they have nurtured a long spiritual tradition of prayer, meditation, and kindness," he explained. "At one time, twenty percent of Tibetans were monks or nuns. The people of Tibet have lived in harmony with each other and the divine for millennia." Tashi breathed a long sigh. "Until this . . ."

He flipped the page to reveal a photo that turned my stomach. A hundred dead monks were piled in the middle of a city square, blood spattered on their faces and robes. It reminded me of photos I'd seen of Jews murdered in Nazi concentration camps. I wanted to throw up. "Why?" I blurted out.

"They continued to practice their religion after the Communists invaded."

I was practically speechless. "That's when the Dalai Lama left?"

"He was twenty-four years old. After trying unsuccessfully to secure protection for his people, he realized there was no hope for him to sustain Buddhism in Tibet at that point. One night he disguised himself as a soldier and slipped out of the monastery with a group of attendants. They trekked on foot for a month over the Himalayas and across a 500-yard-wide river into India. The group narrowly escaped the Chinese army, who pursued them to the very end. India granted them asylum, and now the stronghold of Tibetan Buddhism is in Dharamsala, where the religion remains in exile to this day."

Tashi silently closed the book and placed it back on the shelf. "That, my friend, is why you cannot explore Tibet on your own—especially the parts that Tibetan Buddhists honor as sacred ceremonial sites."

I stared at the book cover for another moment, as if trying to fathom some secret. "Have you ever heard of Mount Lasya?" I asked.

Tashi looked surprised, but recovered quickly. "Lasya? That's the sacred mountain where initiations take place. I've heard about seekers who went there to find the gods. Some came back, and many didn't. The few who returned won't talk about it. It's not a place to take lightly. Why do you ask?"

"Uh, just curious," I lied.

"Just stay with your meditation, Linden," the monk advised me. "What you're searching for is within you."

Tashi rose and left the room. I walked to the map of the world on the wall. There were lots of finger and pin marks on the region of Tibet. I looked closer to see if Mount Lasya was identified. It wasn't. The country was colored red.

II

12

Delhi from the air looked like a crazy patchwork woven without forethought. As I leaned over to peer out the window, I realized I might be annoying the passenger sitting in the window seat, a middle-aged Indian woman with a bright orange sari adorned with hundreds of tiny gold beads. "Sorry, I didn't mean to disturb you," I told her. "I haven't flown much."

The woman smiled. "That's all right," she answered with a thick Indian accent. "First time to India?"

"First time anywhere overseas . . . thanks to my buddy Alex."

"Your friend sent you?"

"This kid Alex, he doesn't talk . . . it's a spiritual thing, if you get what I mean." I figured that being from India, she would understand such religious practices. "Alex discovered that I wanted to come to Tibet to end my life."

The lady's eyebrows arched so high that I thought the little 3-D dot in the middle of her forehead would pop off. "You're going to end your life?"

"Not just my life," I had to explain. "All my lifetimes. You see, I've decided this will be my last trip to Earth . . . I'm sure you're familiar with reincarnation."

She nodded hesitantly, as if to ask, *And where are you going with this?* She was too polite to pose the question, but I knew she was thinking it.

"I'm going to petition the Lords of Karma."

"The Lords of Karma?"

"They dwell in a certain cave in Tibet. I'm going to find the Lords of Karma and tell them not to send me back again. I'm ready to get off the karmic wheel."

Just then the flight attendant came by to tell us to stow our items before landing. I thought my seatmate would use that as an excuse to quit talking to me, but instead she turned back to me. "And you believe the Lords of Karma are going to end all your lifetimes?"

"Yes," I told her. "If you ask sincerely, they will nullify the effects of all your past karma, and you can be liberated and never have to be born on Earth again."

"I see," she replied, closing a book she'd been reading and placing it in her carry-on bag. "And your friend who bought your ticket . . . does he want you to die?"

"Not exactly. He just wants to help me. When he figured out what I intend to do, he wrote me a note asking me if I really wanted to go to Tibet. I told him, 'More than anything.' The next day he gave me this credit card." I reached into my wallet and proudly displayed the card. She didn't seem that impressed; I imagined she had one herself. Probably several.

"Actually, this is his father's card," I had to clarify. "The last time Alex went home he brought in the mail and found an offer for a credit card with no interest for a year. His name is the same as his father's, so he got me a ticket. I promised to pay him back when I get home. I'll ask the Lords of Karma to let me live long enough to pay Alex—that is, his father—back."

By then we were making our approach for landing. The lady just looked out the window until we landed. I think she didn't quite know what to say to me.

When the plane had pulled up to the gate and we were removing our bags from the overhead bins, she remarked, "Good luck with the Lords of Karma."

"Thanks," I answered. "I think I'm good to go."

If you ever want to be motivated to end all of your lifetimes, take a walk along the back streets of Delhi. It has to be the most depressing place on Earth: noisy traffic; suffocating pollution; and sick, homeless, and horribly impoverished people everywhere you turn. The terrible images still linger in my head—old, feeble people; scraggly street kids; guys with stumps for legs; people so skinny that you could see all their ribs. Some parents, I was told, maimed their children so they would fetch more money begging. The horrors of *Slumdog Millionaire* are for real. My heart broke for all of these poor people, and I wished I could feed them or somehow make their lives better. I handed a few of them some coins, but there was no way I could help them all. *If this is what life on Earth is about, I hope they all get to end their lifetimes soon.*

I found a taxi stand and asked a cab driver if he would take me to Dharamsala. His jaw dropped at first, and then his lips curved into a smile—the 500-kilometer ride was fifteen hours and would cost 14,000 rupees—about $300. I started to walk away, and he lectured me on how many kids he had and how fuel prices were ruining his business. Finally we settled on 9,000 rupees. But as I stepped into the cab, I realized I didn't have the cash. The driver pointed to a bank across the street where I could draw on my— well, Alex's—well, Alex's father's—credit card.

I threaded through the insane traffic like a halfback chasing daylight through a crack in a defensive line; then through the bank door seconds before closing time. "You're lucky," the guard told me with a parental glare as he locked the door behind me. I scanned the counter for the friendliest-looking teller and spied a slim young woman with long straight hair, dressed to the nines in a sea-green sari and matching eye shadow. I marched to her window, set the card before her with a flaunted snap, and declared, "I'd like a cash advance on this credit card."

"Certainly," she answered in pretty good English. "May I see your passport?"

"Uh, sure," I mumbled as I pulled it from my fanny pack and handed it to her.

The teller looked back and forth between the card and the passport a few times, and returned both to me. "I'm sorry, sir," she told me. "The name on the passport must be the same as the name on the card."

Eight thousand miles from home with a card worth ten grand, and no way to pull cash from it! I imagined myself washing dishes in a steamy kitchen to the accompaniment of annoyingly nasal singers backed up by rubber-band-sounding instruments on a cheap, static-ridden knockoff AM radio.

"But the owner of the card gave it to me," I argued.

"I understand," she came back in a businesslike voice. "But we have to protect card owners from fraudulent use. Those are the rules."

I looked down the line of tellers to see if anyone looked more promising; they were all closing down. *Now what? Will I have to hitchhike across India? Starve before I make it to Tibet? Will I end up squatting on dirty streets with the emaciated beggars?* I started to feel desperate. "Please, is there anything you can do to help me?" I entreated her. "I have no cash whatsoever."

"I'm sorry, sir." She shook her head again and began shutting down her station.

Suddenly we were startled by someone banging loudly on the bank's front door. Everyone looked up, alarmed, fearing a robbery. I turned to see who it was, and I was shocked to see Alex! I could hardly believe it!

"Let him in!" I pleaded. "He's with me. He has ID."

When the guard decided this wispy monk was no criminal, he unlocked the door. Alex rushed to the counter and, upon my request, produced his passport. I tried to take it from him to pass along to the teller, but he insisted on handing it to her himself. The teller scanned the passport and looked at Alex curiously for a long time. Finally, Alex mimicked a barber shaving his head; obviously, the passport photo had been taken before he'd joined the order. At last the teller nodded as if she understood and forked over about 20,000 rupees. For a moment I forgot they were worth maybe three cents each, and I felt rich.

"What are you doing here?!" I asked Alex as I counted the cash.

My enigmatic friend grabbed a deposit slip, took a pen from the counter, and scribbled: "I was worried about you."

13

Getting out of Delhi was another nightmare. Thousands of cars, three-wheel taxis, trucks, mopeds, bicycles, and rickshaws coming from all directions, honking horns and vying for openings. Hordes of pedestrians, masses of kids riding on the bumpers of buses, and camels and elephants hauling heavy loads. Our cab driver, Jitend, seemed accustomed to the madness; and oblivious to it, he pointed out various religious and cultural highlights. But the long plane ride, compounded by serious jet lag, had frazzled me seriously, and soon I tuned Jitend out and let my head fall against the cab's window.

Moments later I was jolted awake by Jitend blasting the horn at another driver who had cut him off and caused us to miss our green light. I snapped my head up, watching Jitend pound the dashboard and mutter a Hindi curse.

As I lay my head back on the window, I observed an old man lying lifelessly on the sidewalk—a chilling sight. Meanwhile, throngs of people walked past him like a piece of litter. "Jitend," I called to the front of the cab. "That man is just asleep, right?"

Jitend looked over his shoulder and studied the scene for a moment. Then he grew somber and shook his head.

Suddenly something possessed me. I threw open the rear door

of the cab and ran to the man. He was probably seventy years old and wore ragged white dhoti pants and no shirt. His head was mostly bald, and his long white beard trailed onto the dirty sidewalk. A pack of meager goods in a canvas sack was sprawled in front of his pale chest. His eyes were open, and he seemed to be staring off into space. I felt heartbroken, angry, and helpless.

"What's wrong with you people?!" I stood there and shouted. "Don't any of you care? This man could be your father! How can you just keep walking?! Just because he doesn't have a home doesn't mean he's not a human being!"

Lots of people heard me, but none stopped. Some turned and looked. I'm sure they understood me.

By that time Jitend and Alex had caught up with me. "I'm sorry you had to see this," the cabbie told me. "It's just the way life is here. The police will find him and take him away." Alex's face was contorted in sorrow and confusion.

I scanned the row of shops along the street and noticed a small flower stall. I ran to it, grabbed a white rose from a cheap vase, pressed a few bills into the vendor's hand, and dashed back to the old man. I kneeled at his side and gently closed his eyes with my index and middle fingers. I'd never done anything like that before. Cars were now honking as Jitend's idle cab blocked traffic.

"Rest in peace, old man," I said in a low voice. "If there is a God, may he grant you freedom from a world like this."

14

The long drive to Dharamsala seemed even longer in the wake of my encounter with that poor old man. I tried to sleep, but when I closed my eyes, I kept seeing the corpse's color-drained face and vacant eyes. In India, where death is as real as life, you can't escape mortality. Meeting that homeless soul seemed a fitting keynote for my quest, forcing me to think about why death might not be a penalty, but a relief.

For endless hours we bumped along unpaved, rutted, dusty roads, dodging bony cattle and wandering goats. I dozed on and off, hoping every time I awoke that we might be nearing our destination. But the bleak terrain just went on and on.

I looked over at Alex—on one hand, a needy, lost kid, insecure and struggling for direction and maybe sexual identity; on the other, a clever, resourceful, and dedicated friend. Sending me to Tibet when he didn't really know me was a gift far greater than any I'd ever been given. I wondered if he had some ulterior motive—perhaps he wanted me to become his lover. But there was no way I was going to figure Alex out at that moment. I had a bad headache, and my body was battling to catch up twelve time zones. Through my haze I decided that for now I would just be grateful for Alex; and hopefully someday, somehow, I might understand who he was and why he'd shown up.

❋

Finally we rose into the Himalayas, straining up steep mountain grades and negotiating cliffs with terrifying drop-offs. As we narrowly avoided head-on collisions along hairpin curves, I wondered if the Lords of Karma knew of my arrival and were preparing me to loosen my hold on the world I sought to depart.

A forest of spruce trees signaled our approach to the tiny, remote mountain town of Dharamsala. I'd once seen a movie about holy people who made thousand-mile pilgrimages on foot, stopping every step to kiss the earth. When we finally arrived, I understood why: it was not just because the city was sacred, but because any ending to that trek would have been a blessed one.

In spite of my exhaustion, I sensed a tranquility in this secluded haven. The steep upper city, where most of the Tibetans in exile dwell, still retains a nineteenth-century British colonial charm. Temples and schools are artfully tucked into the green mountain walls that lead down, down to a formidable river. A mile above sea level, the town sits in the shadow of massive snowcapped mountains, instilling an inescapable sense of humility.

The cab driver pointed out the Tibetan Institute of Performing Arts, the Tibetan Children's Village, and the Dalai Lama's residence. The renowned spiritual leader, we learned, had departed a few days earlier for a lecture tour in England. If he were home, I would have liked to have picked his brain: *How did you feel when you saw your people decimated? Will this be your last life, too, or will you keep coming back to help people? Have you ever thought about jumping off a bridge? Would you have stopped me?*

We found the headquarters of the dharma center's parent organization, a stately monastery on the outskirts of town. Alex and I entered through portals of gray stone pillars carved with ornate images of Buddhas, gods, and goddesses. Once inside the grounds, we encountered a long array of prayer wheels lining a corridor, with monks slowly walking, meditating, praying, and turning the wheels with their hands. I felt as if we were either going back in time or even rising into timelessness.

We were shown to the guest quarters, probably very nice by Tibetan standards but pretty funky to us: two thin, hard beds; windows that didn't close properly; a rustic dresser with stuck drawers; and a mirror pocked with little black age marks. Alex made a face, but I didn't care that much. I was just glad we'd arrived. Spent, we flopped on the beds, and for a moment this crazy world disappeared.

❁

When I awoke, it was dark. From our window I could see the crescent moon silently ascending over the silhouette of jagged peaks. The last time I'd noticed the moon was from the rail of the Golden Gate Bridge. What a turn my journey had taken since that night!

I sat for a while basking in the quietude of the lingering dusk. The contrast between the insanity of Delhi and the tranquility of this place was staggering. I wished I could just capture that moment and live in it forever. Yet we'd been invited for tea with the head monk, Lama Sungdare, and we didn't want to snub his invitation.

I nudged Alex awake, and minutes later we found our way downstairs to the monastery office, where a solitary monk sat at a flimsy desk reading an old Buddhist text. He was obviously waiting for us, but displayed no impatience at our late entry. The fellow wore the traditional maroon robe and small, round wire-rimmed spectacles. His hair was shaved down to tiny stubble. About my age, he was taller than most Tibetans and seemed more physically fit, the sleeveless yellow monk's shirt revealing some well-defined biceps. He nodded to us and closed his book.

"I am Sonam," he greeted us in a soothing voice as he rose and bowed. "Welcome to our monastery. . . . Did you get enough rest?"

"I guess," I answered hastily, completely forgetting to thank him for the accommodations.

"Where are you from?" he asked, seeming sincerely interested. His Tibetan accent was only slight.

"San Francisco."

"Ah, I visited San Francisco a few years ago," Sonam noted with a boyish grin. "I saw the Giants beat the Dodgers!"

Alex and I shot each other surprised looks. "I followed the Giants when I was . . . uh . . . out of work," I told Sonam. "I used to find leftover newspapers and pull out the sports page."

"What, may I ask, moved you to study Buddhism?" Sonam asked as he began shutting off the lights in the office.

I squirmed a bit. "Well, to tell you the truth, I wasn't just out of work. I was wandering homeless when a Buddhist monk found me."

Sonam stopped his office-closing chores. "I was homeless, too," he told me.

I was stunned, and I'm sure it showed.

"Not by fortune, but by choice," he explained, leaning against the desk. "When I became a monk, I had to wander for one year, begging for food. It was a kind of initiation. I felt terribly frustrated when people wouldn't help me; I was so hungry. But Buddha provided for me."

Me, too, I guess.

Sonam turned off the final light and held open the door. "I will show you to Lama Sungdare's study. He is waiting for you."

Our guide led us down a long candlelit corridor, ancient boards groaning beneath our feet. A collection of old photos and paintings in mildewed frames lined the hallway, but the passage was so dark that I could barely make them out. Finally we arrived at a heavy wooden door draped with a colorful Tibetan *thangka,* a cloth painting of the gods. Sonam knocked softly and listened until we heard a short response from a deep voice. Sonam opened the door, his arm outstretched, bidding us to enter before him.

We found ourselves in an ancient-looking chamber, dark except for the flames in a fireplace at the far end. The amber light illuminated the silhouette of an old man sitting quietly on a couch, staring into the blaze. He was so still that at first I thought he was a Buddha statue. Sonam ushered us to the couch, where the figure slowly stood, frightening me to see it come to life. "Mr. Linden and Mr. Alex, please meet Lama Sungdare, the spiritual director of our monastery." The lama bowed and motioned for us to be seated on some cushions on the floor. Sonam took his place on the floor on the other side of the High Lama.

I strained to make out the lama's features, still veiled in the shadows. From what I could see, he looked quite serious, almost stern. He spoke with a low, gravelly voice that rumbled throughout the room. "Will you be staying with us for a while?"

"Actually, we're leaving for Tibet in the morning."

Lama Sungdare drew a long breath. "We would all like to leave for Tibet in the morning," he noted stoically. "But it is impossible now. You have to stay where they want you to stay and go nowhere on your own."

"Yes, we've heard," I replied. "Isn't there some way to sneak in without being seen?"

Sonam rose to stir the embers, which intensified the firelight, casting an eerie glow on the High Lama. His face, I could see now, was very round, his eyebrows thick, and he had several layers of puffy circles under his eyes.

"Perhaps, but once you got there, you wouldn't easily find sanctuary," he answered. "Communism may have died in Europe, but it lives on with a vengeance on the other side of these mountains. What do you want to do there? Visit temples?"

Alex searched my eyes anxiously, as if to ask, *Are you going to tell him?*

"I intend to find the Lords of Karma in the Cave of Khadroma on Mount Lasya."

Lama Sungdare sat stone-faced for a long, painful silence. Sonam, too, seemed taken aback. Even in the dark I could sense wheels turning in the lama's head. Finally he asked, "And what are you going to say to them?"

"I'm going to ask them to make this my last life," I blurted out. Suddenly the fire flared up, as if some invisible force was affirming —or challenging—my mission. "The pain in my heart is too great to continue this charade we call life," I explained. "I seek true liberation." Sonam's shock seemed to shift to sympathy.

Lama Sungdare, however, kept a poker face. "And how did you find out about this cave? Did you read about it in *Secret Meetings with Mystic Masters?*"

"Yes, yes!" I replied excitedly. "That's where I saw it! Do you know the book?"

The lama nodded. "Yes, I know the book," he stated with a half chuckle, the first time I'd seen him smile. "Some of it is fact, and much is fiction. The foreigners who wrote it passed along what they heard from local people. Fables grow more dramatic and fantastic from generation to generation. Before long you cannot separate myth from reality."

My stomach sank. *Have I come all this way for nothing? Have I pointlessly gotten Alex involved in a mess that could send him to jail for credit card fraud? Does this mean I'll have to keep coming back lifetime after lifetime?*

"Can you tell me how to get to Mount Lasya?" I asked, desperation obvious in my voice. "Maybe I can find the Lords of Karma on my own."

The lama stood up, walked to a wall switch near the door, and turned on a bright overhead light. Instantly the mystical mood of the room evaporated. Then he moved toward the far wall and motioned for Alex and me to join him. There he showed us a large map of Tibet. He traced a circle around the mountains with his index finger and explained, "These are the great Himalayan mountains of Tibet: vast, inspiring, and terrifying. You'll notice the famous ones, like Mount Everest and K2. All of the lesser ones are named as well. Come here . . . Linden, is it?"

I stepped closer to the map. Sure enough, there was Everest. Yes, all the others had names, too.

"Tell me if you see a mountain named Lasya."

I looked closely at all the peaks. And again. And again. Alex tried, too. None bore that name. I scanned one more time. *Nada.*

"So you see, my friend, you have fallen prey to—how do you say it?—'an old wives' tale.' I, too, have heard this story. But I assure you this place does not exist. It is like your 'abominable snowman.' Many people chatter about it, and some say they have seen it—but no one can prove it. So save yourself time and struggle —maybe your life—and give up your ghost hunt now. Everything you seek can be found in meditation. If you wish to stay with us and join our practice, you are most welcome."

I searched Alex's eyes. He looked as confused as I felt.

❀

Lying in my hard bed that night, staring at the ceiling, a million thoughts barreled through my head like runaway trains, rambling in all directions. *Did that book dupe me? Is Buddhism just a big mind game? Is there anything to reincarnation, or is it just a pleasant tale we fabricate to shield ourselves from the fact that when you're dead, you're dead?*

I looked over at Alex, sleeping soundly. He was a nice kid, but I feared I'd dragged him on a wild-goose chase. It wasn't fair to him or his father's money. I couldn't continue without any facts to go on. *Tomorrow morning I'll tell him we're turning back.* The decision afforded me some peace, and I fell into a less-than-restful sleep.

❀

When Alex started to stir in the morning, I sat down on the edge of his bed. I must have surprised him; as soon as he saw me, he pulled the covers practically over his head.

"The game stops here," I told Alex resolutely. "We're heading back."

He gave me a puzzled look. Part of me wished he would plead with me to continue. But I'd already gone that route in my head and hit a dead end.

Sensing my resolution, Alex seemed pleased, and nodded.

I stood up and started to pack. Alex, however, remained in his bed. When I finished and stepped outside to get some sun, he got up and scurried to the bathroom. The kid sure was quirky.

After breakfast, we stood on the monastery steps with our backpacks and waited for the taxi Sonam had summoned for us.

I wasn't looking forward to another butt-wrenching ride. Maybe that was my punishment for such a stupid, harebrained scheme. *Maybe I'm supposed to go back to San Francisco and just meditate until I keel over from boredom. Maybe I'll just go back and jump. This is all getting too complicated.*

When the taxi arrived, Sonam was nowhere in sight. As we descended the temple steps, I looked back several times to see if he would see us off, but apparently he was occupied with other duties. *Has Lama Sungdare forbade him from interacting with us, since we are, in the lama's mind, deluded?* One more glance back and I gave up, disappointed to miss my new friend. Alex and I threw our packs into the trunk, and I opened the door to the backseat.

To my amazement, there sat Sonam. He looked nervous, and motioned me to get in quickly.

"You mustn't turn back now, Linden," he told me, gripping my arm. "Lama Sungdare did not speak truth to you."

I was shocked. "Mount Lasya exists?"

"Yes," Sonam replied, nodding firmly. "That is the spiritual name of Mount Norbu. You'll find that on any map. Only people who understand its significance call it 'Lasya.' I swear to you, I am telling the truth."

I could feel the hair on my arms and the back of my neck standing up. "But why would the lama lie to me?"

"He is sworn to protect the secret of the mountain from people who would misuse or exploit it. But I believe you are sincere, and I don't want you to be discouraged. I want you to make this your last life if that is your true choice."

Sonam placed a small piece of paper in my palm and folded my fingers over it. "Go to the village of Shailesh and find the man whose name is on this paper. He will tell you how to locate the cave. May the blessings of Buddha be with you."

Sonam exited quickly. I looked at Alex, who had slipped into the backseat on my other side. He'd heard everything. I asked him with my eyes what he thought, and he nodded. Sonam was sincere. Mount Lasya and the Cave of Khadroma *did* exist.

The taxi driver stepped on the accelerator, and we sped away. I looked up at the rearview mirror and found the driver's eyes. He knew, too.

I turned to look out the back window. Sonam was ascending the steps to the monastery entrance just as Lama Sungdare was coming out. The two greeted each other with a bow, business as usual.

15

As we forged through rugged mountain roads, we saw determined farmers maneuvering primitive plows behind oxen trudging through hillside fields still largely underwater from recent rains. Toothless old women waved through the windows of adobe-like shanties in small villages. When we stopped for fuel, a dozen wide-eyed kids surrounded the car to gawk at the two white guys in the backseat. I found some chewing gum in my backpack, which I broke into half sticks and distributed among them. You'd think they'd won a Vegas jackpot.

When we passed a big white sign hand-painted with large red Hindi and Tibetan letters, the driver turned and made a dismal attempt at English: "Chinese border—ten kilometer—no can go." A minute later we turned off the main *(ha!)* road and headed down a long soggy lane lined with wild peach trees bursting with stunning pink blossoms. As the mud grew thicker, I began to worry that we'd get stuck. Sure enough, five minutes later we came to a halt. The driver spun his wheels over and over again, spewing muck in every direction. A few neighboring yaks got interested and strolled over to see what was going on.

We all got out of the cab to survey the situation. The entire side of the car was covered with mud, eclipsing its original pale blue

The driver motioned to Alex and me to push. We looked at each other and knew we would soon be layered with goo like chocolate-covered ants. We both made a face and threw our arms up in surrender. Since Alex wasn't strong, I knew the burden would be on me.

We dug our heels into whatever hard ground we could find and leaned onto the trunk. The driver gunned the engine and shot mud at us; some of it hurt. We pushed and pushed until we got a small amount of momentum going. The taxi started to rock a bit, and we got into a rhythm—up and back, up and back, up and back. Finally the car gained traction and lurched out of the bog. But instead of stopping to let us back in, the driver executed a rapid three-point turn. He stepped out of the vehicle, opened the trunk, handed us our backpacks, and stuck his hand out for the fare.

"You can't leave us out here in the middle of nowhere!" I bellowed.

"Walk there!" the driver grunted, pointing down the road and turning his palm back up. I reached into my pocket and gave him what he wanted. As soon as he got his money, he dashed back into the car, floored the accelerator, and clumsily forged his way back through the muck he'd just traversed.

Alex and I looked ahead: road, mud, yaks, and mountains. It was starting to rain.

❀

One hour, four kilometers, and 327 yaks later, we spied a small farmhouse in the distance, a slim gray ribbon of smoke spiraling up from the chimney. We followed a narrow footpath from the road until we reached a yard where a gaggle of gray and white geese waddled over to greet us, squawking wildly. When a huge mama goose went for my knee, I took off my cap and began to swat her. She spread her wings, puffed her feathers, and let me know in no uncertain terms that I was *not* on her invitation list. Finally she relented and scurried to create havoc elsewhere in the yard. Several dogs started to bark, and a few horses in a pasture trotted toward us. No question about it now—company had arrived.

As we approached the rickety porch, I heard footsteps from inside. I tensed, as I feared we might be greeted by some Himalayan hillbilly with a shotgun. To my relief, the door opened to reveal an old Tibetan woman with a round face, large wide eyes, and pure-silver hair in a long single braid. She wore a maroon kerchief and bulky brown jacket, which I'm sure she'd knitted from her own yak wool. She was pleasantly rotund, slightly hunched—and quite surprised to see us.

"Sorry to bother you, ma'am," I began, doubting she'd understand English. "We're sort of lost." The crone looked us up and down, with consternation at first, and then pity. "We're looking for . . ."—I reached into my pocket and withdrew the paper Sonam had given me—"Lin . . . Ling . . . Lingpa."

"Eyla!" the old woman called out in a loud voice. Then she turned and issued a long string of excited Tibetan.

Soon a young woman emerged. Maybe thirty, plain but pretty, she wore a knit hat of the same material as the old lady's jacket, and carried a bowl of rice and some purple stuff I didn't recognize. She looked curious but not frightened.

"I'm looking for . . ." *Oh hell, why even try?* I just handed her the paper. She studied it for a moment, then turned to her grandmother, and they began to speak in animated voices. The younger woman finally turned back to me, pointed to the name on the paper, and said in decent English, "This is my father. He is not here now, but he will be back later. . . . Come in."

I looked at Alex, and we breathed a sigh of relief. Maybe the Lords of Karma were with us after all.

16

Life in the Himalayas has two phases: survival and survival. This family had obviously mastered both. Brutal winters, windstorms, avalanches, torrential rain, and a growing season shorter than a long nap. *How do these people live out here?* But then again, if they knew about *my* life, they wouldn't understand how *I* lived. Ironically, I was at their doorstep because I couldn't figure out how to survive in my own skin.

A thick deerskin rug, a stone fireplace, and a few wrinkled family photos on the mantel made the shanty feel remarkably homey. In a far corner I noticed a child's playpen (Tibetan version: a slight upgrade from a yak fence). A small homemade toy of colored wooden spools strung together on a piece of twine hung over its rail. In another corner stood a small altar bearing a butter lamp, an ash-laden incense holder, and a prayer wheel. They were Buddhists.

"My name is Eyla," the young lady introduced herself as she removed her hat, letting her long, thick dark hair cascade over her shoulders. She looked more like a woman now.

"This is my grandmother, Jangmu," Eyla added respectfully. Jangmu nodded and motioned us toward some cushions on the living-room floor. Alex and I plopped down on them indelicately, savoring the comfort after that dreadful ride and hike. Soon Grandma brought us some yak-butter tea.

"Why do you want to see my father?"

"We were told he can help us get into Tibet," I answered right up front.

Our hostess translated for her grandmother, whose brow puckered. "This is dangerous, you know," Eyla told us.

"Yes, we've heard," I answered, my stomach contracting.

"We have gotten many people across the border," Eyla reported, passing a bowl of berries to Alex and me. We snatched them up like starving street urchins.

"Why, may I ask, do you do this?" I had to inquire.

Eyla sat up straight. "My father was quite young in Lhasa during the Chinese invasion. His father was killed, along with his two monk brothers. He is very bitter and wants to see the Tibetans oust the Chinese. Me, I'm not so angry, but I want to help my people unite with our homeland."

Alex and I sat silently, taking it all in. Seeing a religion torn from its roots and its adherents murdered was hard for me to imagine.

Eyla turned to Alex and asked, "What monastery do you come from?"

Alex, of course, remained silent and looked to me to be his spokesman. "He's taken a vow of silence," I explained. "It makes our conversations real simple."

Eyla passed the news on to Jangmu, who nodded in approval, apparently honored that a monk with such devotion was visiting her home. I guess it didn't matter that he was the Caucasian son of a globe-trotting commodities-exchange mogul.

"And you?" she turned back to me. "Where are you from?"

"Nowhere, really," I replied. "The last place I lived was San Francisco."

Eyla pondered this for a moment. "I understand people in America have many things. I studied English in school, and I've read books and seen movies."

"Many things, yes," I echoed. "But not so much happiness."

"We have few things here," she replied, "but much happiness."

✴

Eyla went out to do some chores in the yard while Alex napped and I helped Jangmu cut vegetables for dinner. I felt uncomfortable to be alone with the old woman, since we had no words in common and the lives that had led us to this odd meeting couldn't have been more different. Yet she seemed oblivious to our differences, softly chanting a Buddhist prayer as she showed me how to chop. When she laid her hand over mine, her touch was of the comforting kind that only grandmothers can bestow. Before long I found myself quietly joining in her simple chant. In spite of Jangmu's age and bent body, I perceived a sparkle in her eyes I'd rarely seen in old people where I'd grown up. Somehow, despite her wrinkles and stiff joints, the fire of her soul still shined through.

Suddenly a deafening downpour began to pound on the roof, and Eyla dashed in from the yard, covering her head with her sweater. "Lots of rain this spring," she announced stoically, shaking the water off. "You may have to wait to travel. You are welcome to stay if you'd like." Briskly she crossed the room and disappeared through a curtained door into her bedroom.

I looked over at Alex, now awake after the commotion. He got up and helped us set the table, displaying astounding meticulousness. He laid the nonmatching silverware out like a waiter in a five-star restaurant, and even returned a few pieces for minor cleaning. I imagined he'd done this a thousand times in his childhood home in Scarsdale, New York; and the process had been more agreeable to him than playing with G.I. Joes.

Finally dinner was ready, and Jangmu pointed us to some rickety wooden chairs. I marveled at how much more this modest place felt like home than the ones I'd lived in, with marbleized hot tubs, keypad-entry gates, and digital security systems. Real security, I began to realize, lives in your head, not around your yard.

A minute later Eyla emerged from her bedroom. She looked so breathtaking that I wondered if I was seeing the same peasant girl who had come to the door a few hours earlier. She wore an embroidered black and deep purple Tibetan dress that was unassuming yet mesmerizing. As the glow of the kerosene lamp highlighted the contour of her eyes in a most alluring way, I realized I was in the presence of an extraordinarily attractive woman. When Eyla took her seat next to me, I felt a bit jittery. Part of me was thrilled, and another part didn't want to deal with the kind of problems I'd gotten into with good-looking women. I was on my way out of this world, and I didn't intend to get involved with anyone or anything that might tempt me to stay.

I took a breath and tried not to stare. When I found my eyes getting lost in the smooth curve of her neck, I fell back on my brief stint of meditation training—which, although I'd resisted it violently at the time, now helped me reel in my wandering mind. I was able to keep my fantasies at bay until Eyla's radiance became a backdrop rather than a distraction.

The rain continued through the meal, its steady cadence almost hypnotic. We talked about our families, our cultures, and religion. "We," of course, meant Eyla and me. Jangmu didn't understand a word of the exchange, except when Eyla would make an effort to translate. Alex, for the first time on the trip, looked bored and bugged. *He'd make a good project for a psychologist.*

After dinner we retired to the living area for tea. Our conversation turned to what I call big-picture talk: *Why are we all here? Are we supposed to be doing something important to help the world, or do we fulfill our purpose simply by being happy right where we are? Why do some people find inner peace, while others are plagued by constant drama?* Jangmu hung in there for a while before she started to nod off; eventually she excused herself and sauntered off to bed. Alex didn't last much longer, crashing in the corner of the living room.

Eyla and I went on talking for another hour, and probably could have continued all night. *Beauty, wisdom, and character—why have I never met another woman who embodied those gifts in such stunning harmony?*

Finally Eyla said, "Well, it's getting late," and began to gather the used teacups. "Thank you for a stimulating conversation," she added as she rose. She scanned the living room and apologized, "I hope you don't mind sleeping on these pillows. They are the best our 'hotel' has to offer."

"This will be just fine," I assured her. After rinsing the cups, she reached into an aged wooden chest of drawers, pulled out a few wool blankets, and cast them over our makeshift beds.

"What will your father say when he comes home and finds two white guys sleeping in your living room?"

"Oh, he won't be back tonight," Eyla answered as she fluffed up some cushions to serve as beds. "He'll stay in the village and walk home in the morning when the rain stops."

"With your husband and child?" *Dude, how obvious can you be?*

"My husband and child?" Eyla laughed. "If you know who they are, please tell me."

"But . . . the playpen?" I asked, pointing to it.

Her laugh downshifted to a warm smile. "That's for my nephew. My brother and his family live in the village and visit us quite a lot."

With that, Eyla extinguished all the lamps and candles except the one near me. She wished me a pleasant rest and retreated into her bedroom.

I gently shook Alex to get up and move to his pillow bed. I covered him with a blanket, slipped into my own "bed," and blew out the final lamp flame. My body was exhausted, but my mind was spinning out of control. I lay restless for a long time. This was all too confusing, like a bad farmer's-daughter joke. Across the inside of my head I read a big cosmic newspaper headline:

Lonely Man Meets Woman of His Dreams on His Way to the Gallows

Funny, in a way.
But not really.

17

I tossed and turned most of the night, trying to quell the fire mounting within me. Being with Eyla reminded me how much I longed to be in a woman's arms. She had a caring heart and sharp mind, and would make a devoted partner. *Is my desire for a lover a natural expression of my humanity, or just another illusion to be dis-spelled? Was I put on Earth to enjoy passion, or overcome it? If God is love, why do so many people get hurt when they love?*

But there was no way I was going to figure all this out, or my attraction to Eyla, right then and there. I was on my way to Tibet for a reason, and to dillydally here would only thwart my quest. Finally I settled into sleep and took refuge in its void.

When I felt a soft and comforting hand gently resting on my chest, I began to stir. I reached up and laid my own hand over it for a long moment. *Ah, sweet connection.* I tried to savor the touch for as long as possible, but alas, the hand delivered a nudge, and I realized I was being beckoned to return to the world. The light I sensed through my closed eyelids told me morning had come. Suddenly my desire to keep Eyla at a distance evaporated, and all I wanted to do was wrap my arms around her and draw her to me. I took a breath and slowly opened my eyes, hoping she would stay close long enough for me to bask in her beauty.

It was *Alex.*

I tossed his hand off and sat up with a start. "What's up?!" I blurted out.

Alex didn't seem much put off by my case of mistaken identity; he might have even enjoyed it. After giving me another moment to fully awaken, he pointed to the kitchen table, where Eyla was setting out breakfast. "I'll be there in a minute," I mumbled.

Alex nodded and left me to myself. *No, this will not turn into Brokeback Mountain.*

I slipped on my jeans and headed for the kitchen, where I found Eyla in her peasant-girl outfit, looking just as she had when she greeted us yesterday. Now I was totally confused. *Did I make up last night in my mind?*

"Good morning, Linden," Eyla greeted me brightly. "Did you sleep well?"

"Uh, yeah," I lied. Somehow it didn't seem appropriate to answer, *Not really. I spent half the night wrestling with my burning desire to make sweet love to you. Did you do the same?* I sat down at the table.

Out the window I saw that the rain had stopped, at least for now. Good chance we could get going to Tibet this morning. Mixed feelings.

Jangmu joined us and smiled as if we were now family. Maybe we were. Alex's mood seemed a bit lighter this morning, probably in anticipation of our leaving; I sensed he didn't want to linger any longer than necessary. Breakfast went quickly—this morning there was no cosmic conversation, and Eyla seemed intent on getting to her duties around the homestead.

"Has your father come home yet?" I asked her.

"Not yet." She shook her head and pointed to a huge bank of ominous purple thunderheads hanging to the east. "That storm will arrive here in about an hour," she predicted. "Then there's no telling when we will see the sun again today. I need to take Jangmu for her walk before I get to my chores. She has breathing problems, and the doctor says she must get exercise each day."

"Would you like me to walk with her, Eyla?" I offered.

"No, no, I'll take her. I do it every day," she replied hastily, without really considering my suggestion. I guessed that the brunt of the work around the farm fell on her shoulders, and she wasn't used to being offered help . . . or accepting it.

"Really, I'd like to." I tried again. "Then you could get your chores done before it rains."

Eyla scanned me for a moment, as if trying to assess whether I was sincere. "Well, all right, thank you," she finally replied. "Just give her your arm to help her steady herself. Once around the pasture will be fine."

I put on my jacket and extended my arm to Jangmu. She hooked hers in mine, and looked like she was having fun. As we ambled through the yard, I gazed back at Eyla, standing at the door watching us. She seemed aglow with appreciation. As for me, it felt good to help the old woman. For the first time in a long while, I put my own self-involved thoughts aside and took pleasure in making someone else's life easier. Maybe that was the point I'd been missing.

18

The squall rolled in just as Eyla had predicted. If her weather report was correct, we'd be stuck there for at least another day. I began to feel both excited and frightened. Would Eyla become my salvation . . . or my undoing?

We spent the morning around the fireplace trading stories about our lives. Jangmu, I think, had fallen in love with me (in a grandmotherly way) and hung out with us as an uninformed listener. I don't think Alex heard much of our talk; he spent a lot of time gazing out the window, waiting for the rain to quit. But it didn't. Finally he excused himself.

I scanned the photos on the mantel and noticed an attractive Caucasian woman in a long ivory dress. "Is that your mother?" I asked Eyla.

"Yes," she answered. Eyla walked to the fireplace, took the photo in her hand, and gazed at it longingly. "She died in childbirth."

These people have it hard. "I'm sorry."

"She was the daughter of French missionaries. She met my father here, and they were married just a few years before I was born."

Eyla's eyes grew sad. "That's why my father is so protective of me," she added, smoothing out a tiny dog-ear on the photo. "It's as if my mother is still living through me. My dad would probably kill anyone who hurt me."

I readjusted my position on the pillows, hoping Eyla wouldn't pick up on my discomfort.

"What about your family, Linden?" she inquired. "Are you close with them?"

Funny you should ask. "We might as well be from different planets," I answered. "Their lives are all about social status and impressing people. My mom cares about me, but she doesn't really know how to love me. My stepfather was a politician, and he sees life as a big power play."

Eyla listened attentively. "And you, Linden?" she asked. "What do *you* want from life?"

Interesting question, considering where I'm going and why.

"To tell you the truth, Eyla, there isn't that much more I want out of life."

She stared at me for a while, as if piercing into my soul. "You've been hurt, haven't you?"

Busted.

"Me? Why do you say that?" I began to feel fidgety and started to scratch the side of my neck.

"I see a man with a big heart in a lot of pain."

Am I that obvious?

Eyla sat by my side, close enough to make me both tingly and nervous.

"Well, if you must know," I confessed, "I was in love with a woman who left me for someone with more money and material comforts."

Eyla laughed. "Why would you want to be with a person like that?" she asked, as if only an ignoramus wouldn't know the answer.

That would be me.

"That's what I keep asking myself."

"Life is different here, Linden," Eyla said. "If you stayed for any length of time, you would discover riches beyond any you could imagine."

Eyla placed her hand on mine, just as I'd felt it with my eyes closed in bed that morning. But this time it was her real hand, not Alex's or a dream. It felt good. Maybe *too* good.

19

The rain continued through the day, a crucible forcing me to deal with my attraction to Eyla. I'd felt remarkably safe with her in the short time we'd spent together, but that wasn't reason enough to get back on the wheel for further incarnations of suffering. Lama Sherap once said that some single acts create lifetimes of karma; if falling for Eyla would keep me coming back, why go there?

As we were cleaning up after dinner, Eyla called out, "Look, the sunset!" I craned to see out the window toward the west, where the sun, sandwiched in the sliver between the cloud cover and the mountains, projected a stunning palette of pink, amber, and lavender rays over the peaks.

"Would you like to take a walk?" Eyla asked. "There's a spectacular view from the meadow just beyond the house."

Moments later we were striding through high, wet grasses like two kids just out of school. We passed a bevy of small redheaded birds perched on some rhododendrons; they, too, were savoring the moment and providing a loud, gleeful score as an accompaniment to the scene.

Eyla guided me to a large rock, which formed a perfect perch to view the spectacle. I found some dry leaves and whisked off the rock with an elegant flair, as if showing my lady to her seat at the opera. Eyla understood the pantomime and smiled. "Thank you, sir," she responded in a lilting voice, and took her seat with an air of grace.

As twilight began to fall, a few stars revealed themselves, followed gradually by hundreds, and then thousands, more. The sky was clearing, it seemed, especially for us. The moon poked up over the eastern ridge, tucking the valley in for the night with a luminous blanket. The scene was out of a fairy tale. Eyla took a few steps out into the meadow, spread her arms, and breathed deeply, welcoming the crisp evening air and contemplating the concert of wonder before us.

Silently I approached her from behind and placed my hands on her shoulders. For a moment I feared I was being too forward; this was not a woman to touch casually. To my surprise, Eyla lifted one hand and rested it over mine. Her touch was both soothing and electric. I began to feel that motor whirring below my belt. *Watch it, Linden, watch it.*

"It's magnificent, isn't it?" Eyla commented, gazing up at the dome of stars.

"Yes, very," I replied as I leaned my head onto her shoulder and rested my cheek against hers. She received the gesture and offered a small nuzzle. *God, this feels good.*

"Do you think you could ever live in a place like this, Linden?"

I drew a long breath. "I don't know," I answered with a certain regret. "I don't know if I could ever live anywhere."

"Why do you say that?"

"I guess I'm just trying to find myself."

Eyla interlaced her fingers with mine. Her hand was firm yet supple. "That's why you took up Buddhism?"

"Something like that."

"My family is Buddhist," she told me. "My father, his father, his father's father—all the way back for more generations than anyone can count."

That was hard for me to wrap my mind around. But then, my father was an alcoholic. So was his father and his grandfather . . .

all the way back for more generations than anyone could count. Eyla's legacy led her to inner peace. Mine led me to the bridge.

"My religion has taught our family how to escape from the world," she explained. "But you know, Linden, I don't know if this is such a bad place. When I see these stars or a Himalayan sunrise or my little nephew laughing, I think that maybe we are supposed to be here. Maybe the answers to life's questions are not out there somewhere, but right here, with people we love. . . . What do you think?"

Eyla turned and looked up at me. As we found each other's eyes, the electricity between us drew us to each other like a magnet. Sensing her permission, I moved closer and gently pressed my lips to hers. They were moist and welcoming. No lipstick. No perfume. Just pure woman. I wrapped my arms around her shoulders and she enfolded my waist, pressing her full body against mine. *Perfect fit.* I held her so close that I could feel her heart beating. *This is heaven. Please don't let it ever end.*

Suddenly I heard footsteps on the wooden porch outside the house. *Holy shit, her father is home!* I turned to look, and was relieved to see that it was just Alex on his way to the outhouse.

I'll never forget the expression on his face as he saw us kissing—it betrayed shock, embarrassment, disappointment, anger. He stood frozen for a moment and then, visibly shaken, scurried back into the house. Unnerved, I started to run after him.

"What's the matter?" Eyla asked, grabbing my elbow.

"I'm worried about Alex," I told her. "He's like a brother to me. I think he got weirded out."

"Doesn't he want you to be happy?"

"Of course he does. . . . It's just that we're on this—well, sort of mission."

"Mission?"

Okay, spit it out. "We're looking for Mount Lasya. The Cave of Khadroma, where the Lords of Karma live. I must see them."

Eyla looked confused, and the romantic mood dissolved. "You didn't tell me that."

"I didn't want to freak you out. A monk at the monastery said your father would know how to get there."

Eyla took a step back, and the sudden space between us left me feeling terribly hollow. "We all know about the cave."

"So it exists?"

"Yes, it is no myth."

"Will you tell me where it is?" I asked, trying not to seem desperate.

"Why do you want to know?"

Let it rip, Linden. No secrets. "I want to ask the Lords of Karma to make this my last life. I want to leave this world behind forever."

Eyla grew sullen, and her countenance darkened. In a flash, that vibrant, radiant woman became a sad and lonely child. "Why do you want to go?" she asked. "What's wrong with here? With me?"

She's not going to make this easy.

"Nothing, Eyla. Nothing's wrong with here, or you. You're an incredibly beautiful woman, and I'm very tempted to be with you. If I were looking for love, I'd stop right here. But something inside me has changed. I've had love, I've had women, and now I want freedom. I'm ready to graduate."

"Now?" Eyla asked, her body practically shaking. "Right *now?* Why won't you give life just one more chance?"

"The lamas say that liberation cannot be postponed. Either you're ready to leave or you're not."

Eyla looked up at me with those wide, deep eyes, as if to plead, *Please, just let me love you.* But I couldn't. I'd come too far to turn back now. "I'm sorry, Eyla. I have to go on. Will you help me?"

Eyla breathed a long, painful sigh. She turned her back to me and stepped out into the meadow a few paces. She gazed up at the mountains and stars as if she were talking to them—or listening —for a long time. Finally, she turned and said, "All right, if that is what you want. I will show you the way in the morning." Then, brushing away her tears, she dashed back to the house without another glance in my direction.

❋

The next fire to put out was Alex. *Jeez, this business of ending your lives sure raises a lot of issues in people.* I found my friend lying on his bed of pillows, staring at the ceiling, looking almost comatose. I sat by his feet and rested my hand on his ankle. "How ya doin', bud?" I asked, trying to act nonchalant, but failing dismally.

He just kept staring vacuously, his jaw clenched and lips pursed.

"Did it unnerve you to see me with Eyla?"

Alex shrugged his shoulders as if to indicate it didn't matter to him. But it did.

"Look, Alex, I'm sorry if that was weird for you to see," I told him, holding his ankle more firmly to try to communicate my sincerity. "I didn't mean to shock you. I had no idea you would show up at that moment." I leaned closer to see his expression; he refused to make eye contact. "I just feel something for the lady. I haven't been close to a woman in a long time—and, well, I guess my heart is still a little broken. You can understand, can't you? Have you ever had your heart broken?"

That got his attention. Alex lifted his head and nodded as if the experience was fresh to him.

"Okay, so you understand," I told him, hoping my apology would comfort him. Still, he didn't look like a happy camper. "Look, in case you're wondering, nothing else happened between Eyla and me. Just a kiss. And nothing else will. I can't turn back now. You and me are on a mission—you know, like *The Blues Brothers:* 'We're on a mission from God.'"

When Alex heard my crappy Dan Aykroyd imitation, he laughed and looked relieved. I felt better knowing he was okay. I couldn't hurt my little brother. It just wouldn't have been right.

20

At first light, Alex and I readied our packs for the difficult journey ahead of us. Still shell-shocked from the previous night's melodrama, I cast open the front door and tried to clear my head with several long, deep breaths of crisp Himalayan air. Yet I couldn't erase the haunting images of Eyla's crestfallen countenance or Alex's stoically clenched chin. *Has any human being escaped the complications of love?*

I turned back for a last look at the interior of the unpretentious home that had afforded such warmth and comfort. Within minutes, ease would be a relic of history, along with my self-aborted romance. I couldn't imagine asking the Lords of Karma to end all of my lifetimes and adding, *By the way, just one more fling on my way out.* Besides, it wasn't fair to Eyla. I cared about her and didn't want to tease her with an affair that was doomed before it began.

"Here is your map, Linden," Eyla remarked as she entered the kitchen, trying to be cheerful, yet her eyes betraying sadness. In her hand she held a blackened piece of paper with gold lettering. I'd seen parchments like this before at the dharma center. The paper was coated with arsenic to keep it from deteriorating, and it was inscribed with gold ink. Eyla unrolled the map on the counter, revealing the secret route to the home of the gods.

"Start from the top of that hill," she instructed, pointing out the window. Alex and I craned our necks to assess the slope; it was rocky, steep, and slick from the previous night's downpour. Maybe 500 feet uphill I could make out a small stone structure.

"At the foot of the Buddha you will see a path," Eyla went on. "It may be difficult to follow at points since the terrain is so desolate. But you will find a rock painted white every few hundred meters should you lose your way. Pay strict attention and you will not get lost."

This could be harder than I thought.

"The ascent will be steep at first, but then the path will take you down into a valley that is lush due to the river that passes through it, engorged with runoff from melted snow. If it is too high to cross, you may have to swim. The water is very cold."

My scrotum started to shrivel just thinking about it.

"On the other side of the river is Tibet. Turn north and hike along the riverbank for about five kilometers until you see a small bridge." Eyla traced her index finger several times over the bridge on the map. "That is the border-patrol station. There you will have to swim again, under the bridge, so the soldiers do not see you. If they do, they will fire on you without any questions."

I looked at Alex, who had inserted his head between us, intent on hearing every word. He was starting to look scared.

"Can't we just stay on this side of the river?" I pleaded.

Eyla shook her head. "The rocks are sheer on this side. There is no place to walk or hold on."

I should have done the ropes course in high school.

"If you make it past the guards, no one will bother you, except maybe snakes or wild boar." Eyla handed me a long, shiny, sharp knife, its handle wrapped in leather.

"Do you really think I'll need this?" I asked, hoping she would break into laughter and confess it was all a joke.

She didn't.

"Maybe, maybe not," she answered, dead serious. "How do you say it? 'Better safe than sorry.'"

Yes, Eyla, that's how you say it.

"If a boar attacks, do not run or it will overtake you and maul you in seconds. Their tusks are a meter long and can easily pierce through cowhide. Instead, stand your ground, and when the beast gets close enough, thrust the knife into its heart. If you miss, it will retain the strength to kill you."

Easy enough, right? Alex was practically quaking. "And the snakes?"

"The knife will not help you with cobras," she explained. "Cobras can smell feelings. If they sense you are afraid, they will strike before you have a chance to defend yourself. Your only protection against a cobra is fearlessness."

I didn't tell her that I always closed my eyes during the snake scenes in *Indiana Jones*.

Eyla leaned in and smoothed the map out. As her face drew close to mine, I wanted to touch my cheek to hers, feel her essence one more time, and give myself a reprieve from the potential horrors that lay ahead. But instead I restrained myself—probably a wise move, considering the agonizing road we'd walked down less than twelve hours earlier.

"The trail will elevate to a ridge," she continued in the forthright tone of a general preparing troops for battle. "After a few kilometers you will come to a rope bridge. This is very old, made of vines and loose boards. Be extremely careful as you cross, and hold on to the railing. Don't shake the bridge, and don't look down. The bridge can hold no more than one person at a time, so do not try to cross together."

I shook my head. Was any of this true? *Maybe she's trying to keep me from leaving—or taking revenge on me for blowing her off.* But the candor in her eyes allayed my suspicions; manipulation was not in Eyla's emotional vocabulary.

"The trail after the bridge will lead you to a circle of seven large stones," she went on. "From that point the summit of Mount Lasya will be in plain view. It is higher than any other mountain in the range."

"Like, how high?"

"Five thousand meters above sea level."

I did a quick calculation in my head—about 16,000 feet. My heart sank. Eyla sensed my frustration.

"But the Cave of Khadroma is not that high," she added mercifully. "Its altitude is perhaps one kilometer above the point where you will first observe the mountain."

Okay, doable.

"How will I find the cave?"

Eyla stepped back from the map and faced us. "Camp overnight near the stone circle. Be sure to be awake before sunrise three mornings from now—the summer solstice. As soon as you sense daylight approaching, stand in the center of the circle and look westward. Behind you the sun will rise between two small peaks very close together. At precisely sunrise, the sun will cast a single ray between the two peaks. Watch carefully where that ray lands on Mount Lasya. That is the exact location of the Cave of Khadroma."

The book said nothing about this.

"Is the cave, like, open and obvious?" I asked, impatient with all the obstacles Eyla had called to our attention.

"A large boulder obscures the entrance to keep the site secret. Mark the rock in your mind before you begin your ascent or else you will not be able to find the cave once you are up on the mountain."

I scratched my head. "And am I supposed to *move* the boulder to get into the cave?"

Eyla took my sarcastic question seriously. "No, that would be impossible. When you reach the boulder, you will see a thin passageway behind it. The opening is invisible until you arrive at that spot."

"Hell, I should have just jumped," I muttered under my breath.

"What?" she asked.

"Nothing," I answered, trying to fathom her dark eyes and wondering if I was crazy.

21

By the time we reached the summit of the first hill, Alex and I were gasping in the thin air. Sure enough, we found a small stone shelter, maybe four feet high, encasing a weathered Buddha. Attached to the primitive shrine we saw a string of flags containing faded prayers etched by those who'd passed this site before us. As the colorful pieces of cloth flapped in the wind, I wondered how many of those pilgrims had their prayers answered—and how many had returned.

I looked down at Eyla's house, miniature now in the distance, and was tempted to turn back. *Am I trading the love of an exceptional woman for a fool's journey?*

"What do you think?" I asked Alex, knowing he wouldn't answer. The kid had become a sort of silent therapist for me. I would think out loud or ask him a question, and in the quiet that followed I would work things out in my mind. "Would a woman distract me from my true purpose, or would she help me fulfill it?"

Alex gave me a long, poignant look, as if I'd hit a nerve equally sensitive to him. Then he averted his eyes and grew still as if he were listening intently inside himself. *Will* this *get him to talk?* Instead, he turned, wrinkled his forehead, and stared back toward Eyla's house. *Is he chickening out? Telling me I would be better off staying?*

Neither, it turned out. In the distance I detected the faint sound of a motor. Over the next minute its volume increased, as if a vehicle were approaching. I thought it was a truck, but there were no roads nearby. The sound grew louder and more rhythmic: *beat-a-beat-a-beat-a-beat-a-beat.* We scanned the distance to the farm. No vehicles in sight.

Suddenly we were accosted by a bizarre and disturbing sight: a helicopter was rising up over a ridge to the south. Like a behemoth surfacing from the depths of the sea, the beast crested the ridge, headed in our direction. *"What the hell . . . ?"* I called to Alex. Just as baffled as I was, he made a confused face, and we both kept watching warily.

As the chopper cut its way toward Eyla's house, she and her grandmother emerged from the shanty, searching the sky. The craft zeroed in on the farmhouse and hovered over it for a minute. It was a dark green American military helicopter with a bold five-pointed star emblazoned on the side. I shuddered as I remembered seeing films of exactly such choppers dumping Agent Orange on defenseless Vietnamese villages, immersing innocent people in billowing curtains of flames.

The khaki monster slowly set down in the field near the house, and two figures stepped out. They approached Eyla and Jangmu, and from the tiny bit I could tell at a distance, began to have an animated conversation. It didn't last long, and ended when Eyla shook her head repeatedly. Finally, the two figures dashed back to the helicopter. Quickly it rose as intently as it had landed.

Alex and I shot each other questioning glances. *Could this have something to do with us? Has the U.S. military somehow gotten wind of our illegal border crossing, and they are trying to intercept us?* No, I reasoned, they don't care about us or the Chinese border that much. No matter their motive, their presence here was not a good sign. We started to hurry down the path.

When the chopper's roar grew louder, we picked up speed. I inadvertently kicked a large rock, jamming my foot. Alex was having just as hard a time and tripped, scraping the side of his face. Running as fast as I could, I looked over my shoulder and saw the helicopter gaining on us. Completely exposed in the rocky Himalayan wasteland, we had no place to hide; it was only a matter of moments until they would be on top of us.

When I felt the wind from the blades blowing my hair, I knew we were sitting ducks. With my heart pounding wildly and every muscle in my body straining to escape, I looked down the trail and spied a fissure in the side of the mountain. If we could get into it, perhaps it would lead to a better-concealed hiding place that the chopper couldn't penetrate. It was our only chance.

I bolted for the opening, Alex beside me, the copter zeroing in on us rapidly. *Jesus, I'm sure they have guns and could fire on us.* But they didn't. They just closed in until the sound of the whirring blades was deafening and the tiny stones on the ground blew in all directions.

Alex and I made it into the fissure, only to find that it butted up against a wall of sheer rock, with no exit in any direction. We were trapped.

22

"You don't need to run," a man's voice boomed over a bullhorn. "We won't hurt you."

I looked at a petrified Alex, his cheek stained with fresh blood from his fall.

"Please step forward," the voice called again.

We turned to see the chopper hovering just above the barren ground, about to set down. I could make out at least two figures through the windshield.

With no other choice, we turned and cautiously stepped out of the fissure. The craft had landed and the blades were winding down, along with the deafening noise and wind. The side door rolled open, and a young black soldier emerged, training a rifle on us. My body quivered and my head throbbed. An older man in civilian clothes followed the soldier; he wore dark slacks, a white short-sleeved shirt, and reflector sunglasses. Another soldier followed him, carrying a thick silver box about two feet square. The three marched toward us.

"Are you Linden?" the non-uniformed guy called out, removing his shades. He was stiff-looking and partially bald, fortyish, with small dark eyes and sallow skin.

I nodded cautiously.

"I'm Dennis Royson, consul at the American Embassy in New Delhi," he shouted. The sound of the chopper blades had died down enough for him to lower the bullhorn.

I shot Alex another wary look. Royson motioned to the soldier to lower his weapon, and I released my held breath. Meanwhile, the second soldier began to open the silver box. Slowly we stepped forward. When we were close enough, Royson extended his hand and offered me a weak handshake.

"Your stepfather phoned us and told us you might be in danger of hurting yourself. He and your mother are very concerned about you, and asked us to intercept you."

Unbelievable. *Un-be-fucking-lievable.*

I looked over at Alex again. He was as shocked as I was.

"How are we doing with the sat phone, Harbuck?" Royson asked over his shoulder.

"Almost ready, sir," the soldier called back, raising a long silver antenna.

"It'll be just a moment," Royson told me almost apologetically. The soldier with the rifle stood off to the side, watching with consternation.

"Okay, sir," Harbuck called back moments later. "We're operational."

Royson nodded, and Harbuck moved the unit toward me, handing me a telephone receiver. I examined it for a few moments as if it were a Trojan horse. Finally I held it to my ear.

"Hello?"

"Oh, Linden, Linden, I'm so glad we found you!" I heard my mother's voice blurt out with her signature histrionics. "We were so worried about you."

This cannot be happening. Not really.

"What in God's name are you doing there?" Bill called out in a castigating tone through the speakerphone.

"Now, Bill, don't be hard on the boy," my mom chided. "We're just glad to hear his voice."

Okay, then, I'll let them hear it: "ARE YOU BOTH FUCKING CRAZY? HOW THE HELL DID YOU FIND ME HERE?"

"I still have some friends in the State Department," Bill answered smugly, oblivious to my yelling. "I made a few calls."

The story of his life. "Did you, like, plant some kind of homing device on me?"

Royson, realizing the conversation was getting personal, respectfully moved away toward the cliff, followed by the pilot. The soldier with the rifle stepped back with the others, but kept his eye on us.

"When we didn't hear from you for a few months, we got worried," my mother explained. "We called that place you were staying and asked them where you were."

"And you got their number *how?*"

"Caller ID the last time you phoned us," Bill explained proudly.

I never should have called them.

"The rabbi there, or priest, or whatever you call him—"

"*Lama,* Mom—he's called a 'lama.'" I shook my head indignantly as Alex looked on. I thought I could detect a faint smile even in his bewilderment. I tilted the earpiece so he could hear.

"That's right," my mom answered, "the *lama* told us you went to India, and he gave us the number of the place you were staying. . . . Did you see the Dalai Lama? I saw him on *Larry King.*"

Now I remember why I want nothing to do with these people. I kicked the dirt at my feet. "And they told you where I was?" I asked, astounded that the dharma center would betray me.

"Well, they didn't want to, but when I told them I was having heart surgery . . ."

"You're having heart surgery?!"

"Well, not exactly. But I have been having some heartburn."

Another lie. *Some things never change.*

"Is it true that you're trying to kill yourself?" Bill asked angrily.

Way to go, Bill. Anger always encourages someone to live.

"Jesus Christ, did he tell you that, too?" I asked, completely pissed.

"He told us some cockamamy story about you ending all of your lives," Bill followed. "What the hell is going on with you?"

I have no patience for these people. I never did. "What is going on with me is that I am sick and tired of living the way I have been. If this is life, then I want out."

Alex huddled closer to me, straining to hear my parents' end of the conversation. Of all the crazy shit they'd ever pulled, this was the *pièce de résistance*.

"But darling," my mother came back, sweet as honey. "You have so much to live for."

"*Now* you tell me?" I shot back snidely. "Where were you when I was growing up, Mother? At mah-jongg games and the mall. You looked the other way when I started smoking pot and snorting coke—but you knew. Why didn't you ask me how I was doing *then*? Where was your 'life is beautiful' rap when I was booked for shoplifting? Were you too busy to visit me in juvenile detention? And where was your charming hospitality when I was picking half-eaten sandwiches out of trash cans in the Haight? No, Mother dear, don't you think it's a bit late to start caring about me? For thirty-three years I've been a burden, a distraction; and now that I'm on my way out, suddenly I'm precious. Get over it. You had your chance."

"Just hang up, Madeline," Bill snorted. "If he wants to kill himself, let him."

"No!" she yelled, tears in her voice. "He's still my baby. I want him to live!"

That got to me a little. I could tell she meant it.

I looked over at Royson, standing at the edge of the cliff, smoking a cigarette. I guessed that dramas were a daily regimen for him.

"Come home, Linden, please," my mother begged. "You can stay with us and use our car."

That got Bill's dander up. "I'm not lending him the Beemer!" he blurted out.

"Of course not!" I yelled. "You hunt me down halfway around the world with a military task force to rescue my butt, but when it comes to lending me your precious wheels, you waffle. Well, fuck you, fuck your car, and fuck your life. You wrecked my life—now deal with your own!"

I tossed the receiver onto the ground, grabbed Alex's arm, and marched toward the trail. Royson had heard me yelling and dashed back to the phone. He picked up the receiver and began conversing with Bill. For a moment I got scared and thought the soldier might fire on me, but at that point I was so angry I didn't care. When we reached the trail, I looked back to see Royson, shrugging his shoulders, speaking in loud tones to Bill. While I couldn't hear his words, I could guess what he was saying: *I've done what I can. My hands are tied.*

We just kept walking.

23

"Sorry you had to see that ridiculous display," I blurted out to Alex as soon as we were out of sight of the goons. I was still pretty riled up. "My real father drank himself to oblivion and left our family in shameful debt. Every day when I came home from school, I found my mother lying in her bed, staring into space with a pile of dirty tissues on the floor next to her."

My sidekick listened attentively.

"Bill was my mother's knight on a white horse. She heard rumors that he was under investigation for accepting kickbacks, but she figured he could provide a stable home for her and her son, so she took what she could get."

I could hear the chopper starting to whir and lift off. Alex seemed more interested in my account.

"Mom feels so beholden to Bill for rescuing her that she's afraid to speak up. She won't even say where she wants to go for dinner—and they eat out almost every night. She's terrified that Bill will dump her back in poverty, so she lets him make every decision for her. But her elegant lifestyle has cost her her voice."

The helicopter motor grew louder, and we both stopped and scanned the sky to see if it would pursue us again. When the volume diminished, we knew it was on its way back to New Delhi.

"I don't know, Alex," I said. "Maybe my mom made the best move she could, considering what she went through. At least she has a comfortable life now. But I can't believe that a marriage is worth losing your soul."

24

The eerie morning fog kept us from seeing more than a few steps in front of us. We had no idea if we were approaching solid ground or a thousand-foot drop. At one point the mist lifted like a curtain rising in a colossal theater, affording us staggering vistas of snow-capped peaks we could practically touch. Then, just as quickly, the shroud closed in again. Here was a land rife with contrasts: danger and allure; heady, intoxicating beauty and rugged endurance; the presence of God and utter abandonment.

As the light fell briefly on Alex's face, I noticed how fair his skin was; he was even younger than I'd thought. Quite the enigma, this young man who'd worn a sacred purple robe when I met him and now baggy hip-hop jeans and a long, loose shirt. Why was he such a devoted friend to someone he hardly knew? Was he living his own quest vicariously through me? Or was he still waiting for me to have feelings for him? Whatever his motivation, he was upending my belief that everyone I'd ever known had let me down.

As we continued uphill, the air thinned even more, and my years of smoking pot and cigarettes compounded my hunger for oxygen. Just as I was about to peter out, we arrived at a summit where we spied the river deep in the valley before us. "Yes!" I shouted, thrusting my hand toward Alex for a jubilant high five.

The descent was easy at first, with no vegetation, only small craggy stones everywhere we looked. But as we approached the river at a lower altitude, the brush thickened. At some point we lost the trail and had to grab on to gnarly tree trunks and branches to keep from slipping down the embankment. It must have taken us an hour to get to the bottom.

When we reached the river, it was swollen and raging, rushing in torrents from distant peaks. To make matters worse, the recent rains had kicked up a huge volume of dirt and debris, turning the water murky brown. There was no way we were going to get across easily, if at all. I wondered if we should wait for the waters to subside—but we needed to be in view of the cave at dawn on the solstice. If we missed that crucial sunrise, our chances of finding the cave were slim to none.

I looked around for a fallen branch thick and long enough to help us steady each other for the crossing, but there was none in sight. Alex walked ahead while I poked through the bushes. After ten minutes I saw him motioning toward a bend slightly upriver that was thinner and dotted with boulders. We might be able to get across by grasping on to the huge rocks one at a time. It seemed like our only chance.

When we reached the bend, my heart sank. The boulders were farther apart than they had appeared at a distance. There was no way either of us could ford between the rocks without being swept away. Alex, however, was undaunted. He reached into his pack and came up with a maroon cloth belt, maybe five feet long, the kind the monks wrapped around their waists for ceremonies. I understood Alex's plan: We would hold on to each other with the belt while one person at a time made his way to the next rock. If the person trudging through the water lost his footing, the one holding on to the rock would secure him with the belt. *Risky, but it could work.*

My mind flashed to the night I stood on the Golden Gate Bridge gazing down at the churning waters of San Francisco Bay. Had my intention to drown myself led to *this* watery grave? But that wouldn't have been graduating, and I didn't want to have to come back and start over. I was also concerned about Alex; I had enough karma to pay off without an angel's blood on my hands.

We tightened our packs so they would rest high on our backs and tied the maroon belt to each of our right wrists, leaving as much length as we could between us. When we felt confident that the knots were secure, we stood streamside, and I said my own rendition of a prayer: *If You're up there anywhere, by any name, please give us a hand now.*

I stepped into the river first. *"Aaaaoooohhhhhh!"* I screamed so loud that the cry reverberated across the valley. If the current didn't drown us, the temperature would freeze us. I forced myself to resolve that this would be over in just a few minutes—one way or another.

The first boulder, about five feet from the bank, was fairly easy to reach. I got a decent grip on a rough handhold and signaled to Alex that it was safe for him to cross. I held firmly to the belt, and Alex stepped across as nimbly as I had. The current wasn't a big factor at this shallow point.

The next rock was harder to get to but doable. The river deepened there, and the force of the current increased, the roar of rushing water almost deafening; if I yelled to Alex, he wouldn't hear me. To make matters worse, underwater rocks impeded my footing. But I took my time and regained it, landing with a calculated fall against the next rock. Alex followed, and I pulled him with the belt. Being smaller and weaker, he had difficulty bucking the current, but the belt plan was working. The little guy looked scared but determined.

When we arrived midstream, the story changed. The distance between the rocks was about eight feet; between them was the deepest and most tumultuous current in the river. Rain began to fall, thickening until it dropped a gray curtain between us and our goal. I tried to see how we might turn around, but at that point backtracking would have been nearly as hard as forging ahead. I looked at Alex and asked him, "Ready?" He nodded.

The moment I stepped into the current, my feet started to sweep out from under me. I gripped the belt tighter and worked my hand up to cut down the length I was holding, which secured me just enough to regain my footing. I eyed the boulder, now about five feet away. I couldn't possibly traverse the distance and still remain connected to Alex. An idea came to me: if I tied the belt onto my foot, its length, combined with that of my body, would give me the span I needed to grasp the next boulder. I worked my way back to Alex and began to untie the sash. His face contorted in fear, as he assumed I was going to try to swim without the belt, which would have been suicide. I pointed to my foot and then, holding on to the rock as well as I could, transferred the knotted loop to my right ankle. Alex seemed to understand the plan, but eyed my effort with mistrust.

I stepped into center stream again and made my way to the farthest point I'd reached on the last pass. The boulder I was aiming for was slick with rain, falling more densely now. I shot a look back at Alex as he grasped tightly to the rock; he nodded as if to give me the green light.

Okay, this is it. Without giving myself another moment to think or bail, I took a shaky step and lurched for the boulder. Instantly my body was sucked into the stream. The weight of the pack on my back pressed me down so hard that I had to fight to keep my head above water. When I did go under, the vicious current tried to drag me away, but I managed to come up for air and fight my way through the torrent just enough to place me within reach of the boulder. I stretched to grab it, my head rapidly sinking and then rising above the waterline. I couldn't spot where any possible handholds were, and had to feel around for them like a blind man. The current continued to pull at me with a vengeance. But I'd managed enough of a hold to stabilize myself.

Then I felt a horrible sensation—the pressure on the belt connecting me to Alex gave way. *Oh God, did he lose his footing and get swept away?* As quickly as possible, I stood up, clinging dearly to the rock, peering through the raindrops to see what had happened. If he were hurt, I would never forgive myself.

It was nearly impossible to see through the thicket of rain, now coming down in sheets. But there, to my relief, I could make out Alex's form still holding firmly to the last boulder. The belt hadn't been long enough for him to cling to the stone and give me enough lead to reach the next one. If he'd held on, I would have been hanging by a thread going downstream, and likely would have dragged him with me. So he had to let me go. *Now how is he going to get across?*

I stooped and untied the sash from my ankle. Then I loosened my belt and pulled it out of the loops in my jeans. I tied the maroon cloth to my belt buckle, increasing the total length by about three feet, just enough to get Alex across. But I still had to figure out how to transfer the line to him.

I reached into my pack, seeking some weighty object. The heaviest thing I could find was a small hardback book of the sayings of Buddha. I hoped I wouldn't offend the Enlightened One by using his book for a sacrilegious purpose, but then I figured that saving my best friend's life wasn't sacrilegious at all.

I tied the belt around the book until I was satisfied it would hold. Somehow my vision pierced through the rain, and I found Alex's eyes. He studied my position and nodded as if he understood my plan. He leaned as far as he could toward me, one arm on the rock and one arm extended to receive the tossed book.

Okay, here goes. With all my might I flung the book across the gap, followed by the ribbon of the maroon and leather belts.

Alex strained to grab the book with his fingertips. He caught it and pulled it to him, dislodged it, and let it go downstream. Then he tied the belt to his wrist. I redoubled my grip and motioned for him to come. He took another step toward me, as far as the riverbed would support him. Then, like me, he had no choice but to lurch forward. But there was another factor I hadn't figured in: Alex was considerably shorter than I was—I could keep my head above water until the final stretch; he couldn't. He was also weaker. It had taken all my strength to fight the current; he had far less. He tried to take one more step and lost his footing.

God, no! In an unforgiving instant, the river began to carry poor Alex downstream. In a heartbeat he was at the length of the makeshift rope, gasping for air. With no time to waste, I leaned with the bulk of my body against the boulder, facing downstream, and tried to pull Alex in. *If I ever needed help from above, this was it.*

The next thirty seconds felt like hours. I had to keep shifting my balance against the rock to stay at its center; if I leaned too far to one side or the other, the river would have sucked me in and that would have been the end of the story. Using all my strength—and then some—I began to pull Alex inch by inch toward me. Gradually the distance between us shrank, and I was able to draw him within reach. As soon as I could grab him, I lifted him to the highest point on the rock to give him a chance to breathe. He was sputtering and coughing, his face blanched and his poor body frozen. *I never should have brought this innocent kid with me. He doesn't deserve this.*

A minute later he calmed down and a bit of color flowed into his cheeks, his shaved head lying against the cold, wet rock. I managed to pull myself to the top of the boulder to steady him. Then I reached into my pack and found a T-shirt that had remained dry in the middle of the other soaked garments, and clumsily wrapped it around his head to try to keep any more heat from escaping his body.

After a few minutes, he looked better. When he seemed to recover his strength, he sat up, looking quite disoriented, his face still drained and his chest heaving. After a while he indicated he was ready to finish the crossing.

With Alex leaning against me, I slid off the rock and we began to forge on. Fortunately, the remaining boulders in the shallower water were easier to negotiate, and minutes later we were ashore.

We dropped onto the bank together, exhausted. When I regained some energy, I dragged him away from the river to a sheltered spot under a thicket and covered him with my sleeping bag. I leaned over him, my chin quivering. "I'm sorry, Alex," I told him. "I'm sorry I brought you here. This is crazy. It's not your fault, and this has nothing to do with you. Please forgive me. If we get out of this alive and there is anything I can ever do to make it up to you, I will."

Spent, Alex forced a small nod. Then he crashed.

25

By sunset I realized that Alex was down for the count, so I rolled out his sleeping bag and guided him into it. Then I slipped into mine, monitoring him until it was too dark to see. He looked better, but he would need a good night's sleep before we could continue our trek.

Soon after nightfall, I started hearing noises in the woods—boars rustling and cobras slithering through my mind. I jumped up half a dozen times and did a 360-degree sweep with the dim light of a candle. Negative. For insurance, I took my knife into the sleeping bag—not that it would save me from a cobra if one found its way in. It just made me feel safer. But it didn't save me from dreaming of wild wolves dragging me into their den and ripping me to shreds. It wasn't my most restful night.

❀

When the symphony of birds woke me at dawn, I looked over at Alex to find him sitting up. I was relieved to see that color had returned to his cheeks and his eyes no longer looked glazed over. We opened our stash of Tibetan flatbread and took out a clump of yak cheese Eyla had packed for us, as well as berries we'd picked along the way. We'd intended to ration our food to make it last over the whole journey, but we were really hungry and consumed a lot of it right there.

Soon we were on our way upstream, trudging on a bank between the river and the forest that afforded us a tiny ribbon of soggy but level ground. Now it was a test of endurance. Trees, rocks, water, and mud. Trees, rocks, water, and mud. At one point I spied a small herd of wild boars rooting high on the hillside, and I froze. One of them looked in my direction for a moment, but then turned back to his meal. Quietly we continued, praying they would take no further notice of us. I didn't feel safe until we'd put a good distance between us and them.

An hour later we caught sight of the border bridge. Sure enough, we spied a small guard station on the Tibetan side of the river. A couple of khaki-uniformed soldiers with rifles stood outside the shack smoking, talking casually, and intermittently gazing up and down the river.

Squatting behind some bushes, we tried to figure the best way to negotiate the bridge. For the next fifteen minutes we kept our eyes on the black-and-yellow-striped gate hanging across the road, which wasn't raised to admit even one car during the time we observed; it was obviously a low-traffic crossing. This gave the soldiers more time to watch the river and likely see us if we were exposed. "What do you think?" I asked Alex.

He shook his head, agreeing with my assessment of the danger. We crouched there for a while, scanning for other possible routes. None revealed themselves, until we heard a car approaching from a distance up road on the Chinese side of the bridge and caught a glimpse of it through the thicket. Here was our clue: if we forged our way through the brush rather than swimming under the bridge, we could reach a section of the road out of sight of the guards, and cross it. Then we could double back through the woods to the river on the other side of the guard station, and continue our trek. Simple and easy enough—assuming no more cars showed up while we crossed.

As quietly as possible we cut through the forest, praying to avoid any unfriendly critters. But it was too late to worry about that now. This whole adventure was founded on conviction . . . or insanity—and in either case, chickening out was no longer an option.

A minute later we spied the road and determined the shortest crossing point. The clearing between the forest and road would cost us maybe thirty seconds of exposure; in the open we would be easy targets. A curve just before the clearing limited our sight distance for approaching vehicles.

We stooped at the edge of the woods and positioned ourselves for our dash. I looked at Alex and asked, "Ready?"

He nodded. I started to count just loud enough for him to hear: "One . . . two . . ."

Just as I was about to mouth "three," we heard a car engine. *No way, the chances are infinitesimal.* The moment I heard the sound, I thrust my arm roughly across Alex's chest to stop him from bolting, which spooked him, as he had started his run. He retreated, and we breathlessly held our position.

Moments later a red Toyota van pulled around the curve, driven by a Chinese woman with short hair, probably in her midthirties. We could make out a small tot in the rear seat. The van slowed as it approached our hiding place and halted a short distance up the road from us. The driver door opened, and the woman emerged. She was nicely dressed in a blue jacket with gold embroidery and sported several flashy bracelets on both wrists. Alex and I shot each other a look of relief. If we'd made our break, she would certainly have seen us and alerted the guards, who would have found us in a matter of minutes and—if reports were accurate—forgone diplomacy in favor of their weapons.

But the woman gave no indication of seeing us. Instead, she walked to the van's side panel and opened it for her child, a little boy of three or so with a Buster Brown haircut, dressed in an Osh-Kosh-like coverall. As the woman slid the door open, I could see an array of garments on hangers in the back; I guessed she was a clothing merchant who did business across the border.

The mother pointed to the bushes, right where we were. *We're done for.* But why, if she'd discovered intruders, would she expose her kid to us? The boy bounded out of the van and dashed straight toward us, followed by his mom. I looked at Alex, baffled.

The mystery was solved when the woman led the boy to a spot just on the other side of the trees in front of us and took down his coveralls, encouraging him to do his business before they crossed the border. I tried to suck in my gut and make myself invisible, hoping they would finish up without incident. It worked.

After the operation was completed, Mom leaned over to help Junior button up, and she casually cast a glance our way.

"*Ayyyyeeeeee!*" she screamed horribly loudly. The woman frantically grabbed her son and dragged him, pants still down, across the grassy area. If you subtracted our predicament from the scenario, the movie would have been pretty funny. But we weren't laughing. We knew exactly what would happen: she would report us to the border guards a hundred yards down the road, they would rush out with dogs and guns, and within minutes we would be prisoners or corpses.

Then Alex did something astonishing: he bolted toward the woman, who was now tossing her half-pantsed son in the backseat and making her own dash for the driver's door. By the time Alex reached the car, she'd turned on the motor and was putting the van in gear to speed off. My first impulse was to make a run for it, grab Alex, and dash for the bushes on the other side of the road. Yet something told me to just stay put.

I watched incredulously as Alex positioned himself in front of the van and placed his hands in a prayer position. *Is he crazy?* I feared the driver would run him over, but she slammed on the brakes and stopped short right in front of him. Yet he remained steadfast. I could hear the woman yelling out her window at him in Chinese. Slowly Alex walked to her window and gave her a long and respectful bow. *What the hell is he up to?* The woman continued to chatter, her voice lower now.

Alex reached into his backpack and pulled out his monk's robe and sash. He was identifying himself as a monk. When the woman saw the attire, she calmed down a bit. Then something amazing happened: A conversation ensued. *Alex was speaking.*

As I observed his hand motions, I guessed that he was explaining he was on a pilgrimage, pleading with her not to turn him in. The woman apparently hadn't seen me, and for all she knew, Alex was alone. A moment later he pointed to the backseat, where the woman turned and reached into a cardboard box, bringing forth a small hand-operated machine that made impressions of credit cards. She looked at him questioningly.

Then Alex did one of the most brilliant things I'd ever seen anyone do, in this life or in as many lives as I might live: *he reached into his backpack and pulled out his MasterCard.*

"Holy shit," I whispered aloud. "The kid is a genius!"

He waved the card in front of the woman and got her further attention. Then he held up some fingers indicating a number, and she held up hers indicating another. Soon it was obvious what was happening: *they were bargaining.* After a minute the woman nodded, stepped out of the van, and set up the machine on the hood. Right there before my eyes, Alex was buying our freedom with plastic. I wouldn't have believed it if I hadn't seen it. After she ran the card, she handed Alex a pen to sign with and then tore off a receipt.

The deed done, the businesswoman flashed Alex a quick smile, and soon the van moved along the road. As soon as the vehicle was out of sight, Alex gestured *Come on!* to me, and we made a wild sprint across the road until we were hidden in the bushes again.

I turned to Alex and high-fived, then high-tenned, him. "Man, you're a wizard!" I told him. "I never would have thought of that!"

He just giggled.

"How much did you settle for?" I asked.

He traced a 1 and two 0s in the air.

"A hundred bucks?"

He nodded.

"Not bad," I agreed. "Hey, how come you broke your vow and talked to that lady, but you never talk to me or anyone else?"

Alex just shrugged and cocked his head as if to say, *Well, you gotta do what you gotta do.*

I figured that if we ever made it back to civilization, I'd write to MasterCard and tell them to add "illegal border crossing" to their list of all the things that money can buy.

26

Eyla wasn't kidding about the rope bridge. When we reached the chasm the next morning, we found a primitive suspension fabricated of heavy vines and flimsy boards. As I leaned over the edge of a gorge perhaps 150 feet deep, then looked up at the shaky apparatus, my stomach went hollow. Many of the long vine rails were rotted from the brutal wind, rain, and sun; rodents had chewed others. The "floor" was a string of rough-hewn planks cut from nearby trees; their integrity was highly questionable. A number of boards were missing, leaving gaps not impassably wide, but affording frightening views straight down to the rocks and rapids below.

We remembered Eyla's advice that only one person should cross at a time. When Alex offered to go first, a wave of guilt began to overtake me. He'd sacrificed so much for me, and I'd done so little for him.

"No, I'll go!" I told him self-righteously. I recognized later that my sensibilities had been compromised by fatigue, hunger, and exposure to the elements. But at the moment my upset seemed justified.

As Alex shook his head and stepped out onto the bridge, I grabbed him by the shoulders, pulled him back, and shook him, almost violently. "I *said* I would go first!" I shouted. "Why are you so good to me?! You make me feel like some kind of coward!" I kept shaking Alex to the point that it scared both of us; more and I might have hurt him.

Finally, Alex broke into tears. I'll never forget the look in his eyes—although I wish I could. Terrible sadness, disappointment, and confusion. Here he'd been the perfect companion, rescuing me physically at half a dozen turns and emotionally a hundred times more, and I returned his kindness with venom. I felt horrible.

I realized I'd gone crazy, and I caught myself. I stopped shaking him, and I told him, "I'm sorry, Alex. I don't know why I did that. You're the best friend I've ever had; I shouldn't treat you like this."

I pulled him close to me, and he buried his head in my chest, sobbing. By that time I felt so bad that I wanted to jump. But I kept my wits about me and just held Alex until we'd both calmed down. After a while he glanced up at me. His eyes were still wet, but he looked better. I believed he forgave me.

I turned and faced the bridge, taking a deep breath and forcing myself not to look down. I leaned my weight onto the first plank, clutching the rail. It held. *Okay, not so bad. Maybe I can do this.* I was tempted to turn and look back at Alex, but only unwavering focus would carry me through this. Another step. *Okay.* And another. And another. *So far, so good.*

A minute later I reached the middle of the bridge. The suspension was the weakest at this point and the bridge most wobbly. Suddenly a gust of wind rushed through the valley, shaking the bridge so much that I thought it would surely snap.

Too scared to move forward or backward, I froze. I couldn't even turn my head. I'd heard about people having panic attacks; now I was in the midst of one. My knees locked, my jaw tightened, and the taste of fear infiltrated my mouth. I closed my eyes and expected to just stand there forever.

I don't know how long I stood there, petrified; time has a way of playing with your head when fear has commandeered your soul.

Yet eventually I knew I had to move. I felt a wave of energy from behind me, as if Alex was sending me encouragement to know that I could do it. *Maybe I can.*

I took a step. *Okay, that's good.* Then another. *You're not falling, Linden. The bridge is holding you. Maybe it will continue to support you. Just keep going.* Small step . . . another . . . and another. After a while, the far side of the bridge, which had seemed miles away, now appeared within reach. The closer I got to the last plank, the easier it became and the faster I moved. Moments later I placed my foot on the bridge's exit step and breathed a long sigh of relief. I turned to look at Alex. He was giving me a thumbs-up.

Okay, Alex, your turn. He looked nervous taking his first step; I could see his knees wobbling. Now I became his cheerleader, egging him on with hand motions. *You can do it, Alex. If I did it, so can you.* Step by step, he moved ahead, holding tightly to the flimsy rails, keeping his eyes trained on me and the solid ground that awaited.

When Alex arrived at the midpoint of the bridge, where I'd frozen, he stopped. I was afraid he'd lock up as I had, but he didn't; he just stopped. Then he did something really weird: he looked down through a missing plank. *No, Alex, don't do that. Just keep going.* But he did do it, and the longer he stared, the more I wondered if I would have to go back and retrieve him. But after a few moments, he looked up. Then he placed one foot on the next plank, past the missing one. His other foot followed, and he was on his way. A minute later he was accepting my extended arm.

The bridge was an initiation. Not just physically. Emotionally. That morning I made up my mind that I would never again take out my frustration on someone I loved.

27

Later that afternoon we rounded a bend and spotted a large stone circle made of seven rocks aglow with life. As we approached the circle, I felt a deep sense of gratitude and humility. This was the place where determined seekers came to change their destiny. *Who has stood in this circle before me? What became of them?* One thing was for sure: anyone who got this far had a steely intention that would be hard for any god to deny.

We dropped our backpacks and stepped into the center of the circle. Standing erect, we closed our eyes and tried to feel the energy. At first I felt nothing, but after a few minutes a strange tingling began in my lower spine. A few seconds later it became more palpable and pulsed upward. When the current reached my neck, I felt a sharp pain, as if the energy had hit a block it had trouble passing. I took another breath, and the current ascended to the top of my head, where it seemed to burst like fireworks.

At first this wave delighted me, like a mild drug or subtle orgasm. I started to giggle. However, when the energy intensified and grew hot, I became frightened. *Maybe this is how the Lords screen the purity of aspirants; if they don't make the cut, they get zapped.* If that was the case, I figured, bring it on. *I came for a purpose, and I am not leaving until I accomplish it.* When I surrendered and relaxed, the current ran for another minute and then dissipated.

I opened my eyes and turned to look behind me. High above, just as Eyla had foretold, I saw two peaks protruding like the humps of a giant camel. At dawn the next morning, the sun would shine between those peaks and illuminate the cave of the Lords of Karma. I would ascend the holy mountain and beseech the gods to end all of my lives. Part of me was excited, while another was petrified. I felt like a man on death row at his own request.

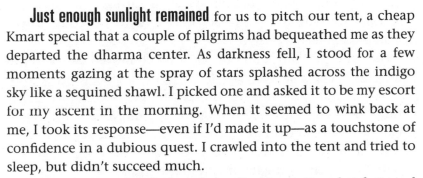

28

Just enough sunlight remained for us to pitch our tent, a cheap Kmart special that a couple of pilgrims had bequeathed me as they departed the dharma center. As darkness fell, I stood for a few moments gazing at the spray of stars splashed across the indigo sky like a sequined shawl. I picked one and asked it to be my escort for my ascent in the morning. When it seemed to wink back at me, I took its response—even if I'd made it up—as a touchstone of confidence in a dubious quest. I crawled into the tent and tried to sleep, but didn't succeed much.

The rain came just before dawn. It pitter-pattered at first, and then escalated to a roar. With each new surge, my heart sank more; I needed that precious ray of sunlight to designate the cave's location. From time to time, I poked my head out of the tent, only to find a sinister shroud obscuring the stars. The wicked sky dumped ruthlessly on everything as thunder rolled through the valley like a lion's roar. Alex awoke, and we huddled in a corner of the tent, avoiding a few bad leaks. He looked as worried as I felt.

Fifteen minutes later, shades of pale light began to penetrate the edges of the tent door. I crawled to the door and opened the zipper. Still no sun to be seen; the sky was simply getting lighter as dawn approached. The rain had diminished to a sprinkle, and a heavy cloud cover lingered over the valley.

I crept out of the tent, muddying my hands and knees, and stood up. *Come on, Lords. . . . Come on, star. . . . Come on, whoever out there can help me.* I turned to survey the sky behind the mountains, struggling to detect some hint of direct sunlight. There was none.

In the far distance, eastward behind the twin peaks, I spotted a small patch of blue. The clouds had yielded a tiny opening. *Maybe . . . maybe . . .*

Alex emerged from the tent and found his way to my side. I pointed out the patch of light to him. We both stared at it like two lottery-ticket holders anxiously waiting for the final, crucial number to be announced.

The small opening in the clouds didn't expand as I'd hoped, but it did drift toward the mountain. The murky blue morphed to a brighter shade, and then light—magnificent golden light—streamed through. If the timing—and our karma—was right, we might have our ray. But was it too late? Were we seeing the dawn, or had the sun already risen?

The wind picked up, and the clear patch moved closer to the peaks. *Come on, come on, come on.* Then it happened: The tiny patch—the only opening in the entire sky—positioned itself behind the peaks and filled with gold. The morning sun threw a single shaft of light directly between them, as if the finger of God was pointing expressly for us. Quickly Alex and I turned to see where the ray fell on the mountain to the west.

It touched a boulder about a third of the way up the ridge. I made a mental note of which boulder was the right one, for there were several near it and I knew that once I scaled the mountainside, the correct site would be hard to discern. A small rock slide had halted just above it, and below it stood an evergreen tree. The areas to the left and right were fairly devoid of vegetation.

I looked back at the sky and saw that the clear patch had moved on, leaving most of the sky still under cloud cover. But the crucial moment had bestowed the all-important signal. I looked up to see if my star was still visible, but it wasn't. I thanked it anyway.

"I'm ready," I told Alex resolutely. He nodded, and we cast each other one more long glance. We both knew there was a chance I wouldn't return. If the Lords exacted their due on the spot, this would be our last moment together. I thought it poignant that my one true friend in life might have shown up at its very end.

I reached into my pack and extracted a candle and some matches, praying they'd stayed dry. I would find out. I faced my silent companion one more time, gave him a firm hug, and turned to ascend the mountain of the gods.

29

Clawing my way up the mountainside was no easy task. The rain had slicked the little grass there was and turned the exposed soil to mud. *Another initiation.* I did my best to keep my eye on the target boulder, but it grew indistinct as I worked my way through a thicket of trees. Every few minutes I looked down toward Alex, who pointed with hand signals and redirected me when I veered off course. As I gained altitude, though, he gradually diminished from sight until he eventually disappeared. *Just me and the mountain now.*

I must have climbed for two hours; distances are deceptive in the wilderness, and what at first seems doable can turn into an ordeal. *Did they move the cave on me?* As I looked up at the rock I'd been aiming for, I found no evergreen below it. *Maybe it's a trick of perspective.* When I moved closer, there was still no tree. Another few steps revealed no rock slide above. I'd been climbing toward the wrong rock!

I looked around and spied another boulder that might be the one. It took me about fifteen minutes to reach it. When I arrived, there was no aperture behind it. *Maybe the right rock is higher up the hill . . . maybe more to the side . . . maybe this whole trip is a foray into illusion.* I trudged upward for another ten minutes, losing energy rapidly in the lean atmosphere. I saw a large boulder to the left and one to the right. I tried both of them. *Nada.*

Exhausted, I flopped down, leaned my back against a tree, and gazed down at the river, its steady voice rumbling through the valley. I tried to guess where Alex was and thought I knew, but I couldn't see him. Gasping for breath and sweating profusely, I could go no farther without some rest. I stretched my neck, turning my head from side to side to alleviate my stress.

As I looked left, I noticed that the area was relatively clear of rocks or vegetation. I saw the same when I turned my head to the right. I looked back to the left, then again to the right. *Could it be?* I stood up and surveyed the area. Clear to left, clear to right, tree to my back. Directly above me, boulder.

Boulder.

I scurried to the huge rock, about fifty feet uphill from me. Either there was a cave behind it and my 8,000-mile journey would have meaning, or I would find bare mountainside and my expedition would prove a fool's errand.

I reached the boulder and touched it; it was cool and slick from the morning rain, but I sensed no magic. I closed my eyes and said a prayer. When I opened them, I noticed some markings on the face of the rock. They were covered with dirt and moss, which I rubbed off with my hand. After a minute of scratching, I could make out the imprint—it was the "Om" symbol. Someone had been here before me and etched it. I took the crucial step and peered around the back of the boulder. *There was a cave.*

30

I craned my neck to see inside. The opening took a turn about fifteen feet from the entrance, beyond which I could not see. The dark felt eerie and menacing. Part of me screamed to turn back, but sheer adrenaline drove me forward.

As I took my first step inside, I felt the temperature drop and the humidity rise. I touched my hand to the cave wall; it was wet. Slowly, carefully, I penetrated the dark. As the outside sounds diminished to silence, all I could hear was the crunching of my shoes on loose pebbles on the cave floor. I expected bats to fly out at me at any moment—or worse. Each step grew louder and echoed through the cavern. I started to feel chilly.

I reached the point where the cave made a turn and the outside light pierced no farther. I took out my candle and matches and hoped that my efforts to keep them dry through our wet ordeal had worked. I tried to strike a match. *No luck—too damp.* I threw it down and tried another. It produced a little spark. *Please don't let me down.* One more try. *Ah, there.* I touched the burning match head to the wick before it changed its mind. The wick sputtered a bit. After a few moments, it ignited.

As I moved ahead, I could hear my heart pounding. My knees were rubbery, and my breath grew shallow and rapid. Every horror movie I'd ever watched—every bony hand clutching an unwary victim's throat in a haunted basement, every slasher/psycho/demented-ghoul face I had ever seen—flashed before me until I thought I'd pee my pants. *Keep moving, Linden, just keep moving.*

After another minute I began to relax a bit. Nothing had grabbed me; maybe nothing would. I circled 360 degrees, holding the candle up at arm's length to scan the cave. Just rocks. Then a thought even more terrifying than lurking demons gripped me: *What if there's nothing to this place? What if it is just a myth? What if I came all this way for an old wives' tale? That* would be tragic.

Suddenly something brushed against my face. "*Unnnhhhhhh!*" I cried out as my body stiffened and a terrific rush of fear shot through me. I turned and started to bolt, and stumbled. I fell with a grunt, scraping my chin on the cave floor—it burned bad. Somehow I managed to clutch at the candle and keep it from rolling into the dark and extinguishing. I looked back into the abyss, but heard and saw nothing.

Slowly, trembling, I raised myself to my knees and stood up. Every impulse in my body screamed, *Run like hell!* But something forced me to stay. *Am I a hero or an idiot?*

I made my way back to where something—or someone—had touched my face. Still shaking, I held the candle up to cast some light on the upper portion of the cave. There I saw a cloth suspended by a vine tied to rocks on both sides of the cave. I lifted the light closer to the cloth. It was a Tibetan prayer flag.

This is the place.

As I moved forward a few more paces, my foot kicked something solid. I got scared again, but felt more confident after having seen the flag. I lowered the candle and discovered a wide, almost round rock at the center of the cave floor. This was no natural phenomenon. Someone had placed the stone there. I lowered the candle and examined it. It looked like a river rock, maybe twenty inches in diameter. *Who put it here? And why?*

I moved past the rock and lifted the candle, casting its flickering beam on the cave ceiling, now just a foot above my head. The walls converged before me; the cave was coming to an end. *Is this the end of my journey?*

One more step and I lowered the candle. There was an altar—a large, flat rectangular stone had been set on top of some smaller ones. On it was melted candle wax. *Someone has been here.* On another stone sat a Tibetan prayer wheel. On another, a bell. I was in the right place. *Now, where are the Lords of Karma?*

31

"Sit down, please," I heard a voice speak from deep within the cavern.

No, no, it came from my mind.

"Your journey is done."

Is it the Lords of Karma or merely my wishful thinking?

I set the candle on the altar. The light splashed on the back of the cave and then spilled up, back, and over me, adding warmth to the spooky space. Someone had inscribed a symbol on the cave wall above the altar. It was a circle with eight lines radiating out from its center, like spokes of a wheel, each line extending beyond the circle's circumference. In the center of the large circle there was a smaller one. In the dim light I tried to figure the symbol out, but couldn't. For now, it lent a comforting note.

I lowered myself to the rock, running my hand over the outside of my pocket to make sure I still had the matches in case the candle blew out. The stone was cold and hard, slightly damp. I folded my legs into a half-lotus position and looked over my shoulder to see if anyone was there. Only dark.

I closed my eyes and tried to settle into meditation. When I felt calmer, I started the mantra: *Om mani padme hum. . . . Om mani padme hum.* I relaxed a bit more. *Om mani padme hum. . . . Om mani padme hum.* Suddenly it seemed as if someone else was chanting with me. I opened my eyes to check if anybody was there. No one. The candle flickered, and the cavern grew brighter. *Om mani padme hum. . . . Om mani padme hum.*

Then I could swear I heard more voices joining me. *Om mani padme hum. . . . Om mani padme hum.* I opened my eyes and looked over my shoulder again. Still no one. *Okay, just go with it. . . . Om mani padme hum.* Now lots of voices. This time I didn't even bother opening my eyes. The journey was inward.

On the inside of my eyelids I could see the afterimage of the candle, a tiny throbbing yellow-gold dot. As I became fascinated with it, it took on a stronger glow and grew larger. Was it actually expanding, or was I just concentrating on it more deeply?

Then the light morphed to a sort of vertical oval, the larger part at the top. I could make out some shapes within it—several distinctly darker areas—two dots about one-third of the way from the top; another halfway down; and another, wider dot one-third up from the bottom.

Am I hallucinating? Delusional? Or is something very weird happening?

The dots within the oval began to take on their own shapes, darkening as they went. The uppermost dots spread into two horizontal almond shapes. The middle one elongated vertically and widened a bit at the bottom. The lowest dot spread side to side and turned up slightly at its outer edges.

It was a *face.*

Startled, I opened my eyes and started to stand up. But the feeling accompanying the face wasn't scary, but pleasant. I felt drawn to return.

I sat down and closed my eyes again, wondering if the face might have disappeared. It hadn't. It was even clearer. The eyes darkened, the nose became more defined, and I perceived a space between the upper and lower lips. As the features filled in, I saw, to my astonishment, the face of a very old Tibetan man—roundish, with leathery brown skin and deep wrinkles. The face, although a bit stern, had a benevolent air to it. I wasn't afraid anymore.

The face transformed from two dimensions to three and became animated. I was seeing a real person now, not a picture. The ancient eyes glimmered with life. The lips turned up in a faint smile, and the head bowed to greet me.

"I am Akar, Lord of Karma," I heard a voice speak.

This is it.

"Am I making you up, or are you real?" The conversation was mind to mind.

"I assure you I am quite real. At least as real as anything else you have made up."

"Are you *the* Lord of Karma? Or are there others?"

"There are many. We are of one mind, yet we come in many forms."

This is too weird.

To the left of Akar another face began to appear in the same way, but more rapidly. It was thinner and had softer features—it was a woman. Her countenance was fair, and she had a covering over her hair, like a nun.

"And you are . . . ?"

"I am Teresa of Avila."

"You're not Tibetan."

"The Lords of Karma are not limited to any one religion or race," she answered in a kindly but authoritative tone. "Our truth is universal. We appear and communicate with you through language and images you recognize."

I had a flash of my Catholic elementary school that I'd hated. *You'd think they'd send someone I had a pleasant association with.*

Another image began to appear to the right of Akar; this one downloaded the fastest. It was a Chinese man with a Fu Manchu mustache. He was younger than the others, yet his eyes spoke of ancient wisdom. The sage simply nodded. No words. Just very present. In my mind I heard the name "Chuang-Tsu."

"We know why you are here," Akar stated.

Okay, then let's get on with it. "I want to break the cycle of birth and death," I declared. "I want this to be my last life."

The Lords of Karma were silent. Were they just listening, or were they having some kind of silent conference?

"Do you understand what this means?" Chuang-Tsu asked.

"I think so."

"If we agree to help you, you will leave this world soon and this will be your last life on Earth," Teresa asserted firmly. "You will never be born again in a human body, for any reason. Your decision is irrevocable."

"I understand."

Silence again.

"Then state your intention plainly," Akar commanded with a military air.

Keeping my eyes closed, I stood and spread my arms. I felt a bit wobbly, but steadied myself. "I, Linden Kozlowski, choose this to be my last life on Earth." My words boomed out, echoing off the cave walls and, it seemed, through the mountains and valleys below. "I will not be reborn, and I will not return to Earth in a human body. This is my sovereign and irrevocable decision, forever."

Another silence, this time shorter. "So be it," declared the Lords of Karma in unison. Then they disappeared as mysteriously as they'd arrived.

When I arrived back at the stone circle, I found Alex waiting. The expression on his face when he saw me approach spoke of deep relief, coupled with anxiety. Although he uttered not a word, I swear I could hear him say, "Well?"

I looked him straight in the eye and stated, "It is done."

To my surprise, my little brother just lowered his head and nodded slightly. Then one small, lone tear fell from the inside of his left eye to the corner of his lip.

I wished he would have been happier.

33

Our return journey was easier. We knew where we were headed, the river's flow had abated to a sane level, and the border-station road was without upwardly mobile clothing merchants. It seemed that the universe was applauding my commitment. I felt heady, even smug, as I assumed that the Lords of Karma had pulled some strings on our behalf.

Alex, however, seemed despondent. He dragged along, smiled little, and rarely looked me in the eye. I tried to cheer him up with one-sided banter, but he seemed not to hear a word. Maybe the kid had some emotional problems he'd never told me about. But then again, he never told me *anything*.

We reached Eyla's house in two days, rather than the three it had taken outbound. She was pumping water from the well when we arrived. Her face lit with surprise, she dropped her bucket, threw her arms around me, and hugged me warmly. "Thanks be to the gods for your safe return!" she exclaimed. *"Pa lags!"* she called out, summoning her father, who'd finally returned after being stranded in town.

Lingpa looked much as I expected him to—sixtyish; tough-skinned; strong, sure hands; no awards for charisma. He was taller and leaner than most Tibetans, almost gaunt, wearing a fedora-like hat and a simple gray jacket. He greeted us politely, yet watched me like a hawk.

I can't say that I blamed him. Part of me still longed for his daughter. When I saw her—especially after having run the gauntlet of my own private *Survivor* episode—she looked even more ravishing than I remembered. Her sparkling exotic eyes, golden skin, and childlike smile all made a tempting vision of this rare blend of earth mother and sensual goddess.

But everything was different now. I wasn't just trying to find a way to exit this world; I had a one-way ticket off the planet, which the Lords could redeem at any time. I wouldn't take the risk of hurting Eyla by starting a romance with her, and I certainly didn't want to create any karma that would force me back onto the wheel of birth and death. Not to mention having to deal with her possessive papa, who would have surely hastened my departure if I messed with his daughter's body or mind.

A welcome change of clothes, hot bath, and Grandma-cooked dinner made the ramshackle cottage feel like a luxury resort. Lingpa wasted no time grilling me about our quest. I was reluctant to reveal the intimate details, but since Eyla had told him where I went and why, I figured I owed him some explanation.

"You're lucky," he remarked after I recounted my tale, setting down his mug of *chang*, a barley-brewed Tibetan moonshine. "Not everyone finds the cave."

"And even fewer return once they do," Eyla added.

"I know," I answered soberly. "I think the gods were with us."

Alex had tuned us out; I was almost getting used to it by now. Half the time he seemed needy, and the other half cold and distant.

"Did they tell you how long you would stay?" the old man asked.

"In India?" I asked naïvely.

"No," Lingpa replied, shaking his head with an almost sardonic half smile that gave way to a serious look. "In this world."

I hadn't thought about a timeline.

"Or how you would leave?" Eyla asked.

How I would leave? I didn't really want to think about that. I'd been thinking more about being done with life in general, not my exit scene.

Eyla and her father exchanged a serious look, as if they were silently asking each other, *Who is going to tell him?*

Finally Lingpa spoke: "We knew someone else who returned from the cave. A Tibetan monk living in Manali. He went for the same reason you did."

And?

"The Lords of Karma told him how he was going to die," Eyla put in.

This is getting uncomfortable. But I'd started this train of thought just by being there, and I had to finish it. "And how was that?" I gulped.

"They showed him a picture of his stomach," Lingpa answered.

"It was black and shriveled, like an old ravaged cloth," Eyla added.

How dainty.

"So what happened? Did a car drive over his stomach?" I asked, trying to be funny.

Our hosts weren't amused. "A month later he got food poisoning at the temple and died," the old man answered.

My stomach went queasy. "Did any of the other monks become ill?" I asked, hoping for some logical explanation. "I mean, they all ate from the same pot, right?"

"Only *he* died," Eyla explained.

At that moment I realized I'd placed myself in a strange predicament: I wanted to die one day—but not just yet. In the time since Tashi had plucked me from the bridge, my life had gotten better. I'd met people who genuinely cared about me, found unprecedented loyalty in Alex's friendship, and made the acquaintance of a gentle yet powerful lady light-years ahead of any woman I'd ever known. And as much as I hated to admit it, the meditation and chanting had helped tame my restless mind—just a bit, but enough to lighten my load. I would be sad to leave just now. Maybe later, when I had time to prepare, but in a *month?* The Lords had said only "soon." That could be a day, or a month, or in the big picture of a life, a year or years. *Maybe I can petition them to just let me finish out this lifetime.*

But no, the deal was done, and I wasn't going back on it. If they took me in a month, they took me in a month, and I would accept that.

Well, maybe.

34

I had a hard time falling asleep that night. Still disturbed about the food-poisoning story, my mind conjured up all kinds of horrible images of how I might be offed. I felt slightly nauseated, but I figured it was just the power of suggestion. *Will I now just worry myself to death?* I took a few long, deep breaths and finally drifted off.

Through the portal of deep sleep, I found myself back in the cave. The faces of Akar, Teresa, and Chuang-Tsu were as vivid as when I'd sat with them in person. "Do you have a plan for how and when I will die?" I asked the council directly.

Silence followed, like the dark that settles in a theater just before the curtain rises. Then I saw a scene in which a hawk was soaring high above an ocean. Flying at different altitudes below were seven seagulls. As if on cue, the hawk swooped down and devoured one of the gulls—then another, and another, until all were gone. His mission complete, the hawk ascended to the sun and disappeared.

The dream wasn't scary, nor was it pleasant. It just *was*, like an unbiased news report.

A rooster crowing from the yard woke me. It was still the middle of the night.

35

As we stood at the door ready to leave the next morning, the longing in Eyla's eyes mirrored my own. We both knew I would never see her again. I simultaneously wanted to thank her for showing me a vision of an extraordinary woman, and rail at the gods for the untimely introduction. I wanted to hold her in my arms one last time and feel the smoothness of her skin against mine. Yet Lingpa's glare and Alex's jealousy forced this out of the question. With a polite bow and thank-you, I turned and walked away from Eyla and, symbolically, all women. Maybe even life.

❈

The temple at Dharamsala looked much as it had when we left it. It was *I* who wasn't the same. Lama Sungdare seemed surprised to see us, yet greeted us cordially. "Where have you traveled since we last saw you?" he inquired, Sonam at his side.

I was still angry at the lama for deceiving me, but my indignation was offset by a sense of self-satisfaction in having proved him wrong. "We visited various temples," I lied, "and stayed with some charitable Buddhists."

"That's good," he replied, apparently convinced. "Very meritorious for your karma."

Which will all be done quite soon.

As the lama continued on his way down the hall, Sonam took me aside and whispered, "What happened?"

Unlike Lama Sungdare, Sonam deserved the truth. "I met the Lords of Karma," I told him.

Sonam's eyes nearly bugged out of his head. Like any good Buddhist, he tried to regain his composure, but he couldn't conceal his excitement. "And did they grant your wish?"

"They did," I answered.

The young monk grew pensive and nodded. He took both my hands in his and told me, "Then may the blessings of Lord Buddha be with you. May your soul find everlasting peace."

❀

Our time at the temple was anticlimactic. More chanting, bowing, and meditating. After a week I felt bored with all the talk of karma and reincarnation. I was done with my incarnations and wanted liberation more than religion. *Game over.*

After dinner one evening, Sonam, Alex, and I sat together sipping tea in the study, flanked by ancient Buddhist texts. I removed an old book from a shelf and studied the worn cover. "This religion goes way back, doesn't it?"

"About 500 years before Christ."

"Sometimes I wish I could meet Buddha," I told the monk. "I wonder what he would say about life, death, and our world situation today."

Sonam scanned the shelves thoughtfully. "I believe Buddha would say today exactly what he said 2,500 years ago."

"And what's that?"

"'If you do not get it from yourself, where will you go for it?'"

That was a bit daunting to hear, since I had just trekked halfway around the world to meet three spooks in a cave.

"Well, that's appropriate," I replied, "considering I'm ready to go back to the States."

Alex shot me a nasty glance. *Maybe I should have discussed my plan with him first.*

"Excuse me a moment," Sonam said as he rose and made his way out of the study.

As soon as he was gone, Alex flashed me another mean look, as if to say, *What's up with you?*

"I need to get back, Alex," I told him in a hushed voice. "I'm getting antsy here."

Alex sighed and squirmed in his chair.

A minute later Sonam returned with an envelope in his hand. He sat down next to me and carefully removed a small object from the envelope. It was an ancient, fragile leaf, decayed with many holes, just intact enough for him to gently cup it. "This is a leaf from the Bodhi tree," Sonam explained.

"The tree Buddha sat under when he became enlightened?" I asked, remembering one of Lama Sherap's discourses.

"That's right," Sonam replied, pleased that I knew. "Buddha spent his early life in luxury as a prince. Then he renounced his royal riches and immersed himself in severe austerity. Eventually he realized that neither opulence nor self-abnegation was the goal of life. He sat under the Bodhi tree and meditated until he recognized his true spiritual self. That is when he became the Buddha."

Sonam held the leaf up to the light. Its skeletal pattern was artistic.

"You mean this leaf has survived twenty-five centuries?"

"Not that long." Sonam smiled. "But the tree is known and revered, and lives to this day. When I made a pilgrimage to the sacred Bodhi tree several years ago, I received this leaf from a monk who meditates there."

Sonam placed the delicate object in my hand. "I want you to have this, Linden," he told me.

I was shocked. "Are you serious?"

"Yes," he answered with a firm nod. "Take this wherever you go to remind you that Buddha and his enlightened mind are always with you."

I felt unworthy to receive such a generous and meaningful gift. But I realized that my friend truly wanted me to have it. "Thank you, Sonam," I replied. "I will treasure this." Then I had to ask,

"Do you think that Buddha's life story was really what people say it was?"

Sonam took a long sip of tea. "The details of his life are less important than what he lived for," he answered. "A man's story is worth telling only if the truth he discovers is greater than the pain that led him to seek it."

36

The next afternoon as I was cramming my jeans into my backpack, Alex slipped into the room, clutching a brightly colored brochure. Excited, he placed the trifold in my hand, his face revealing the first real spark of enthusiasm I'd seen since I'd come down from the mountain.

"What's this?" I asked, not bothering to read it.

Alex motioned for me to just look at it. RANI PREMA RESORT, the headline shouted, AN INDIA YOU WILL LONG REMEMBER. Below were a half dozen attractive photos of an upscale tourist hotel.

"I've already seen an India I will long remember," I told Alex.

Not dissuaded, he swung his arm as if to say, *Let's go!*

"You want to go to this place? What for?"

He shrugged his shoulders, and his eyes lit up. By now I could read his body language. This I interpreted as *It just sounds like fun.*

I read the description and perused the photos. "This looks like a ritzy place, man . . ."

Alex reached into his pack and produced his (father's) trusty credit card. Wow, had we gotten a lot of mileage out of *that.*

"I don't know, Alex," I whined. "I'm pretty much ready to head back."

The kid's eyes dropped, and I could feel his disappointment. *Okay, okay, maybe here's my chance to pay him back for all he's done for me.* I glanced at the brochure again and then at his eager face.

"Okay, buddy, I'm in," I told him.

Alex flashed a huge grin and ran off to get Sonam's help to change our travel plans.

37

Rani Prema was even more opulent than Alex or I had bargained for. In picturesque pastoral hill country called Arunima, a few hundred kilometers northeast of Mumbai, the hotel sported immaculately manicured grounds, spacious rooms with vaulted ceilings, and rich Venetian tiling. Not to mention towel warmers and bidets. The contrast between the luxury at hand and the third-world accommodations we'd gotten used to was mind-boggling.

Practically all of the resort's occupants were couples—wealthy professionals from English-speaking countries, plus a handful of upper-class Indians. Realizing how weird two mendicant Buddhists would look, we ditched our robes and donned our civvies. But our jeans and dirty, hole-ridden sweatshirts were even more incongruous than the religious attire. So Alex made a visit to the hotel's gift shop and returned with a fashionable set of resort wear for each of us. *I hope Alex Sr. has a good cardiologist.*

We were assigned to a dinner table with three snobbish couples who spent most of their time vying to impress each other with their credentials and travelogues. ("You haven't lived until you've taken the Black Sea cruise on the *Nautica*.") Alex and I remained quiet and occasionally raised our eyebrows at each other as their conversation grew more and more pretentious. We were quite the anomaly, and I'm sure they thought we were gay.

Finally one of the gentlemen, whom I'll call Baron von Harrumph, decided to draw us into the conversation. "So what brings you fellows to India?" he asked in a haughty tone. "Holiday?"

Okay, I'll have to participate. I lowered my voice a few notches and answered, "I'm Dr. Sidney Hartha—call me Sid. I'm a primate biology professor at Stanford, and this is my laboratory assistant . . . uh . . . Igor."

I wish I had a video of the shocked look Alex shot me. But now, under the scrutiny of our tablemates, he had no choice but to play along. "Igor" offered a polite smile and a calculated nod.

I persevered with the charade: "We're doing a research project on the mating habits of the Arunachal macaque, a monkey recently discovered in the Manipur province."

Alex tossed me an even more inquisitive look, as if to ask, *Where did you get* this *from?* I leaned over and whispered to him, "I read it in a magazine in the men's room." I turned back to the good baron and asked him (attempting to imitate his air of intimidation), "I assume you've heard of it?"

Not wanting to appear uninformed, he replied, "Why, of course."

"And you . . . Igor . . . are you enjoying your visit?" the baron's wife, Cleavagella, inquired.

Alex, of course, remained silent and deferred to me as his spokesman.

"You'll have to forgive Igor for not speaking," I apologized on his behalf. "He had a lip operation the day before we left the States, and the doctor forbade him to talk for one week."

Alex, now into the improv, rubbed his mouth as if he was still in pain.

"Beats a chatty bride, you know," I joked. They all laughed.

I didn't think anyone really believed us; I'm sure they thought we were gay anyway. Ultimately, I couldn't care less; this was my last life, and if they wanted to suffer under terminal snootiness, that was their karma. Maybe in order to learn compassion, they would have to be reincarnated as homosexuals. Or Buddhists.

❁

After dinner, I needed space to clear my head of the bragga-docio. Alex decided to peruse the gift shop; only now did I realize how dangerous he was with plastic. The young man was creat-ing some serious karma with his father, which, I imagined, might impel him to return for numerous incarnations to pay it off. I figured he was next in line for the Cave of Khadroma.

I decided to stroll around the grounds for a while and take in the heady scent of the azaleas at the height of their bloom. The aroma led me to a little lake at the heart of the resort, where I stood on a small bridge and watched a couple of swans preen each other. *Is Rani Prema real,* I wondered, *or just a well-created fairy tale? Is the world simply a distraction from inner peace, as the Buddhists sug-gest, or is God speaking to me through the beauty before me?* For the moment I was happy to just watch the swans. *Maybe that's all there is to life: enjoy the show at hand.*

From a distance I could hear the old English grandfather clock in the lobby chime nine times; I'd been wandering for nearly an hour. As night began to fall, so did the temperature. I pulled up the collar of my thin cotton shirt and started back to the room.

As I threaded through the maze of flagstone pathways, all the fine tea I'd imbibed at dinner started to catch up with me, and I quickened my pace. Luckily, a maintenance worker drove past me in a golf cart, and I flagged him down.

"May I help you, sir?" he asked with impeccable courtesy.

"Is there a restroom near here?" I replied, trying to play down how much I needed to go.

The worker surveyed the area for a moment and shook his head. "No, but I will be happy to drive you to your room if you like."

"That would be just great," I answered, and hopped aboard.

When I arrived back at the bungalow with not a minute to spare, the lights were out; Alex was likely still back at the gift shop doing damage. As for me, my bladder was about to burst, and I had one objective. As quickly as possible, I shoved the key into the lock, wrenched the door open, and dashed for the bathroom. *Hurry—before there's an accident . . .*

I flung the bathroom door open and was shocked to see Alex standing in front of the bathtub, naked from the waist up. That was not the issue. The issue was that *Alex had tits.* You know . . . *breasts.* My immediate thought was that some disoriented guest had randomly wandered into the bathroom. But when he—or she—turned his—or her—head, it was *Alex.*

Horrified, Alex shrieked, grabbed a towel to cover up, and stood quaking as if I were a frothing Rottweiler. *Poor Alex,* I thought. *You have some terrible genetic deformity that grew these globules on your chest.* But then as I quickly surveyed the curves of Alex's torso, still mostly exposed in spite of the towel, the unbelievable fact was unmistakably obvious: *Alex was a woman.*

Alex's eyes turned saucer sized, and I fell back against the wall, my jaw hanging. We both stood there for the longest moment in history, shocked and confused. I finally pulled it together enough to mouth, "Holy shit! You're a *girl!*"

"Holy shit—yes, I am!" she shot back. I never thought those would be the first words I would hear Alex speak or that they would be uttered in such a high voice.

"Why didn't you tell me?"

Alex's chin furrowed and she stiffened. "Because the Buddhists would never let me into that dharma center if they knew I was a woman . . . and . . . and . . ."

I motioned with my head to encourage her to keep going. "And what?"

". . . and because I fell in love with you, you big, stupid jerk!"

This was definitely getting weird. I wished she would have just stopped before the "and."

"You *what?*"

"It started when I saw you in the garden with that kid," she answered, pulling the oversized towel up to cover herself better. "You—big, tough, suicidal Linden Kozlowski, King of the Homeless, 'I don't give a shit about anybody or anything; I'm outta here'—you have a heart of gold. You think cosmic, you feel deeply, you're not afraid to go for what you want, and you have a tender side that no one sees—not even you. Do you realize how rare it is for a guy to gently show a five-year-old how to plant a seedling? And the guts to chastise the whole Indian nation for leaving one of their own to die in the street? You have no idea what an amazing guy you are, Linden—or what a loss it would be to scratch you from the world. *That's* the guy I fell in love with—if you must know."

Come on, Alex, don't mess with my head—not now. "Then why didn't you say something way back then? Why this charade during all we've been through?"

Alex stepped toward me and squared her jaw. "If I'd told you, you would have blown me off. You were burned, and obsessed with that stupid bimbo who used and abused you. I didn't stand a chance to penetrate your armor."

She was right. When I'd met Alex, I wanted nothing to do with any woman. I would have dissed her in a heartbeat.

We both just stood there silently for another long moment, staring at each other, tense as hell.

"So now what?" I finally asked in a quieter voice.

"I don't know, Linden. What do *you* think we should do?" she answered almost indignantly. "Shall I put my baggy clothes back on and go on acting like your little brother?"

I shook my head and shrugged my shoulders. At last I mustered a reply: "Maybe we could start over."

Alex just smirked. "No, that won't really work." She shook her head. "Now you get to die because you gave up on life before you met me."

No, no, that's not what I meant to do.

"I-I'm sorry, Alex," I stammered. "I had no idea . . ."

"I'm sorry, too, Linden," she shot back. "I *had* an idea . . . but I was wrong—dead wrong."

38

That night Alex and I lay in our beds a few feet from each other, as we had a hundred nights before. But now everything was different. Alex's revelation had turned my world upside down, and my mind had no box to hold all that she'd laid at my doorstep. I tossed and turned all night, and I doubt Alex got any more sleep than I did.

When morning came, I walked over to her bed and sat at the foot. "Is Alex your real name?"

"Short for Alexandra." She looked tired, and her eyes were red.

"And your dad?"

"He's Alex."

So that explained how she'd worked her scheme. "Will he be pissed about the credit card?"

"Totally . . . but we'll pay him back."

Upon hearing that, a wave of angst engulfed me, for two very reasonable reasons: first, I doubted I would be around much longer, and repaying Mr. Leister for all we'd spent was highly unlikely; and second—believe me, this was far scarier—"we'll" sure sounded like we were an item now. *Did our shared travails qualify us as a couple?*

Alex sensed my discontent. "Are you all right?" she asked.

Not really.

"Well, it's just that I don't think that anything in my future is a healthy investment," I answered, "basically because I don't *have* one."

Alex sat up and propped her back against the wicker head-board. The light streaming through the window fell on her face at just the perfect angle to accentuate her feminine features. *How could I have been so blind?*

"Linden, do you really believe what happened to you in the cave was real?" she asked. "I mean, the Lords of Karma and your decision to end all of your lives?"

I can't believe she's questioning me after all we went through. "Well, yes. . . . Don't you?"

"I don't know." She shrugged. "I wonder about it."

Her comment ticked me off. "But you came with me on my journey. Christ, you *funded* it!" I started to raise my voice. "We nearly got killed at several turns. You were in this with me all the way. And now you doubt my purpose?"

She sat up straighter. "I was in it with you not because I want you to die, but because I want you to live," she answered. "I believe in you, Linden. I want to be with you."

This is all coming at me too fast.

"So you mean that if I decided to go to, like, dentistry school instead of the cave, you would have gone with me there?"

"Linden, I would have gone with you to the moon to find green cheese if that was important to you."

I didn't know what to say. Part of me felt furious that she doubted my mission, and part of me wanted to cry in the face of loyalty I'd never before known.

I stood up, paced nervously for a few seconds, and leaned both arms against the back of a chair like a cop interrogating a suspect.

"Then who do you think I met in the cave?"

"Maybe yourself," she answered as if she'd given this a lot of forethought.

I shook my head. "But . . . all the other people who have gone there . . . all the teachings of Buddhism—of Buddha himself—do you think it's all bullshit?"

"Not at all," Alex replied. "I think there's a lot of truth in it. But I also think we have choices about how we live our lives; and no Lords of Karma, psychic reading, past-life residue, astrological configuration, or anyone or anything else has more power over our choices than we do."

Dear Lord, women confuse me. This one masquerades as a guy, follows me to the ends of the earth, tells me she is in love with me, and then insinuates that my mission might have been delusional. *Now I know why people become monks.*

"And what will happen now, Alex?" I asked.

"Well, for one thing, I'd hate to see you off yourself just to prove you're right," she retorted.

"I would never do that!"

"Subconscious intention is powerful, Linden," Alex argued. "You can attract all kinds of experiences with your mind without knowing you're doing it."

"Like how?"

"Like my friend Becky who was so afraid that her boyfriends would leave her that she started fights that *made* them leave her. She still doesn't have a man in her life, and she blames *them*. But *she* was behind all of her breakups."

I resumed pacing back and forth. "I don't know, Alex. . . . You can take this psychological stuff too far."

Alex motioned for me to sit down on the bed next to her. I hesitated for a moment, then joined her. "Let me ask you a question, Linden," she said. "What would *you* like to do now? Do you want to live or die? Do you really want to end all of your lives, or would you be willing to give life one more chance?"

I closed my eyes to think. It was a hard question, *really* hard. I'd spent so much time and energy trying to end it all that changing my mind didn't seem like an option. My head demanded that I forge ahead and not be distracted. But my heart felt otherwise. For the first time in a long time—maybe ever—I saw some beauty and value in life. Just a spark, like the last ember that flares up before a fire goes out—but enough to make me reconsider my decision.

"I don't know, Alex. I can't say for sure," I answered with uncharacteristic humility. "What do *you* think?"

She sighed and looked me straight in the eye. "I think we should just go on living as we would choose. If you die—or I do, for that matter—well, that's life . . . or death. But I see no value in trying to stop something that could be great if we let it."

Maybe she had a point.

39

"Where are you going?" Alex asked as she watched me toss a can of peanuts from the minibar into my backpack.

"I just need to get outside for a while," I told her as I fumbled with the zipper. "I'm sort of on overwhelm."

Alex nodded. She'd been with me long enough to know that I needed space to process stuff.

"I'll see you later," I said, trying to close the bungalow door behind me without sounding like I was slamming it.

For half an hour I walked aimlessly around the resort grounds, mulling over the events of the last twelve hours. I began to envy the Linden who'd stood on the bridge, ready to jump—at least he knew what he wanted and had a plan. Now I was caught between a possibly desirable life and an impending death with questionable aftereffects.

As I passed the lobby, I smelled some noxious exhaust fumes coming from a hotel courtesy bus sitting at the curb. MUMBAI AIRPORT SHUTTLE was painted on its side in broad letters; below, the driver and a bellhop were loading luggage. A short line of passengers was beginning to board.

As I watched them step inside, something pulled me to follow them. *Are you crazy?* a voice in my head reproached me. *You can't just walk away from Alex like this—not now.*

148

Why not? I argued with myself.

She's been there for you. She sees the best in you. She's in love with you.

But she lied to me. She's not the person she told me she was. She had an ulterior motive.

The line was shrinking. In a minute all the passengers would be on board and the bus would drive away.

I moved toward the door.

Don't do this, Linden. You'll just be creating more karma. Your situation will only get worse.

I continued past the front desk, past the bellhop stand, past my past.

I reached the bus as the last passenger, a frail Japanese woman wearing a fisherman's hat, was taking her seat. Just as the driver was about to close the door, he saw me and kept it open. I approached and looked into the bus. "Are you coming?" he asked with a thick Indian accent.

I stood there for a long moment, thinking.

I stepped onto the bus.

40

As we approached Mumbai nearly three hours later, I figured that Alex was wondering where I was. I felt hollow. I didn't want to hurt her. She was a good person. She meant well. *Maybe she'll understand. Maybe this is better for her, too.*

This was the most time Alex and I had been apart since the beginning of our trip. *Weird,* I thought. *I spent three months with Alex as a male co-worker and dorm mate and was in his company 24/7 traveling for almost a month, and we got along really well. Suddenly "he" is a girl, and within one day I need to get away.*

The Mumbai airport was teeming with people hurrying, saying emotional good-byes, and dragging huge valises behind them. As I squeezed into the line to exit the bus, I noticed I was drumming my fingers on the seat beside me, something I do when I'm nervous. My departure was starting to feel real. Moments later I stepped down to the pavement and watched the other passengers follow the driver to the underbelly of the bus, where he opened the baggage compartment and started to unload suitcases. I was the only passenger who didn't line up for luggage. Hell, I didn't even have a change of clothes.

As I entered the terminal, I caught myself looking behind me, waiting for Alex to catch up. I felt extremely odd, almost naked, to be traveling without him—uh—her. *What is she doing now? Is she worried about me? Does she think I just went for a long walk and I'll be back soon?* Much as I hated to admit it, I missed her. But I'd get over that. Twenty-four hours from now I'd be 8,000 miles away, and Alex and I would have no idea how to contact each other ever again.

I found the Air India international check-in counter and took my place in line behind an elderly couple. The wife sat in a wheelchair, which her husband pushed from behind. He wore a small plaid golf hat and walked with a hunch. She held an exotic-looking purse in her lap, obviously a treasured souvenir from this trip, and her blue flowered dress hung neatly below her knees. When their turn came, Sam and Sadie (the names I picked for them in my mind) strained to hear the agent explain the departure process, asking him to repeat the instructions a few times. I began to feel impatient, but I imagined these folks were someone's grandparents, and that helped me relax.

When I finally reached the counter, I was greeted by a tall, handsome agent with a mustache and thick jet-black hair combed back very neatly. I figured he was an actor who was working for the airline until he got his big break. "I'd like to get on the next flight to San Francisco," I told him, fumbling to produce my crumpled ticket.

The agent studied the computer monitor intently, scratching his cheek.

"There is a flight connecting to San Francisco, departing in fifty minutes. I have a seat for you, but you'll have to hurry."

I'm really leaving. Without Alex.

"Sir?" the fellow called to me, stirring me from my reverie. "If you want that flight, you'll have to go right now."

I forced a breath. "Uh . . . okay . . . I'll take it."

The agent's fingers raced over the keys, the printer whirred, and seconds later he handed me a boarding pass. I thanked him, threw my pack over my shoulder, and dashed toward the security line, nearly bumping into several people and shooting brief apologies over my shoulder.

Twenty minutes later, the immigration agent was asking me what my occupation was back in the U.S. I told him, "Near-death-experience researcher." He gave me a strange look, but seemed tired enough to not care, and stamped my passport without further questioning.

Soon I was streaking past a blur of shops, snack bars, and talking heads on TV monitors, all the while praying that the plane was still boarding. Finally I reached the gate, panting heavily, only to find hordes of people still sitting in the waiting area. The status board behind the counter indicated that the plane's departure had been delayed by thirty minutes. *The gods must be with me.*

I took a seat at the end of a row and caught my breath. Soon the agent announced preboarding for passengers needing special assistance. I glanced to my right and saw Sam and Sadie taking their places in line a few feet from where I was sitting. Sam seemed to recognize me from the check-in counter and offered me a little smile. I reciprocated.

Five minutes later the line hadn't advanced, and I noticed that Sam looked tired. I leaned over, tapped him on the shoulder, and invited him to sit in the empty seat next to me. He liked the idea and explained his plan to Sadie, who told him to take care of himself; she would be just fine.

"Ahhhh," he let out as he plopped down. "What a schlep to get here!"

"Where you from?" I inquired.

"Originally New York," he answered in a Yiddish accent that could have made him a caricature. "Moved to San Diego in '79 . . . terrible how crowded it's getting. Have you driven the I-5 lately? . . . Huy!" The old man reached into his jacket pocket, removed a handkerchief, and began to dab his brow.

I nodded to let Sam know I was with him. "You and your wife on your way home from vacation?"

"Not just a vacation—our fiftieth-anniversary honeymoon!" He beamed with pride.

"That's wonderful."

"My wife has wanted to visit India her whole life. We never had a lot of money, but I told her, 'Sweetheart, if we make it to our fiftieth, I'm taking you to the Taj Mahal.'"

Sam leaned closer to me. His eyes were glassy with age, with little red patches on the skin beneath them. I had to hand it to him for taking such a big trip. "Fabulous, I'm telling you." He shook his head in awe. "Some maharaja built the place for his wife."

I'd heard something about that, and I nodded.

"I told my wife, 'If I had that kind of gelt, I would build this for you.'"

My chest started to warm a bit. "So you still love her?" I asked him.

"Yes, sure, I still love her," he answered with a knowing smile. "Do you know how hard it is to find a good woman these days?"

Funny you should mention that. I gazed over at Sadie in her wheelchair. She seemed relaxed, trusting that Sam wouldn't leave her stranded.

"Do you mind if I ask you a personal question?"

Sam shrugged his shoulders. "Sure, sure, you can ask," he answered, dropping the *re* from his "sures" in a Brooklyn kind of way.

I leaned in to be certain he could hear me. "Have you ever wanted to leave Sadie?"

"Sadie? Who the hell is Sadie?"

Oops. Imagination spills too freely into reality. "Sorry," I came back quickly. "I meant your wife . . . have you ever wanted to leave her?"

"You mean Selma? My wife?"

Ah, not far off, was I?

"Yes . . . Selma . . . your wife."

Sam cast his gaze to the ground as if tapping into a long and rich memory bank. Then he straightened and leaned back toward me. "I wanted to run away a hundred times," he confessed. "And once I did . . . but I came back. I used to blame my wife for not being perfect—but, you know, neither am I. You have to take the good with the bad." Sam lowered his voice, as if to tell me a secret. "Let's face it . . . I don't know how much longer either of us will be here. I have a heart condition, and she don't walk so good anymore. That makes every moment precious. I don't want to miss even one."

Sam gazed lovingly at his wife. "She's my best friend . . . and we have each other. That's all that counts."

He was interrupted by a loud voice over the PA: "We are now ready to continue preboarding . . ."

When Sam didn't seem to hear the announcement, I nudged him and pointed toward the gate. Grateful for the heads-up, he rose, tipped his little golf hat to me, and found the handles of his wife's wheelchair. Ever so slowly they sauntered along, and a minute later they disappeared down the Jetway.

His words echoed in my head: *That's all that counts.*

As soon as the preboard was complete, the agent called for passengers seated in rows forty-one to fifty. That was me. I stood and took my place in line. When I arrived at the entrance to the Jetway, the agent extended her hand and asked, "May I have your boarding pass, sir?"

I hesitated for a long moment. I could feel people getting antsy behind me.

"Your boarding pass, sir," she repeated. "I'll need it now."

I looked down the Jetway. It was a lot longer than I'd anticipated.

I stepped out of line.

41

As I tiptoed into the bungalow, the blue numbers on the alarm clock shined 1:43 in the darkness. Alex was sleeping, or appeared to be. I'm sure she heard me, but she probably figured it was best to just let me be. I quietly set my pack on the floor next to the door and kicked off my shoes. I dropped my jeans beside the couch and slipped into my bed.

Alex never asked me where I'd gone that day, and I never told her. Some things are better left unexplained. Sometimes what you end up doing is more important than how you got there.

42

Breakfast the next morning was basically silent. A couple of times I started to speak, but in light of the storm we'd both just weathered, anything I thought of saying seemed dumb. Alex just stared into her asparagus omelette, I into my grapefruit crunch. I remembered a story about a family who had invited the father's boss and his wife over for dinner. Just before the guests were to arrive, one of the kids discovered a gaping, bleeding rhinoceros head lying in the middle of the dining-room table. Not knowing what to do with it and having no time to clean it up, they decided to just leave it there and hope no one would notice.

"How's your omelette?" I finally asked. *Dumb, dumb, dumb.*

"All right," Alex replied, equally uneasy. "How's your grapefruit?"

"Okay, I guess."

For the first time during the meal, our eyes met. Alex inhaled as if she were about to speak, but then froze.

"Go ahead, say what you want to say."

She seemed relieved by my permission. "I'm sorry I lied to you, Linden," she told me. "I didn't know any other way to be with you."

"I understand. . . . Forget about it."

Uncomfortable silence. Another few disinterested bites of breakfast.

"I *can't* forget about it," she finally said. "I feel like I made a fool out of myself telling you I was in love with you."

Ah, the rhinoceros head will have its way.

"No, no," I tried to comfort her. "I thought about it. It was a compliment." Inwardly I reaffirmed my decision to never tell her I had been one Jetway away from never seeing her again.

Alex smiled and let out a sigh. *Good call, Linden.*

"Actually, I kind of missed you yesterday," I told her.

Did I really say that?

Alex lit up. "Really?"

"Yeah, we've spent so much time together that it felt strange to be apart for the day." *How weird would it have felt to be apart forever?*

"Thanks for telling me. . . . I felt that way, too."

Alex reached across the table and took my hand. It was the first time she'd touched me since I'd discovered she was a woman. It felt a bit creepy, and I stiffened. I closed my eyes and tried to relax. As I let go, her touch felt more natural. I reached out with my other hand and took her hand in both of mine. My mind was going nuts with objections, but somehow it felt right.

As we touched, I could feel Alex as a woman. In her eyes I saw depth and tenderness. I felt safe with her, an ease I'd wished I had with other women but never did. We kept looking into each other's eyes for what turned into a long time. Then something really strange happened: I felt a strong sensation in my chest, like an old, hard stone starting to chip, then crack. I could feel my heart—not my physical heart—my *heart.*

I can't remember the last time I felt this. When I was a kid? Ever?

Alex sensed that something was happening inside me; I think I may have started to tremble. At first she looked worried, but there was nothing she could say or do. I had to feel what I had to feel. Naked. Scared. Excited. Embarrassed. Humbled. I started to sweat.

Alex took a napkin from the table and wiped my forehead. I broke into a nervous smile. *Breathe, Linden, breathe.* When my flush receded, I leaned toward Alex, drew her hands toward my face, and placed them on my cheeks. Her palms felt soothing. My mother had touched my face like that when I was very little. She stopped, I think, when I started school. Until that moment with Alex, I hadn't realized how much I'd missed it.

I closed my eyes and basked in the warmth of her hands. Her fingertips were calloused from our journey, yet her palms were soft. I sensed that she'd closed her eyes, too. I felt secure in the darkness; maybe she did, too.

I moved Alex's hands to my lips, and I began to kiss them softly. *What the hell do you think you're doing?* a voice chided from a deep crevice of my psyche. But it was too late to pull back now. My lips were trailing along her fingers, not so much kissing, but caressing and smoothing. We were having the conversation with our bodies that had felt too uncomfortable to have with words.

I opened my eyes and watched a small, soft smile spread over Alex's lips, more genuine than any smile she'd offered before. In all the time I'd been with her, I'd never seen her happier. After a while, she took my hands and placed them, palms together, against her right cheek. It, too, was soft and warm. I melted a little more. I was starting to feel out of control. Part of me wanted to run out the door, but what we were doing felt good. I didn't want the feeling to end.

I looked into Alex's eyes and saw not a little brother or a threatening man-eater, but a sensual woman. I let my shoulders drop. Slowly our faces drew closer together. I was getting lost in her eyes. *There is so much more to her than I realized.* Finally we met midtable, and our lips touched. At first it felt more like a meeting than a kiss. We just held the touch for a long time, as if both of us were reluctant to go further, but more reluctant to go back. Soon we were leaning more firmly into each other, and I began to feel tingly. The energy started to overtake me. Our kiss grew stronger and deeper and went on and on. I'm sure people were gawking, and it created a stir in the dining room. I didn't care.

I cupped my hands around Alex's cheeks and chin. She dropped her hands to my shoulders and drew me close to her. We kissed harder. Longer. People looked more. I cared less.

The wall had crumbled.

43

Alex signed the tab, we rose in synchrony, and we slipped out of the dining room, trying not to attract any more attention. I took some comfort in thinking that there might be a few couples in the hotel who could understand what was overtaking us. Not that *I* did.

Alex and I walked hand in hand back to the bungalow, mostly looking down at the ground, without a word between us. Occasionally we would glance at each other and flash a short, nervous smile. When we reached our room, I opened the lock easily enough, but the door was swollen with the humidity. I leaned Alex against it, pressed my full body against hers and kissed her hard. She received my advance and pressed her body to mine, tentatively at first, then more firmly. There was no question about it now—Alex was a woman. At last the door gave way, and we practically tumbled into the bungalow. I kicked the door closed behind us.

We were making love before we even had our clothes off. It was a physical thing, sure, but something more was happening between us. Some invisible force was moving us without our controlling it. We were part of a dance that seemed impromptu, yet orchestrated; scary, yet exhilarating.

As we fell into bed, I had the oddest sensation that we'd done this before. This wasn't a new meeting, but a reunion, as if it had been planned for a long time and the universe was just waiting for us to catch up with the program. How, during all the time we'd spent together, could I have overlooked that Alex was a gorgeous, alluring woman?

As we moved deeper into our merging, I realized how lopsided my life had become—terribly weighted toward loneliness, dry masculinity, and living in my head while denying my heart. Opening up to Alex restored a softer element that had cost me dearly to ignore. Was my long and painful struggle to find myself simply my quest for balance? Now with a vibrant, sensual woman in my arms, I felt nourished in a way I could never have found by myself. Finally, my mind gave up, and I surrendered to the magic enfolding me. For the first time in a long, long time, I felt whole.

44

We spent most of the next three days in bed making love, napping, reading to each other, discussing cosmic ideas, and talking in a mock Indian accent irreverently suggestive of the other guests. Laughter returned to my spirit and, Alex told me, light to my eyes. I thought I'd been in love before, but my connection with Alex opened a door I didn't even know existed. If Vicky was a bad dream, Alex was waking up.

"This is like a scene in a movie," I told her as we woke up on our final morning at Rani Prema. Alex set a pillow between us, propping our heads up so we could face each other nose to nose.

"How's that?"

"Well, you know how in every romantic movie there's a segment where the couple is falling in love?"

"Like?"

"Like a montage of scenes where they're washing the car and squirting water at each other. Or riding a motorcycle, their hair blowing in the wind. Or strolling along a beach at sunset, holding hands, trailed by their big, friendly golden retriever. Meanwhile Barry White is singing some corny love song in the background."

Alex smiled. She'd seen those movies, too.

"It feels like that's the scene we're in now," I told her. I wondered if the phrase "falling in love" was too loaded. I was just talking about the movies.

"Okay, count me in," Alex said, appearing neither shaken by the phrase nor enamored by it.

Just then the chambermaid knocked. "Housekeeping! Do you want your room serviced?"

We looked around. We'd been holed up like John and Yoko for three full days; towels needed to be cleaned, and the toilet paper was almost gone. Alex giggled, "I guess we should give them a shot at cleanup."

"Yeah," I agreed, "let's get outside before they send in a search party."

❀

Twenty minutes up a hiking trail, we were privy to a panoramic view of the lush valley that cradled the resort. We could see emerald hillsides, a small river meandering through the plain, shirtless farmers in their fields, and in the far distance, children walking to school. For a moment I had the sense that the world, in spite of all my resistance, was all right. Even the people living down the road in tin shacks weren't outside of love's embrace. Their joy depended on nothing material, and they were free in a way that people with lots of stuff couldn't claim.

"Hey, Linden, they have a garden!" Alex shouted as she rounded a bend ahead of me. I caught up and saw a plateau with long rows of colorful vegetables. We ambled along the path and let ourselves in through a rickety wooden gate, where we beheld well-kept beds of lettuce, beets, tomatoes, potatoes, cabbage, and an assortment of vegetables and herbs I didn't recognize. When I spotted a row of succulent snow peas, I plucked two ripe pods and handed one to Alex. She bit into it with a loud crunch, her eyes bulged, and she let out a long *"Wwwwooooowwww!"*

"Do you like our garden?" a voice asked from behind us.

Startled, we turned to see a dark-skinned Indian man in his mid-forties, slightly paunchy, with a small patch of gray at his hairline.

"Sorry if we picked without permission," I offered.

"That's all right," he answered with a smile, a small gold cap on one of his front teeth glistening in the sun. "If you didn't eat it here, you would have gotten it in the dining room."

I had to restrain myself to keep from cracking up. The guy's accent was identical to the one Alex and I had been impersonating. I flashed a sneaky glance at her. She understood.

"I am Ramesh, head gardener," he told us proudly as he approached us.

"Nice garden you have here."

"Would you like a tour?"

Of course. As we wandered through the beds, Ramesh pointed out his favorite plants like a schoolteacher showing off his best students. He was especially pleased with the okra and cauliflower. When we arrived at the lettuce patch, I noticed some pest damage. "You know, Ramesh, if you place a saucer of beer at the base of the lettuce, the slugs will go for it and leave the lettuce alone," I told him.

"Really?" Ramesh returned. "You're not pulling my rope?"

Alex and I had to stifle our laughter again. "You mean, 'yanking my chain'? No, really," I assured him.

"And if you plant some garlic around the cabbage rows," Alex added, "they'll resist bugs, too."

Strolling through the rows, we were entranced by exotic vegetables we'd never seen before, like north Indian black chickpeas, ridge gourds, and parsley-like ajwain. Ramesh picked up on our excitement; we were like kids in a toy store.

Finally, we returned to the garden entrance. "You two know your stuff," Ramesh told us as he opened the gate. "If you ever want a job here, we can use you. We'll give you room and board and a small salary. You can stay as long as you want."

A generous offer. "Thanks, but we have tickets to go back to America tomorrow," I told him.

"Okay, safe travels," Ramesh wished us in his comical accent, flashing us a thumbs-up before he went on with his rounds.

❀

As soon as we got back to our room, Alex flopped on the bed. "What did you think of his offer?" she asked, folding her hands behind her head.

I plopped down beside her. "You mean to stay here?"

Alex cocked her head like a puppy asking for a treat. "It could be fun."

"But we're flying out tomorrow."

"Yes, but to what?" she retorted quickly. "We have no jobs, money, or place to stay. When my dad gets back from his European jaunt, he'll discover that we've pumped our way through Asia with his plastic, and cancel our card. You have no burning desire to see your mom and stepfather, do you?"

I grimaced. "About as much as I yearn for the Chinese border guards . . ."

"So what do we have to lose, Linden?" Alex turned and faced me directly. "We love this place. Any room they give us will be ten times as nice as all the places we've stayed put together. Besides, who knows how long you'll be around? Or me? Let's live the good life while we can."

Suddenly it hit me: "You don't want to go back to the States, do you?" I asked her.

Alex heaved a sigh. "Not really."

"Why not?"

"I don't feel connected to anyone back there."

"What about your dad?"

Alex's face flushed. "My dad hurt me awfully," she answered. I could see a vein start to pulse on the side of her neck. This was a first—Alex upset, and me the rational one.

"Did he, like, beat you or abuse you or something like that?"

"Worse," she replied, contorting her face. "If he was mean to me, at least I would have had a relationship with him. His crime was terminal absence. He spent most of his time jetting around three continents fattening his portfolio and cavorting with high rollers and hookers. When my mom finally divorced him, he had the deep pockets for lawyers and she didn't, so he got custody, and my brother, sister, and I ended up in his big, empty house."

"An empty house? With all that money?"

Alex sat up and shot me the stink eye meant for her father. "He had plenty of stuff, all right—a world-class wine cellar, state-of-the-art home theater, red vintage Jaguar . . . and on and on, *ad nauseam*. The house felt empty, Linden, because he was never there. We were raised by our au pair and the property manager. They were nice enough, but no substitute for a real father."

"So this trip is like flipping your father the bird," I concluded. "The Buddhist lifestyle flies in the face of his materialism, and maxing out his credit card hits him in the pocket, where it hurts."

"Oh, it would take a lot more than we've spent to hurt him," she snickered.

"Exactly. Simply being here with me is an act of rebellion. I'm the opposite of everything he would wish for you."

"Well, maybe," Alex answered, still huffy. "But I wouldn't be here if I didn't love you. Nobody in her right mind would go through what I've gone through just to spite her father."

I decided not to pursue the issue. Apparently we both had pasts we were trying to leave behind.

45

India is a study in contrasts. Searing heat followed by monsoon onslaughts. Opulent castles towering over depressing squalor. Frail, loincloth-clad yogis meditating in remote ashrams, while tattooed, pierced kids cruise neon-bathed nightclubs. Old women selling homegrown vegetables laid out on city streets in front of office buildings where their computer-savvy kids are answering tech-support calls from Americans trying to install wireless routers. A nation of 1.2 billion, with perhaps the richest spiritual tradition in the world, marred by a long history of political assassinations. The site on planet Earth where truth is simultaneously the most obvious and the most obscure.

The Rani Prema Resort, quietly tucked away from poverty and politics, became my oasis. How I got there still seems unbelievable to me. Yet for the first time in my life I felt a sense of peace that lasted for more than a fleeting moment. Perhaps my life could work—if I were allowed to live it.

❀

"Your hair is growing in," I commented as Alex leaned over to harvest some cinnamon.

"Five months is a long time for a hair," she called back over her shoulder with a chuckle.

"I must say I find you more attractive as a woman than as a man," I replied.

"Well, that's a relief!" Alex exclaimed as she stood up, forming a picturesque image against a backdrop of burgeoning saffron.

"Hey, you two!" Ramesh called to us from his pickup truck. "Will you close the gate when you're done? I have to go into town to pay my wife's electric bill." He threw his hands up and added with resignation, "I have to take care of my karma!"

We nodded and waved our quirky boss on his way. "Speaking of karma," Alex remarked as she tossed a handful of cinnamon sticks into a basket, "have you had any visits from the Lords of Karma lately?"

Her question took me by surprise. "Not really. . . . Why do you ask?"

"I don't know—it was such a big thing for you, and you haven't said anything about it for a while."

I put aside the basket of minty pudina I'd just picked. "To tell you the truth, Alex, I really haven't thought much about it. Maybe they've given me a reprieve."

"That's good," she replied, a smile spreading over her face. "I'd like to keep you on Earth for a while."

I started to bend down to pick up the pudina, but Alex's question had stirred me up. I stood back up and faced her. "But, since you asked, there is something that's been bugging me . . ."

"What's that?"

"Do you remember my theory about how all those falling-in-love movie segments are the same?"

"Yeah, sure." Alex giggled. "That was clever."

"Well, there's another piece to the formula, just as predictable."

"What's that?" she asked, taking a swig from her water bottle.

"The shit hits the fan."

Her brow creased. "Like . . . ?"

"Like one of the lovers gets a horrible disease, or a secret skeleton from the past comes back to haunt them, or the woman finds out the guy has a wife . . ."

Alex's jaw dropped in feigned horror, and she made an angry face. "You're not secretly married, are you?"

"Oh yeah, I've been meaning to tell you—I have a thing going with Ramesh. . . . Come on, Alex, I'm being serious now!"

Alex moved the cinnamon basket aside and took a few steps toward me.

"Well, our time together has been so magical that . . . that . . ." I faltered.

"Just spit it out, Linden."

". . . that sometimes I'm afraid the other shoe will drop."

Alex seemed unfazed. "And how might that happen?"

I wished I hadn't opened my mouth, but it was too late to stop now. "What if the Lords of Karma hold me to my vow? I gave my word, and they don't take that lightly. There are a million ways people could die. I heard about a guy who tripped and fell with his face in his dog's water bowl and drowned."

Alex burst out laughing. "Come on, Linden, get real, would you?"

"The law of karma is *real,* Alex," I argued. "In a way, this scene seems too good to be true—you and I together in this enchanting place. No responsibilities, no worries, no families to hassle us. We have a great thing going. In those movies this would be a perfect setup for a crash—"

"But this *isn't* one of those movies, Linden," Alex interrupted, her eyes afire. "This is *our* movie, and we get to produce it however we want. I love you, and I'm not about to lose you to some cosmic karmic bogeyman."

"I'd like to think that, too, Alex—but what about destiny? Don't you believe we set things in motion that we have to face later?"

She nodded. "Sure, but we can also make new choices that affect what comes around. I don't think this is about facing destiny, Linden. I think this is about facing yourself. If you made a choice due to fear and you keep making fear-based choices to escape your first one, I don't think you're advancing much spiritually. I think some religions and philosophies just keep people going in little circles. If there's a wheel you want to escape, escape the one you've drawn around your mind."

46

The son of a Brahman priest and a hairdresser, Ramesh Chand embodied a curious amalgam of spirituality and materialism. He would recite a long litany of Hindu prayers upon awakening each morning and then log on to the Internet to bet on horse races. He believed that his gods helped him win, and attributed his losses to bad karma from a previous life.

One evening while I was having a beer with Ramesh in his bungalow, I reached for a magazine on his coffee table and found a family photo album underneath, which I started flipping through. Ramesh pointed out his son, an astrophysicist; and his daughter, who worked as a makeup artist in the Indian porn industry. "'Just keep staying on that side of the camera,' I tell her," he clarified. "She had a job taking reservations for United Airlines, but porno pays more. It's all about economics, you know."

Whatever.

Leafing through the album, I saw Ramesh's wife, who left, he explained, when she got fed up with his gambling. ("I never really lost any money—just my family.") Most of the photos showed his family posing proudly in front of their over-the-top Mumbai home, the color of which was something like "Pepto-Bismol/neon iguana." I practically had to avert my eyes to avoid the kind of retinal damage you might sustain from looking at a solar eclipse straight on.

"She got the house, but I landed here at the resort. I made out better, don't you think?"

Duh.

I turned the page quickly. Ah, a soothing panorama of regal mountains blanketed with verdant forest. "Where's that?" I asked, far more interested in this view than the gaudy city digs. Ramesh pulled the album toward him and studied the photo. A small smile played on his lips, and I saw pleasure in his eyes that had been absent a moment earlier. "That's our country place in Melghat, a few hundred kilometers from here. My uncle left it to me a few years ago. He had a long feud with my father, but he always liked me. I'm not sure if he willed it to me because he loved me or he wanted to spite my dad."

The property looked really sweet. Rolling hills with sweeping vistas, fruit trees, a garden, and a small but nicely kept house.

"I hardly ever get up there," Ramesh explained almost wistfully. "It's so far, and I'm so busy. What a shame—a great hideaway just sitting there." He turned the page quickly, I imagined, because he felt sad that he didn't get to be in the one place that would probably clear his head of all the bullshit he'd gotten immersed in.

The next photo showed Ramesh with a thin old man in a white dhoti, standing in front of a Hindu temple. "That's my father, bless his memory," Ramesh said. The two were posing before a wall painted with quotes from the Hindu scriptures and adorned with photos of gurus. Amid the array, one symbol vaguely jogged my memory, but I couldn't quite place it. I thought and thought, to the point that I felt irritated. To quell my anxiety, I rose to grab another beer from the fridge. As I passed the kitchen window, I surveyed the mountains surrounding the resort. *Mountains . . . mountains . . . the cave . . .* That was it! The symbol was the one I'd seen on the wall of the Cave of Khadroma.

I rushed back to the photo and studied it. *Yes, that was it.* "What is that symbol, Ramesh?" I asked. "I must know!"

"Which symbol? There are a bunch of them."

"That one there," I replied impatiently, pointing to it. "The one over your father's left shoulder."

Ramesh studied the image again. I hoped he wasn't too drunk to answer.

"That's not a Hindu symbol. It's Tibetan."

Of course. "I know, I know. . . . What does it mean?"

"Our temple was decorated by a yogi who studied in Tibet. He painted that image."

"Okay, okay. What does it mean?"

He shrugged his shoulders. "I don't know. My father never explained it to me."

My heart sank. *So close and yet so far.*

Tired, soused, and disappointed, I decided it was time to head back to my room. I thanked Ramesh for his hospitality, told him I would pray that his daughter stayed in the makeup department, and closed the door behind me. As I left, I peeked in the window and saw Ramesh opening up a racing page on the Internet.

47

After hearing Ramesh's horror story about his tanked marriage, I was glad to wake up next to Alex the following morning. As soon as I saw her eyes open, I reached to pull her toward me.

"Uh-uh," she protested, pushing my hand away. "Sorry, hon—I don't feel so good." She tried to say it diplomatically, but didn't quite hit the mark.

Here it comes . . . the other shoe is dropping. My imagination fast-forwarded to her long, lingering illness and me shouldering her coffin.

"My stomach," she moaned, moving her hands to her abdomen. "I never should have had that spicy soup last night. I'm just not cut out for Indian food. Where's a good Mocha Frappuccino when I need one?"

I withdrew and gently held Alex's hand.

"Just get me the hot-water bottle, would you?"

I went to the kitchenette to boil some water, and then retrieved the thick red rubber bag from the cabinet below the bathroom sink. Minutes later I laid it against Alex's belly and invited her to rest her head on my lap. I rubbed her forehead like my mom used to when I wasn't feeling well; that was always a soothing memory for me.

"Ah, that's better," Alex cooed and closed her eyes. Drifting off to sleep, she looked like a little girl. I could picture her at age seven, tucked under the covers, hugging a stuffed animal. When I moved to get up, however, Alex opened her eyes, which bulged like the possessed little girl in *The Exorcist.*

"Out of my way!" she yelled as she threw off the covers, ditched the hot-water bottle, and dashed for the bathroom. She slammed the door behind her with her foot, but not before I saw her drop to her knees in front of the toilet bowl. The sounds that ensued were ungodly. *Poor Alex.*

Five minutes later she emerged, pale as a hospital sheet. "God help me, Linden," she groaned. "If this is paying off karma for something, I will soon be totally liberated." Alex threw herself back on the bed and stared at the ceiling for a long time, alternately closing her eyes, trying to sleep, and opening them when she couldn't. Finally, she announced, "That's it! I refuse to lie here like a fucking invalid." She rose and started dressing.

"Where are you going?"

"To see the resort doctor. . . . One thing you may not know about me, Linden: I have a low threshold for pain. I can suffer to help someone I love, but when it comes to suffering for *me,* I see no purpose. I'll see you in a while."

She was out the door before I could say a word. I jumped up to follow her.

❀

Dr. Amrita Reddy was on call in Bungalow 12, a two-bedroom unit allotted to her by her son, Jaya, assistant manager at Rani Prema. Dr. Reddy had retired from her medical practice a few years earlier and decided she would live the good life while she could. The resort gave her a small stipend to be available to their guests, who suffered mostly from Delhi belly and internal curry burns. Few of the guests were daring enough to injure themselves rock climbing or spelunking, so the outer limits of her practice were joint pain and irregularity.

When the doctor emerged from her quarters, she struck me as an Indian version of Aunt Bee from *The Andy Griffith Show*. Endearingly portly, with a prominent nose and pulled-back graying hair, Dr. Reddy carried herself with likable dignity. Her choice of a floral sari rather than a lab coat made us feel more like her friends than her patients. The physician shooed the resident tabby cat from her desk, received Alex kindly, ushered her into the examining room, and closed the door behind them, leaving me in the frayed wicker chair to babysit my morbid thoughts.

To distract myself, I perused the makeshift library of books left by tourists: predictable romance novels; *Reader's Digest* condensations; and the perennial favorite, *Windows 95 for Dummies*. Much of India was like slipping into a time warp.

The longer Alex remained in the examining room, the more anxious I grew. I'd inherited my mother's "There's a dark cloud in front of every silver lining" mentality. If a pessimist sees the half-empty portion of a glass of water, my mother would see the crack in the glass through which any remaining water might escape. Now that I had the world on a string, I had plenty to lose. I kept checking the small travel alarm clock on the doctor's desk. Twenty-five minutes gone. *What the hell are they doing in there?*

Five minutes later the door opened. I tried to read the two women's faces. They looked serious but not pained. The first chance I got, I caught Alex's eyes, but she didn't hold my glance long enough for me to get a reading. The tension was killing me.

"See me again in two weeks," Dr. Reddy instructed Alex. *Does that mean something is wrong that needs to be checked, or something is right enough that it doesn't demand immediate attention?* My mind was spinning out.

"Well?" I asked Alex as soon as we were outside.

"I'll tell you when we get back to the room."

I couldn't tell if Alex was feeling good or trying to paste a pleasant demeanor over a grave situation. Our walk back to the bungalow was agonizingly silent.

❀

"Okay, what's up?" I demanded as I closed the door behind us.

"Sit down, Linden," Alex ordered, kicking off her shoes.

Oh God, that's not a good prelude. I took a seat in the armchair.

To my surprise, Alex didn't sit on the edge of the bed opposite me, as I'd expected. Instead, she approached the armchair, lifted her skirt, spread her legs apart, and straddled me. *Sex? Now? What the hell is she thinking? Does she want one last fling before launching into the great beyond? Is this her version of* Dr. Strangelove?

Alex kissed me hard on the lips, so hard that she pressed my head into the back of the chair. *Is she wigging out in the face of a dire diagnosis?*

She sensed my tension and rubbed my shoulders softly, as if to say, *It's okay, relax.* But I couldn't relax. I needed to know what was happening to her.

Alex leaned back far enough for me to see her eyes. She looked serious, very serious. Then the corners of her mouth turned up into a nervous smile. *Some people mask pain with false joviality.* I was totally bewildered, and she was freaking me out.

Alex leaned toward me until her lips were practically touching my ear. Then she whispered, "We're going to have a baby."

48

Fatherhood had never been a possibility I took seriously, especially since my father deserted me. Hell, I could hardly deal with my own life, let alone be responsible for a child's.

"You're making this up, right?" I snapped at Alex.

"No, Linden, I'm not making this up. *We are going to have a baby.*"

She said it again. I tried to wrap my mind around the idea, but there was no compartment for it. It was like hearing, "You've just been elected to fly to Jupiter."

"Are you sure?" was all I could think to say.

"The doctor did the test twice. Two stripes means baby. There were definitely two stripes. Besides, she can tell. She's had five kids."

I just sat there, stiff as the big statue of Abraham Lincoln at the Lincoln Memorial. But not nearly as calm.

"Well, aren't you happy?" she asked, giggling nervously.

"I . . . I don't know, Alex," I had to tell her honestly. "I think I have to believe it first. That could take years."

"Well, you better hurry up. We have about seven and a half months."

I don't know if I can describe what went on inside me, but I'll try:

First, absolute terror. *What do I know about being a father?* I liked playing with the kids from the park across from the dharma center, but that was for all of twenty minutes at a time. Then they went back to their mothers, and I went back to my garden. *Can I handle any more time than that?*

Then, a deep sense of shame and inadequacy. Six months earlier I'd been a bum panhandling in the Tenderloin district, eating leftover sandwiches out of Dumpsters, peeing in alleys, and relieving my sexual tensions in my cardboard "boudoir." *What kind of kid would want a father like that? What kind of kid* deserves *a father like that? How can I bring a child into a world that he or she may one day be praying to be liberated from?*

Next, a huge sense of pressure. *How will I support a wife and child? Did I say "wife"? Will we have to get married now?* My mind went full tilt—like the cartoons where Daffy Duck runs into a wall and a reel of symbols spins through his eyes like a slot machine, until he keels over. I was close.

Alex sensed my anxiety and clasped my shoulders more firmly. "Come on, big guy, snap out of it. You'll be a great dad! I told you I fell in love with you when I saw you with that kid in the garden."

She doesn't know who I really am. She doesn't recognize my hidden terrors and shortcomings and issues. "You don't understand, Alex," I argued. "I'm not cut out to be a father."

Alex smiled a knowing smile. "That's what half the men in the world say. Then they just do it. Some of them really like it."

Some. Not all.

"But what about us, Alex? Where will we live? How will we pay for our family? We can't live off your father's credit card forever."

Alex's face turned serious, and she averted her eyes as if I'd hit a nerve. "What's the matter?" I asked.

"My father already canceled the card." She sighed as she got up and then flopped down on the couch.

"How do you know?"

"He told me."

"You *talked* to him?"

"I got an e-mail."

"An e-mail? How? Where?"

"At the resort office. They have an Internet station that employees can use. I e-mailed him a couple of times, just to let him know I'm okay."

I started to feel nauseated. And it wasn't from morning sickness.

"Are you going to tell him you're pregnant?"

Alex rolled her eyes. "Are you serious? He'd be on the next plane over, have you arrested, and snatch me up personally. Daddy's little girl, you know . . ."

I let my head fall back on the chair and stared at the ceiling. "That puts us in an even worse position, Alex," I complained, shaking my head. "I knew he'd pull the plug sometime, but the timing couldn't be worse! How are we going to survive?"

Alex glared at me. "Linden Kozlowski, I'm surprised at you! We've both just been on the most incredible adventure of our lives, totally taken care of at every turn—we've been sheltered and fed; met the coolest people; and survived raging rivers, wild beasts, Chinese soldiers, and rickety bridges . . . and just look where we are now!"

I scanned the plush couch, marble countertops, and Italian-crafted overhead fans. Out the window I observed a hand-carved statue of Krishna playing his flute, an aromatic Arabian jasmine hedge, and lavish waterways meandering through impeccably landscaped grounds.

"We're living at a romantic resort, eating gourmet food, getting out into nature every day, and spending the best time of our lives with each other," she went on. "How much better could it get?"

She was right. *Someone or something is taking care of us.*

Then I remembered what I wished I could forget: *I may be gone soon.* I'd made my vow to the Lords of Karma. I was going to die and never, ever come back to Earth. Now I wouldn't be leaving just a screwed-up world behind. I'd be leaving a woman I loved and a child who needed me. If I left now, I would be more despicable than my father. *This changes everything.* I couldn't leave now. I had to stay.

Alex watched my face. "Now what, Linden?"

"My vow," I reminded her. "I don't know how much longer I'll be here. I don't want to leave you and the baby."

I tried to camouflage my remorse, but couldn't. Alex took me in her arms and started to kiss my face like a baby. She kissed my cheeks and my eyes and my forehead and my nose. "Linden, Linden, Linden," she said in a soft voice. "You don't have to go anywhere. It's time you got over this horrible fear of karma. No one is taking you away. If you want to stay, you can and you will."

I wished she were right. "You don't understand, Alex," I argued. "You weren't in that cave with me. I know you think I made it all up, but it was real. The Lords of Karma were there. They heard my vow, and my decision was recorded. These were not people. *These were gods, Alex. Gods.* They're powerful. Don't underestimate them. They'll take me where and when they choose."

49

From that day on, I didn't take Alex or anything about our relationship for granted. I began to savor every moment. Our talks, our meals, our lovemaking, our time in the garden, and our evening walks all became precious. My senses were heightened, and every experience intensified: the amber and burgundy sunrise; the chorus of larks greeting the morning; a tiny new pepper popping out from a stalk; kids giggling on a tire swing; the tingling of garlic *roti* bread against my tongue; plopping into bed, good-tired after a day in the garden; falling asleep gazing into Alex's loving eyes. *Where have I been all my life?*

A couple of nights a week I'd hang with Ramesh in his bungalow and down a couple of Kalyani Gold beers with him. It felt good to have a guy friend; men understand each other. One night while watching the original *Godzilla,* I asked Ramesh, "Do you like being a father?"

He took a sip from his bottle and answered, "Sure—best thing I've ever done."

I was surprised. "But you've worked hard all your life to support your wife and kids; and now you're divorced, your wife has your house, and your daughter works in, well . . . was it all worth it?"

Ramesh set his beer down and put the movie on pause. "Sure, there are hard parts," he told me. "But I love my kids, and I'm proud of them. When I see them happy, I know I was born for a good purpose."

"So you'd do it all over again?"

Ramesh laughed. "That's the *only* thing I would do over again," he answered. Then he pressed a button on the remote and caught the final shrieks of Japanese hordes stampeding through the Ginza district.

"What made you ask?" he asked over his shoulder.

"Alex is pregnant," I told him straight up.

Ramesh paused the DVD again and turned to me. "Really?"

"That's not the kind of thing a guy would make up, is it?"

Ramesh's face lit up. "That's wonderful, Linden!"

I tried to force a smile, but I don't think I was convincing. "I guess so," I half-whined. "It's just that Alex and I haven't been together for that long, and I don't know how long I'm going to be around. I want my kid to have a father."

Ramesh gave my knee a comforting pat. "There are no guarantees about anything in life, Linden. You just have to play it as it comes." He reached for his beer. "My son, Rupesh, was a surprise."

"Really?"

"My wife and I weren't getting along, and when we found out she was pregnant, we had a big fight. She wanted to have the baby, and I didn't want her to have it. So I prayed to our family's patron god, Ganesha, and he told me to let God's will be done."

"And it worked out?"

"It *more* than worked out." Ramesh smiled. "The minute I saw Rupesh, I loved him. Now that he's grown, we're like best friends."

That was comforting. "Well, maybe I could be a good father—I guess."

"If I could do it, Linden, so can you."

Ramesh raised his Kalyani to toast, and I lifted my bottle to meet his. I didn't tell him about my deal with the Lords of Karma. If we were going for a miracle, it would have to be across the board.

50

The next night I took Alex on a dinner date in the fine dining room. It was a splurge on our meager salary, but when your days may be numbered, money becomes a detail rather than an issue. We topped off the meal with champagne. "To us," I toasted, "and our family!"

"To us and our family!" Alex echoed, our glasses clinking.

I took her hand, found her eyes, and blurted out, "Let's get married!"

Alex practically choked on her champagne. "You want to get married?"

"Yes, yes, I do, Alex. I want to get married. I want to marry you."

I stood up, raised my glass, and shouted to everyone in the dining room, "I want you all to know that I want to marry this woman! I am totally in love with her and our life together. I am also in love with our baby." I pointed to her tummy.

The startled patrons shut up and gave me their attention. Then they smiled. Alex looked embarrassed, but I could tell she loved it.

I dropped to one knee, took Alex's hand, and asked her, still loud enough for everyone to hear, "Alex Leister, will you marry me?"

Alex smiled as a few small tears ran down her cheek. "Yes, Linden Kozlowski," she answered, not as loud as I'd been. "I would be honored to marry you."

All the patrons broke into cheers and applause. But they didn't matter. Only Alex, and the two of us, and our baby mattered.

That was our wedding. We never went to a church, temple, dharma center, cave, or the all-night Chapel of Elvis. We didn't need to. Our vows couldn't have been any stronger or clearer, and God couldn't have heard them more plainly.

51

"Are you Alexandra?" the man in the dark blue uniform inquired with a pointed glare. Standing beside Alex at our bungalow door, I searched her eyes anxiously.

"That's right."

"I am Agent Sharma of the India Immigration Authority. May I see your passport and visa?"

Over his shoulder we could see a police car at the roadside, a cop smoking a cigarette in the driver's seat.

"Sure," Alex answered soberly and stepped back from the door. We both knew precisely where this was heading. She reached under the bed, slid out her bag, and rummaged through one of the pockets until she unearthed the documents. *Now for the onslaught.*

Sharma flipped through the papers. "Your visa expired on December 12th, Miss Lee . . . ? Lay . . . ? Leister. Today is February 20th. You have overstayed your visa more than two months."

"I know, officer, it's just that—"

"May I see your documents, sir?" he asked, turning to me.

I silently strode to the closet, found my fanny pack, and removed my passport and visa. The officer repeated his inspection.

"You are also staying here illegally, Mr. Koz . . ."

We both just stood there without a word. *What could we say that he hasn't heard a thousand times before?*

"In light of your violations, I must order you to leave the country immediately," Agent Sharma stated pompously.

"Can't we apply for an extension?" I pleaded.

"You could have done so before your visa expired. Now it's too late. Do you have your return tickets to the United States?"

Both of us fiddled with our papers and produced them.

"Good. Now please get your things together."

"Now?" Alex asked, dumbstruck. "You want us to leave *now?*"

The officer stood erect and didn't flinch. "If you do not depart immediately, I will arrest you and you will spend time in jail before your deportation. It's your choice."

"But we have friends here," Alex begged. "And jobs. And a life."

"Have you been working illegally, too? That is another offense."

I could see we would get nowhere with Mr. Anal-Retentive. I looked at Alex and could tell she agreed. We sighed and dejectedly began to pack. He could have at least given us time to say good-bye to our friends.

"Officer Chitra and I will escort you to the airport and make sure you are on the next flight out," Agent Sharma informed us. Then (in a very British manner) he added, "I trust your journey home will be pleasant."

Well, thank you very much. That makes up for you being a dick.

It took us half an hour to get all of our gear together while Sharma waited outside the door. No discussions, no slack, no chance to slip away.

As we exited our beloved home, I realized that it was the only one that ever felt safe to me. But now even that had been wrenched away. If I wasn't so pissed off, I might have bawled.

Officer Chitra started the ignition as Sharma held the back door open for us. It was a real police car with bars between the front and rear seats and on the windows. *Jeez, do they really think we're criminals?* As we slid into the backseat, Alex asked Sharma,

"How did you know we were here?"

He hesitated for a moment as if deciding how much to tell us. "Your father phoned us," he answered as he shut the door with a thud.

52

As usual, the Mumbai airport was brash and chaotic, a highly incongruous sea of people surging in all directions. Stocky women in designer saris, sourpuss men in business suits, Sikhs wearing turbans, and elderly tourist groups with matching neon-chartreuse name badges. Americans on a spiritual pilgrimage to India. Indians on a financial pilgrimage to America. East meeting West in passing without either recognizing its own gifts.

Officer (please-don't-squeeze-the) Sharma would win no prizes for warmth, sharing all of three comments with us during the three-hour ride. But Sharma wasn't in his profession for the joy of it. He was a government cop, and, as he explained to us with neither judgment nor pity, he was just doing his job.

Immigration Man escorted us to the ticket counter and gave the airline agent his rap. We were obviously not the first deportees. The agent checked our tickets and informed us that we needed another $307 each to cover the difference between our original tickets and that day's flight. "Sorry, we have no more money," I explained, hoping that would be an excuse to stay.

"I have a credit card number to pay for the difference," the officer interjected with a kind of sadistic enthusiasm. The credit card account obviously gave him a sense of power.

"Whoa, they even have deportation plastic here!" I whispered to Alex.

Yet he produced no card. Instead, he read from a small piece of paper, enunciating each number ever so clearly, flaunting his English. When he finished, the airline agent asked, "And in whose name is the card, please?"

Officer Sharma did not, however, cite the Indian Immigration Authority as the card owner. "Mr. Alex Leister," he read proudly.

Jeez . . .

"That explains it," Alex said in a low voice, leaning toward me.

"What's that?"

"Dad has lots of dealings in Asia. I'm sure he expedited our departure with a few well-placed phone calls and gifts."

"And shall we bill Mr. Kozlowski's ticket to the same card?" the agent asked.

"Yes," the officer answered. (I'm sure that wasn't in Alex Sr.'s instructions. But he would be privy to his own generosity in about thirty days.)

As we presented our passports, a long line of Indians behind us were breathing down our necks (some actually approached the counter and read our information over our shoulders as if they were reviewing their own bank statement). A minute later we received our tickets: Air India Flight 9683, Mumbai to Dubai, departing at 8:35 P.M. Connecting to United Flight 977 to San Francisco. And should we feel moved to take a little detour in the United Arab Emirates? No worries; a local officer would meet us upon our disembarkation and make sure we were on our connecting flight.

Officer Sharma ushered us to the waiting area—two hours until departure. Apparently Indians were used to lines and waiting. Some were already camped by the gate, perusing the daily rag, listening to iPods, munching on little snacks of curry-coated dried peas, reading racy romance novels, supervising unruly children, and sleeping. India is all about masses of people. Everywhere.

When I had to go to the restroom, Sharma waited outside with Alex for my return. He did likewise for Alex. He and Mother India were clearly intent on our imminent departure.

53

"**Ladies and gentlemen,** Air India Flight 9683 to Dubai is now ready for boarding. We will begin with families with children, those needing assistance, and . . . *blah* . . . *blah* . . . *blah*." Alex and I gathered our gear and mobilized toward the Jetway. On the other side of the panoramic window sat a huge gleaming Boeing 777 being loaded with meals and luggage. I noticed a name painted on the nose of the plane: *Jataya*. I don't know why that caught my eye. It just did.

We bade a welcome farewell to Officer Sharma, who had kept us in his eagle sight for the duration of the wait (except for brief interludes of checking out non-sari'd chicks, some of whom we guessed had been worked on by Ramesh's daughter). Again, he wished us a pleasant journey, and we told him (under our breath) that we hoped he'd have sex in this lifetime. I'm sure the venerable constable remained at the gate until the plane's wheels were up.

We approached the agent at the entrance to the Jetway and handed him our boarding passes. As I glimpsed his face, he seemed both strange and familiar. Strange because he wasn't a typical Indian, probably not Indian at all. His skin was lighter than many Indians, thick and leathery, and he looked much older than most gate agents, deep wrinkles etched between his eyes and temples.

He resembled a mountain man more than a city slicker. As I caught his eye, I sensed a certain wisdom. *Why did he seem familiar?*

Alex and I took our places in the line that had backed up down the Jetway, the walls decorated with large romantic posters of the cities Air India flew to. When we reached the San Francisco ad, I stopped cold. The poster, of course, featured the Golden Gate Bridge. The last time I'd been on it, I was going to jump. My life in the city had been hell, and I left because I wanted to die—forever. Now returning to San Francisco, I wanted to live. I wanted to be with Alex and our baby. I wanted to grow old with her. I wanted to discover what life could be like without miserable depression. I wanted to know who I could be if I wasn't the loser I'd always believed I was. I wanted to know why I was born, not why I was going to die.

But I'd *agreed* to die. What a strange twist of destiny! As I gazed at Alex's growing tummy, now almost four months along, I realized that my angst had been growing within me simultaneously. If there was a God—or gods—out there somewhere, I sure could have used a hand right about now.

The flight attendant at the aircraft door greeted us and directed us to our seats. We made our way down the skinny aisle, waiting for people trying to shove all their worldly possessions into overhead compartments too small to fit their seriously oversized carry-ons. Finally we found our seats. We were lucky at the last minute to get two together, a window and an aisle. *Maybe the gods are smiling on us and this trip is the springboard for a new life.*

Eventually all the material goods of the Indian nation were stuffed overhead and we settled in. I buckled my seat belt and glanced across the aisle, where I saw an odd-looking woman wearing a dark shawl covering her head, leaving only her face exposed. She seemed familiar, too, jogging some vague memory, like the ticket taker. As we made eye contact, she nodded and smiled slightly. *Am I in some kind of* Twilight Zone *reality warp where everyone I knew from another life has squeezed through some cosmic wormhole to haunt me? Is God playing with my head for sport?*

As we taxied for takeoff, a flight attendant passed through the aisle checking that all seat belts were fastened. *What's a Chinese guy doing working for Air India?* Looking more like a coffeehouse poet than a flight attendant, he wore a small beard, and his hair—longer than most in his profession—was pulled back into a small bun. I thought I knew him, too. I started to feel really anxious.

"What's the matter?" Alex asked, sensing my disquiet.

"Nothing . . . nothing," I lied. "I guess I'm just a little nervous about heading back."

Alex squeezed my hand to comfort me.

The flight attendant noticed me getting fidgety. "Is there anything I can help you with, sir?" he asked, leaning over with a smile.

"No, thanks," I answered in a perfunctory tone. The fellow nodded and started to move on.

Well, since he asked . . . I tapped him on the arm, and he turned back.

"That name on the airplane's nose, Jataya, or something like that. What does that mean?"

The man nodded again as if he'd expected me to ask. Being that he was Chinese, I didn't think he'd know the answer. But he did. "*Jataya* is the Sanskrit word for a sacred hawk or vulture," he explained. "It's from the Hindu epic *Ramayana*. That's the name of the airplane we're on."

Hawk . . . hawk . . . hawk. . . . When had I been thinking about a hawk?

I searched my memory bank. *Scanning . . . scanning . . . scanning.* Then I remembered. *No, it couldn't be.* My dream . . . the one about the hawk eating the seagulls. I stiffened and whispered, "No way!"

"Now what?" Alex asked.

"Do you remember the dream I told you about? The one where the hawk ate the seagulls?"

"Sort of."

"What month is this?" I asked, the tension in my chest spreading to my stomach.

"It's February . . . Linden, what's going on?"

"What month did we get to the resort?"

"Let's see—I think it was July."

I counted aloud on my fingers. "August, September, October, November, December, January, February . . . that's seven months."

"So?"

"Seven months—seven seagulls. The hawk flying over the ocean devoured seven seagulls—*we have to get off this plane right now!*"

"Linden, what *are* you talking about?" I could feel perspiration surfacing on my forehead. Alex started to squirm.

"Don't you see, Alex? My dream was prophetic. I asked the Lords of Karma how and when I would die. They showed me a hawk devouring seven seagulls. The name of this plane is 'hawk,' and we just had seven amazing months together. We're about to fly over water. *Alex, this plane is going down, and it will take us with it, along with our last seven wonderful months.*"

I was scaring her. "Okay, Linden, just try to relax," she said, attempting to allay her own anxiety as much as mine. "I'm sure there's some explanation."

By then the plane was hurtling down the runway. Frantically I pressed the call button. The flight attendants were all in their jump seats for takeoff. The Chinese guy was facing us from his position near the galley. He heard my button go off and saw the light over my head. He caught my eye and pointed to the illuminated FASTEN SEAT BELT sign. He would remain seated until we were in the air, as would I, a prisoner of my own misguided intentions.

I began to sweat profusely. Alex looked really worried. She put her arm around me and held my hand tightly. She then stroked my shoulder and arm gently, like a mother trying to soothe a terrified child.

The takeoff seemed to last forever. Would the crash occur then, or would we plunge to a watery grave 500 miles out over the Arabian Sea? If I could have gotten up and run with all my might, I would have. But we were trapped.

Finally, the plane gained altitude and began to level off. The Chinese flight attendant released his shoulder harness and approached me.

"Is something wrong, sir?"

"We *have* to turn this plane around!" I told him. "We are doomed!"

"Why do you say that?" he asked with a dubious look.

"I had a dream . . . a hawk ate seven seagulls . . . this plane is the hawk. . . . You've got to tell the captain to turn around now. All of our lives depend on it. Not just mine. *I don't want to be responsible for killing 300 people.*"

The flight attendant turned to Alex. "Does your husband have a history of flying anxiety, ma'am?"

"No, no, nothing like that," Alex answered, more frightened by my histrionics than an impending crash.

"Listen to me, sir," the flight attendant said in a confident tone. He'd been through this before with fly-aphobics. "Just try to relax. I'll get you some aspirin and water if that will help. The course is in the hands of the pilot. Our flight plan is laid in. There is no turning back now. You'll be well taken care of." He touched me gently on the shoulder, nodded, and headed for the galley.

That nod . . . that nod . . . I *knew* that nod. I'd seen it before . . . *in the cave.* The nod of the Chinese sage. I knew the flight attendant looked familiar—it was Chuang-Tsu. My body started to shake. Alex grabbed me tighter. She looked terrified now.

"That was the Chinese Lord of Karma!" I told Alex in a voice loud enough that the guy sitting in front of me turned around. "Something is going on here . . ."

"Oh, Linden," Alex practically moaned. "Please let me help you. Please let *someone* help you."

I wished someone could have. But this event was orchestrated from a very high level. "And the guy who took our boarding passes . . . he was no Indian. He was Akar, the Tibetan Lord of Karma."

I looked across the aisle at the woman in the shawl. The nun. "I saw that lady in the cave, too, Alex. She was Teresa, the nun. She looks like one now, doesn't she?"

Alex gazed at the woman, who was reading. For the first time since I'd known Alex, she was at a complete loss.

"I'm not losing my mind," I practically yelled, fumbling with my seat belt and standing. "I asked the Lords of Karma for a sign, and they gave it. This is it. We're not going to make it over the water. You and I and our baby are going to die in a horrible plane crash. And there's nothing we can do. Did you hear the flight attendant say, 'Our flight plan is laid in. There is no turning back now'? That had a double meaning—he was saying that I'd sealed my destiny. *I have sealed my destiny.*"

The flight attendant returned, followed by a huge guy with a shaved head. He was Arabian, at least 250 pounds—some kind of thug or bouncer. He grabbed my shoulders and pressed me back down into my seat. There was no resisting this goon.

"Sir, I am an Air Security Constable empowered by the United Arab Emirates to maintain the safety of this aircraft," he told me. "I am trained in the martial arts, and I am carrying a weapon. If you create any further disturbance, I will disable you. Do you understand?"

I wanted to get up and twist this devil's head off. But he was far bigger—and stronger—than I was, and I could hardly move. He wasn't kidding. He would break my neck if he had to.

I shut up.

When he felt me give in, he released me. "Now do you think you can relax and cooperate for the rest of the flight?"

Our flight plan is laid in. There is no turning back now. It was a done deal. Even if the goon erased me, the flight would continue on. Everyone was going down, no matter what I did. There was no use resisting. The die was cast.

I nodded.

"All right, then. I'm sitting three rows behind you, and I'll be watching you. Have a nice flight."

I collapsed back against my seat. Alex, completely pale, tried to comfort me. It was just a matter of time.

54

I prayed like a madman. Maybe I *was* a madman. Now it wasn't just my death I'd set in motion; I would have the blood of the woman I loved and our unborn child on my hands. *Please, God, if there is any way to reverse my decision, please do it. I was a fool. I didn't understand my life. I didn't appreciate what I have. Do You have compassion in Your heart for fools? Do You punish people for choices made out of ignorance?*

Suddenly I realized I was talking to the God I was taught as a child, not the deities I'd learned of in Buddhism. Was fear shaking me to my emotional foundation? Or simply moving me to innate wisdom?

I took Alex's hands and found her eyes. She looked like a basket case.

"Alex, if anything happens to us, just know that I love you with all my heart. You're the best thing that ever happened to me. You've been nothing but kind and loving to me, and I screwed it all up. I hope that someday, somehow, you can forgive me. I don't think we have much time left together, but I vow to find you in heaven. I'll marry you there and be yours forever. I can't believe how stupid I've been to miss the gifts I've been given. And *you* are the best of all."

Alex began to sob, then practically bawl.

I turned to her tummy and placed my right hand gently on it. "Little one," I began, quivering, "thank you for coming into our lives. You have changed me even before you were born. Please know that your father loves you. If I had the chance to love you in person, I would be the best father in the world. I would help you find the gratitude for life that I missed. Please forgive me for taking your life away before you had a chance to live it."

I thought Alex was going to faint. Finally, she collected herself enough to say, "Linden, I don't know what's going on with you. With every cell of my being, I hope you're wrong. I love you, too, with all my heart, and I vow to be with you in this life or any other."

As we held each other, I felt the depth of the love we shared, which extended beyond anything that happened to our bodies. I'd heard about spiritual love many times, but now I felt it from the inside out.

Then something clicked within me—a strange sense of well-being, as if everything was going to be all right. I looked around the cabin and saw other passengers talking, laughing, and eating. Some were watching DVDs on their laptops, others were reading novels, and children were coloring. No one else on the plane appeared to be worried or stressed. Maybe, in spite of my fears, everything would be okay. We would land in Dubai and then San Francisco, and this crazy episode would be behind me. Alex and I would find a place to live and start a new life.

I sat back in my seat and closed my eyes. I felt relaxed for the first time during the flight, and I drifted off.

55

I awoke when I felt my equilibrium shift. I looked out the window and saw that the plane was making a long, wide turn—a minor course correction, I figured. But a minute later we were still turning, now at least ninety degrees away from our original bearing. We weren't heading toward Dubai anymore. Then the announcement came:

"Ladies and gentlemen, this is the captain. You may have noticed that we are making a turn. That's because we have lost use of our generator, which powers our electrical needs. Fortunately, we have a backup generator for situations just like this, so there is nothing to be concerned about.

"Since safety is our number one priority, I have decided to return to Mumbai. I do not want to take you across the sea without a backup generator. When we arrive in Mumbai, we will replace the defective equipment and start our journey again. I apologize for the delay, but I think you will agree with my reasoning. I repeat, there is no cause for alarm. Relax, and we should be landing in about an hour."

I felt a chill and looked at Alex. She tried to play it cool, but I could read behind her veneer of composure. Neither of us said a word; we just acted as if everything was all right, reading magazines and surfing the audio channels. Meanwhile, we held each other's clammy hands.

"Linden, there's something I need to tell you," Alex finally spoke up.

"What's that?"

"I like being a woman."

"You like being a woman?"

"Yes, I like putting on makeup, brushing my hair, and wearing frilly stuff. I like being a woman."

I turned and faced her directly. "Why are you telling me this now?"

"Just so I don't have to sit here and be scared shitless."

Got it. "Anything else?"

She swallowed and nodded. "The Buddhist monk thing wasn't really for me. When you met me, I was going to quit soon. I asked to be transferred from Ojai to San Francisco so I wouldn't be stuck in the L.A. basin when I left. It was a little sneaky, having the dharma center pay for my travel, but I didn't have any money, and it was my way of taking care of myself." Alex looked sheepish to be revealing her guilty secret. I placed my hand on top of hers to comfort her.

"Then why'd you stay?"

"I felt more for you in the first day I saw you than I ever felt for Buddhism. I saw something bigger in you than you saw in yourself. I still do."

How far and wide would I have to search to find a someone who loved me like this?

"How about you?" she asked. "Is there anything you want to tell me?"

I gulped. But I figured that with the end staring us in the face, I could tell her the whole truth. "I was scared shitless most of our trip upriver," I told her. "I continued because you were strong for both of us."

Alex smiled bittersweetly. "I guess we're doing sort of a confession, huh?"

"I guess."

I leaned my head back and tried to relax. As the minutes ticked by, I began to feel more confident that we would make it. For a long time I kept reading the same magazine pages over and over, retaining not a word. Finally I looked out the window and could see the lights of fishing boats in the far distance. We were approaching the coast. *Thank goodness. We're going to land.*

The intercom chime sounded, and the head flight attendant reached for the phone. *The captain is telling the cabin crew to prepare for landing.* After a short conversation, she summoned two other flight attendants standing nearby. I looked behind me toward the galley, where several more were conferring. Something was up.

"Ladies and gentlemen," the captain's voice returned over the PA system, this time more grave. "This is the captain again. Something highly unusual has occurred. Our backup generator is faltering. We're trying to revive it, but if we cannot, we will lose all electrical power on the aircraft. I have to tell you honestly that this is a serious situation, and we are setting into motion emergency-landing procedures. Please pay strict attention to the instructions from our flight attendants. We will do our best to land safely, but that depends on how long our power holds out. We will be turning off the cabin lights and all nonessential electrical equipment. This is a real emergency, so we ask you to do your best to stay calm and cooperate. I repeat, this is an emergency."

My heart leaped to my throat and I began to feel sick to my stomach. Alex clutched my arm as a wave of panic rippled through the cabin like rank smoke. The faces I could see registered shock and horror. An eerie murmur went up. People started holding hands, even across the aisles. Anxiety ruled.

I looked over at Teresa the nun, or whoever she was. At that exact moment, she turned her head to look at me, as if she knew precisely what was going on inside me. I tried to peer into her eyes, hoping that she might somehow relieve my dread. She appeared quite calm, in contrast to the other terrified passengers. She seemed to be saying to me, *Death is not what you think it is. Trust the choice you have made.*

The flight attendants went into their emergency-landing spiel, advising us to remove eyeglasses, shoes with sharp heels, and any pointed objects. We were ordered to pull the life preservers from beneath our seats and put them on. Everyone quickly reached to do so, fumbling in panic. We were to lean forward as far as possible, cross our arms, and brace ourselves on the back of the seat in front of us. As the able-bodied passengers went into action, the elderly were at a loss, and children began to cry. I could hear someone a few seats back throwing up; the stench soon penetrated the air. It was hell.

When the cabin lights went out, the darkness deepened the fright. The floor lights that guide passengers to the emergency exit doors went on. *No one ever gets to use those lights,* I knew. *Nobody survives a plane crash.* As the aircraft started to shimmy and rock, several women began to shriek. The floor lights illuminated the flight attendants' faces just enough for me to see their angst; they were as helpless as the passengers, and no amount of training could quell the horror of impending death. The children cried louder. I could feel the plane losing altitude rapidly; my ears began to throb with intense pain. I looked out the window. We were still far from land. This was it.

56

As our altitude dropped more quickly, I could see the whitecaps on the ocean hurtling up to meet us. Alex squeezed my arm so tightly that it hurt. The cabin was filled with a sinister silence, except for some people praying out loud: Hindu prayers, Muslim prayers, Christian prayers, and prayers by people who had never prayed before.

Alex leaned forward, but I didn't bother; I didn't expect that my position on impact would protect me. I held her frozen hand in mine and placed my other hand on her tummy. I knew I couldn't save our child, but I thought maybe I could give it some comfort in this field of horror. Imagine—*me* comforting someone on death row.

I looked out the window and saw that we were still over water. In the far distance down the coastline, I could make out city lights, but there was no way, at this velocity of altitude loss, we would make it to the runway. We would crash in the ocean, where 300 lives would come to an abrupt end, catapulted by my death wish. *Did they have their own?*

I guessed we had maybe thirty seconds left until impact, considering how fast we were falling. I reached to draw Alex's chin up, and she straightened to look at me. Her ashen face was wet with perspiration, and her jaw was clenched. I'm sure I looked worse.

Then, in that moment of impending calamity, something extraordinary happened: I saw her soul. It was as if a veil between the worlds lifted, and the truth of the spirit became perfectly evident. I could see that part of a human being that is bigger, deeper, stronger, and more real than everything that comes and goes, including the body. I saw the essence of the being who would live beyond the crash. I knew she saw the same in me. We sat together in that state for what felt like a long time, but which I'm sure was quite brief.

They say that just before you die, your whole life flashes before you. That was what happened to me. I saw all the experiences dispassionately, as if watching a movie. I observed myself building a Lego house in kindergarten; my dad as he shut the door behind him on his way out of my life; my first kiss, with Rebecca Hosling; the night Bill beat me with a fireplace poker; and on and on . . . right through finding Vicky in the car with her lover, climbing the rail of the bridge, meeting Alex, entering the Cave of Khadroma, and the day Alex told me she was pregnant. All of it streamed by in a matter of seconds, like fast cuts on an MTV video. Strangely, when I thought of my parents, I felt no animosity toward them, just compassion for the pain they must have been in. I realized I had inherited my terror of life from them, just as they'd inherited it from their parents—and all the way back. There was no blame, just lost people trying to escape their suffering.

I wanted to say to my parents—even my father: "It's all right; I understand; you were doing the best you could with what you knew." I, too, had done the best I could with what I knew. For the first time in my life, I had compassion for myself—the very element my world had lacked.

Then something very odd happened: I felt a jolt beneath me. Not the ocean, as I expected; rather, the plane seemed to be resisting the fall. We weren't losing altitude as rapidly as we had been a few moments earlier, and our airspeed dropped. I looked out the window and saw that we were just a few hundred feet over the ocean. Apparently the plane had salvaged enough power to brake the descent a bit. But we weren't out of danger by any means. The runway was still miles away, and we would crash on the reef or shoreline before we reached it. *Are we being saved, or has our sentence been intensified?*

I returned my gaze to Alex, still stone silent. But I could read her thoughts: *Is there a chance we'll make it?* I had no answer, except hope, fervent hope. Hope that my silly death prayer might be nullified and my life prayer might be answered. That God's idea of grace could be bigger than my idea of karma. That mercy would triumph over foolishness. I gazed at Alex and was bathed in the intense love I felt for her at that moment. We were in God's hands.

Suddenly a blue light caught my eye behind Alex. *Is this the light people see when they are about to go to heaven? The sacred corridor reported by those who have survived near-death experiences?* But this light wasn't soothing and welcoming like those I'd read about. This blue light was blinking. And there were many more. Interspersed among them were red and white lights—also numerous, also flashing. These lights, I realized, weren't ushering us through some cosmic portal. They were blinking through the window. As I shifted my focus, I saw a long line of emergency vehicles poised along the runway. *The runway—are we that close?*

"Alex, we're landing!" I yelled. She turned to look out the window, her eyes dilated with amazement. Shaking and shivering like a fragile leaf in a maelstrom, the plane kept dropping until its rear wheels touched down—clumsy and jarring, but unspeakably welcome. Moments later, the front wheels followed. A symphony of sirens wailed in the distance. Fire trucks moved toward us, and a massive emergency ground team swung into action to respond to the crash. But, in spite of all my ominous expectations, it never came.

57

You would have expected a huge cheer to rise from all the passengers. But no, everyone was still too stunned to celebrate. *Will the plane catch fire? Will we make it to the gate?* When death stares you in the face, you don't forget it quickly. No one would feel safe until our feet touched the ground. And then maybe not for a long time.

Alex and I fell into each other's arms and held each other tight. All too slowly, the plane rolled to the gate, until the door finally opened and I knew we were safe.

Then I started to laugh—raucous, uncontrolled laughter, more gut releasing than humor. I once heard that the body throws off stress in four ways: laughing, crying, shaking, and sweating. I'd done the other three; now laughter was my final recourse. As passengers crowded the aisles, rushing to exit, I just sat and let it rip. Alex stared at me curiously, as if to ask, *What on earth are you laughing at?*

Finally I calmed down enough to ask Alex, "Do you realize what has happened?"

What? she flashed me a look.

"We're back in India, and Officer Sharma won't be here to greet us. Or anyone else. We don't have to go back to America, or face your father, or explain anything to my parents, or see anyone from our old life ever again. We can stay here under the radar, have our baby, and live as we choose."

Alex understood and began to laugh with me. People stared. They couldn't even imagine the miracle that had just happened: The Lords of Karma hadn't called me to the gallows as I'd expected. Instead, they'd pulled off an astounding coup in our favor.

III

58

The mountains of Melghat are thick with rain forest, ringing with the song of Indian warblers and home to a rare giant bee that produces vast volumes of honey. Deep within its folds, tigers roam freely in a sprawling sanctuary, while rare forest owlets watch from above. Our cottage, small but adequate, was perched high above the jungle, offering striking vistas in all directions.

Each morning Alex and I strolled through the mango, banana, and orange groves on the property and plucked breakfast from the trees. We lived outdoors more than in, and my body felt healthy for the first time in years. Our life couldn't have been sweeter. If, as some say, life is a study in contrasts, our trip to hell had set us at the threshold of heaven.

"I've been thinking about that plane-crash episode," Alex remarked as we leaned against a banyan tree at sunset one evening. "Look where it led us, Linden: Ramesh gave us this spectacular place to caretake; it might as well be ours. He lets us keep the income from the fruit we harvest, which is just enough to take care of our needs. No one knows we're here except him. Even more important, we grew so much closer to each other during those terrifying hours. Maybe our relationship will be better for the rest of our lives because of it. I think the whole idea of God being a nasty Karmic Cop is something people made up. Maybe the hand of love is behind everything and we just don't see it."

"Yeah, that sure sounds a lot better than 'God created you, and He loves you so much that He will let you suffer for eternity because you're stupid.'"

I took in the scene for a final moment, the parting kiss of light on the landscape evoking the otherworldly luminescence of a Maxfield Parrish painting. The purple lotus blossoms in the nearby pond were prayerfully folding themselves in for the night. Benevolence had set its hand upon our world.

"Ready to head back?" I asked, extending my hand.

"Sure," Alex answered, giving me hers. As I helped her stand up, she grunted, "I sure am glad we're in the land of the sacred cow—I'm turning into one!"

We started up the hill toward the house, but soon I realized that Alex had fallen behind for a moment to catch her breath. When I turned to wait for her, I beheld an alarming sight: A large cobra had slithered out of the high grass and was headed straight for her. Her back was turned to it, so she had no idea it was there.

My first impulse was to shout, *"Jump away!"* but I remembered Eyla's admonition that a snake would attack if it sensed fear. The cobra was now in striking distance, and any sudden movements or frantic energy would surely rile it.

"Alex . . ." I called to her as calmly as possible, hoping that my fear wouldn't provoke an attack.

"Yes?" she answered, oblivious to any danger. The cobra began to coil its body and rear its head.

"Do you remember a time when you felt really peaceful?"

She thought for a long, nerve-racking moment. It was all I could do to keep from screaming at her.

"When I used to visit my grandma when I was a kid."

Slowly, methodically, I picked up a rock at my feet. "Tell me more . . ." The cobra held its position, poised to strike.

Alex smiled. "With Grandma Maggie I always felt like I was enough just as I was . . . like I didn't have to prove myself."

Mentally I took aim. "Good, Alex. Now do me a favor. When I tell you to, jump to your left, real quick."

"What are you up to, Linden?" I could see the snake's fangs and pointed tongue, even from a distance.

"This is a game . . . just keep thinking of Grandma Maggie and then jump."

Alex rolled her eyes.

"One . . . two . . . three—*jump!*" I called out.

Alex played along and took a big leap to her left, just as the snake was about to strike. In a split second, I hurled the stone at the cobra and hit its coiled body. It got spooked and slithered back into the bushes.

When Alex saw me cast the stone, she finally caught sight of the cobra. "My God, Linden! It was right next to me!" she shrieked, dashing to me, her hands on her heart and her chest heaving.

"Lucky I saw it, huh?" I took her hand. She fell onto my chest and rested her head there. I stroked her hair, keeping an eye out should the snake reappear. It didn't. "Let's get back," I said. "We've had enough excitement for one sunset."

But apparently not. Halfway to the house I sensed a disturbance in the sky above me—I figured it was probably a bat fluttering around, as they did at this hour. When I looked up, I saw a large hawk circling over my head, about to dive-bomb me. I grabbed a shovel that was leaning against the garden fence and waved it between me and the bird. The hawk retreated for a moment but then redoubled its efforts and attacked with a vengeance. As fast as I could, I ran with Alex to the porch, trying to beat the bird away with the shovel. The hawk refused to relent until we were inside and I'd slammed the door behind us.

I braced myself against the closed door; now it was my turn to pant, my neck and underarms drenched with sweat from the snake's threat and the hawk's attack.

"Are you okay?" Alex asked.

"Yeah, yeah, I'll be all right," I answered almost automatically. But after a moment's thought, I turned to Alex and told her, "Actually, I'm not okay. . . . I can't go on like this, Alex."

"Like what?"

"Like, wondering if the Lords of Karma are going to collect their due at any moment."

Alex let out a disgusted groan. "Are you still on that old wives' tale?"

I could feel my blood pressure rising. "It's not an old wives' tale! It's real to me."

Alex looked frustrated, like someone who'd gotten rid of a disease and then noticed it had come back. "You haven't said anything about this for a long time."

"I've tried to keep it from coming between us . . . but it's always in the back of my mind."

Alex stepped closer. "What happened today doesn't mean the Lords of Karma are coming to get you, Linden," she told me in her most rational voice. "Shit happens."

"But a *hawk,* Alex? That was no accident!"

She glared at me. Over our months together, I'd learned what her looks meant. She had an upset, argumentative look; and a more serious, grounded look, like "I don't intend to deal in bullshit here." This was definitely the no-bullshit look.

"Come on, Linden, get with the program, would you? We're here. We're alive. We love each other. We're having a baby. We're happy. Why question a good life?"

Her logic made sense, but I wasn't convinced. "I know, Alex, but I made the vow with my whole heart, and the Lords acknowledged it. Maybe we just had a stay of execution and the blade will fall at any moment."

"Please, Linden, just hear me." Alex raised her voice. "No bogeyman is after you. Even if you invited him and changed your mind. Do you hear me? *No bogeyman is after you!* If anyone is after you, it's *you,* and I wish you would get over it already."

I squared off to face her. "Maybe you're right—but I have to know for myself. Otherwise I'll go on wondering if something bad is going to happen to me or you or our baby or all of us. If I don't find out for sure, I'll keep looking over my shoulder for the rest of my life. And I'll be no fun to be with."

"You're *already* no fun to be with!" Alex blurted out and stormed into the bedroom.

I stood there by myself for a while, pissed off and confused. Then I followed Alex into the bedroom and found her curled on the bed in a fetal position, crying into a pillow. I hated to see her like that. As delicately as possible, I sat down next to her and placed my hands on her back. A moment later she turned and faced me, her hair disheveled and her face wet. "So what are you going to do, Linden? What will it take for you to get over this terrible obsession that's ruining your life—and now mine?"

I was quiet for a while, appearing to ponder the question. But I'd already thought this out. "I have to go back to the cave. I have to ask the Lords directly. The solstice will be here in another week, and if I wait, I may not be able to find the cave again for a year."

Alex shook her head from side to side adamantly. "Don't do this to me, Linden," she pleaded. "Please don't bring your warped ideas of self-punishment into our relationship and our family. We have too much going for us. You're a good person, Linden. Sure, you've made mistakes—but we all have. God doesn't punish people for not being perfect. God just wants us to do the best we can, even in our abysmal humanness. Nothing bad is going to happen to you. Would you *please* just get it? *Nothing bad is going to happen to you!*"

I wished I agreed with her, but I didn't. "You might be right, Alex. But I just have to know it for myself. Once and for all, I have to know."

She stared at me intensely. Daggers. "Linden, I don't want you going back to that cave," she insisted. "The trip is too dangerous, and I'm in no condition to go with you. I can't stay out here and manage this place by myself. I'll have to go back to Rani Prema or someplace where I might be caught and deported. If something happens to you, you'll leave me a widow and your child fatherless. You can make the prophecy come true with your own pigheadedness. I beg of you, don't make something bad happen because you want to be assured that something bad *won't* happen."

Now I was really stuck. If I went, I could hurt Alex and our child terribly. If I stayed, I would worry for the rest of my life and not be present with the woman and family I loved. I saw no easy way out.

59

The journey back to Dharamsala was shorter but far more difficult. Shorter because I knew the way and what to expect. More difficult because I'd left the woman I loved in tears, along with our unborn child, whom I might never meet. My mother used to tell me I was obstinate, and she was right. For sure I'd made lots of bad decisions, and maybe this was one of them. But at least they had been my own. If I died now, at least I was honest in my choices.

Either way, this trip would be my last gamble. If the Lords of Karma told me that my vow was irreversible, I would surrender to my fate. If they released me from my oath, I would put my worries behind me and give my family my full presence. Now I wanted life far more than death, but I wanted to live it fully. This was my way—headstrong though you might judge it—of facing my fear and busting through it.

❀

When Sonam saw me enter the monastery office, he lit up. "Welcome back, my brother!" the monk exclaimed with his toothy smile. As his laugh resonated through the room, I realized that of all the religious people I'd ever met, the Tibetan Buddhists seemed the most genuinely happy.

When several monks passing the office saw me, they began to chatter in hushed but animated tones. "What's up with them?" I asked Sonam.

He looked embarrassed. "After you left, I told Lama Sungdare and some other monks about your visit to the cave. I wasn't gossiping; I thought your experience might help them. I didn't think you would ever return here. I'm sorry, Linden—I did not mean to violate your trust."

That didn't matter now. I didn't really care if anyone knew. I was doing what I had to do, and they—including the old lama—could think what they wanted.

"Have you come to meditate with us for a while?" Sonam asked, offering me a plate of small Tibetan candies that resembled little clusters of dried dates.

"Actually, I'm on my way back to the cave," I answered as I picked a couple of sweets from the plate.

Sonam's eyes bulged. I had a way of blowing his mind.

"Why would you do that? Didn't you get what you wanted?"

The question I hated to hear. "Yes, I got what I wanted. But now I want something else. . . ."

"What's that?"

"I want to reverse my decision," I told him. "I want to live."

It took Sonam a few moments to regain his composure. "Let's get you to your room. Get some rest and we can talk more later."

He ushered me to the very room where Alex and I had stayed during our last visit. As I entered, I remembered: *The last time I was here, Alex was a guy.* How weird to be here now without him—that is, her. I plopped down on the thin mattress and let layers of muscles unwind from the bumpy trip.

As I studied the patterns on the timber ceiling, I saw Alex's face. At first it was the young, enigmatic guy who'd shadowed me on my journey of a lifetime. Then the face morphed into Alex the woman—my lover, my wife, the mother of our child. My chest started to swell with emotion. *What the hell am I doing here now? Am I nuts? Forsaking the love of an amazing woman so I can fulfill some selfish, testosterone-driven mission?* I shook my head. *How could*

I have been so deluded? I started to get up to retrieve my pack and turn back, but I was too tired. Lying down felt too good at the moment. I would take a nap and decide what to do after I got some rest.

60

The knock on the door was unmistakable. "Mr. Linden," a young monk's voice called, "would you like to join us for the evening meditation?"

I sat up, scanning the room to try to get my bearings.

"Uh . . . yeah, sure. I'll be right there."

I peered through the window; it was almost dark. I'd crashed for nearly three hours.

Bleary-eyed, I found my way downstairs to the meditation hall and took my seat on a zafu toward the rear of the room. A minute later Lama Sungdare made his entrance and strode down the aisle. As the lama passed, he made eye contact with the students, offering a slight smile and graceful nod. Finally, the elder took his place at the head of the hall. Tonight an empty zafu sat next to his.

The High Lama lowered himself onto his cushion and looked out over the audience. Then he pointed toward me, motioning me to come forward. Startled, I looked behind me to see who he was summoning. No one was there. I pointed to myself questioningly. He nodded.

What could he possibly want?

I rose and made my way to the small platform at the front of the temple. All eyes were on me. The empty zafu loomed ominous;

it was usually reserved for an esteemed guest or the High Lama's assistant. *I am neither.*

"Please sit," he invited me. It was really an order. I complied.

As I surveyed the group of about fifty monks and students, a queasy feeling swelled up in my gut. Some of the monks had been practicing meditation for twenty-five years. *What am I doing in front of them? Will I have to give a talk? Is the lama going to embarrass me?* I wanted to bolt, but forced myself to stay seated.

"Tell us, please, Linden, what brings you back to our monastery?"

I'd never seen a public interview like this at the dharma center. I tried to think of an explanation that was clever or at least plausible. I couldn't. Then I did something unbelievable: I told the truth.

"I am going to the Cave of Khadroma to visit the Lords of Karma," I stated.

The lama was visibly disturbed. I cast a quick look at Sonam, who was sitting up straight and visibly nervous.

"Ah, yes, I believe we spoke about this the last time you were here," Lama Sungdare replied, recovering admirably. "I explained to you that this cave is just a myth. Why do you keep looking for it?"

I shot another glance at Sonam, who appeared petrified that I would reveal his complicity. I wouldn't.

"The cave is not a myth, Lama Sungdare. I've been there."

The High Lama arched an eyebrow. "And what happened in the cave?" he asked, as sarcastic as a lama might get.

"Three Lords of Karma appeared to me," I answered. I scanned the assembly. The monks' faces were rapt.

Lama Sungdare nodded as if he was humoring me. "Why did you go there?"

"I went to ask the Lords of Karma to end all of my lifetimes so I could forever escape the wheel of birth and death."

"A noble intention," the lama replied. I couldn't tell if he was taking me more seriously or mocking me. "Did they grant your wish?"

"They did."

I wish I had a video of that room. I don't imagine the monks had had such a good show since a squirrel had found its way into the hall during meditation and crawled up one of the monks' pant legs.

"If you got what you went for, then why are you returning?"

Drop the bomb. "I want to ask them to reverse my decision."

Lama Sungdare reeled with astonishment. "You want the Lords of Karma to undo your sacred vow to renounce life on Earth forever?"

"That's right." I nodded.

"Why do you ask this?"

My mouth grew dry. If I spoke the truth, it would fly in the face of everything the dharma center—and all dharma centers, all Buddhists, and maybe even Buddha himself—stood for. It would be like giving a giant finger to the fundamental principles these people held dear. Here they were sitting in deep meditation day and night, some for an entire lifetime—maybe *many* lifetimes— trying to escape the wheel of rebirth. *I am about to take a hatchet to their sacred platform.*

I studied the eyes riveted on me. "I am asking this because I fell in love with an amazing woman, we're having a baby, and I've decided that life really is worth living."

Dead silence.

I felt totally vulnerable, just waiting for the angry mob to storm the platform. But the monks didn't budge. Instead, they sat there respectfully. I mustered the courage to look Lama Sungdare straight in the eye. I didn't mean to challenge him. I just had to speak my truth.

In true Buddhist form, he remained (or at least appeared) dispassionate. "And your wife, Linden, does she know about your quest?" he asked.

"Yes, absolutely, Lama. In fact, you know her."

I didn't think he could arch his eyebrows any higher than he had the first time—but he did. "I *know* her?"

"Yes. My wife is Alex, the guy I came here with last year."

I don't know if a lama has ever fainted in front of his disciples before, but this one came very close. The venerable elder's brain appeared to short out like a computer under siege from a spilled latte. He just sat there, unable to mouth a word in response. I looked out over the audience; they bore the same deer-in-headlights stare. I waited a few choice moments and then figured I should put them out of their misery.

"Actually, you see, Alex wasn't a guy. He was a woman who dressed up as a man so he could be a monk. But then he—I mean, she—fell in love with me and decided to remain a Buddhist so she could be with me. When she got pregnant, she told me she really enjoys being a woman, and Buddhism was more of a phase. I'm going back to see the Lords of Karma so I can know for sure if they're going to hold me to my vow, or if I have a shot at living the rest of my life with the woman I love."

The only way I can describe the feeling in the room at that moment is *once-in-a-lifetime.* Or many. Buddhists, you see, are very mellow. Very, very mellow. They're supposed to take everything in stride and not display strong emotional reactions. I, however, was yanking their chains to a prodigious degree. Not purposely. It's just what happened.

A student in the back of the room—the one white guy, obviously from some Western country—raised his hand, and Lama Sungdare called on him. I'm sure the lama was relieved to be off the hook for the moment.

The student bowed his head and asked in a proper British accent, "What did the Lords of Karma look like? Were they breathing fire through snorting nostrils, with blood dripping from their teeth?" When the other students began to titter, I realized he was goofing on me.

I was tempted to shoot back a snotty answer, but another voice in my head asserted itself: *Don't go there, Linden. Don't stoop to his level. Take the high road.* I took a moment to compose myself. "One was an old Tibetan," I answered. "He had wide, dark eyes; deep wrinkles; and a colorful round Tibetan hat. Another was a white woman, wearing a shawl over her head like a nun. The third was Chinese, younger, with a Fu Manchu mustache."

Lama Sungdare's eyes lit up, and for the first time since we began our conversation, he looked happy. *Thank goodness—he believes me.* My shoulders relaxed, and my fingertips began to warm. The elder raised his arm to summon Sonam, who hustled to the platform. The lama whispered in his ear; Sonam nodded and briskly left the room.

Another student raised his hand, and the lama called on him. This fellow was more sincere. "Buddhism requires celibacy on the part of monks who intend to achieve enlightenment," he noted. "Do you think you can be liberated if you're married?"

If I could answer that question definitively, I would win a Nobel Prize.

"I can't really say for sure," I had to answer honestly. "I just know that for the first time in my life, I feel happy. If the purpose of life is happiness, then I have to believe that what I'm doing is good. If the purpose of life is suffering, I've failed. But I can't believe we're here to struggle. I know pain happens, but I think we bring a lot of unnecessary suffering upon ourselves. I just cannot believe God created a world the purpose of which is to escape."

The students sat silently, taking in my words. *Are they getting my drift? Surely they've grappled with the same issues.* Yet the monks remained true to their meditative presentation, and it was practically impossible to read their reactions. I just had to hope that what I'd said had made some sense to them. And if not, at least I made sense to *me*.

While I'd been speaking, Sonam returned with a package under his arm wrapped in an old maroon cloth. He handed it to Lama Sungdare, who carefully unfolded the cloth and examined the objects it contained. Sitting next to the lama, I could see that they were pictures in very old wooden frames, cracked and mildewed. The High Lama methodically dusted them off and turned one toward me. "Is this the man you saw in the cave, Linden?"

I couldn't believe it. The subject of the photo looked remarkably similar to Lord Akar (and the boarding agent at the airport). "Yes, it is!" I answered, astonished.

A small smile grew on the lama's face as his gaze rested on the audience, milking the moment. "I am sorry to disappoint you, Linden. This is not a Lord of Karma. This is a photo of Lama Chodrak, one of the monks who founded this monastery over a hundred years ago."

Before I could respond, Lama Sungdare turned another photo toward me. "Does she look familiar?"

Damn if it wasn't Teresa, the nun.

"This is Katrienne Maes, a Belgian woman who lived in Tibet during World War I. She fled the war in Europe and took refuge at our monastery. She was a nurse who helped many of our predecessors."

This can't be happening.

You can probably figure what came next. Lama Sungdare showed me the third picture—not a photo, but a lifelike artist's rendering of Chuang-Tsu, the Chinese sage. Not an exact likeness, but close enough.

"Huan Li was a Taoist who adopted Buddhism over a thousand years ago. His brilliant teachings and pure heart have earned him a place in our community. He is respected as an enlightened being, almost as much as Buddha."

Lama Sungdare laid the three pictures at my feet, faceup for me to inspect, like a lawyer presenting his triumphant evidence to a delusional witness. Stymied, I just kept scanning the pictures. They bore an uncanny resemblance to the spirits in the cave and the people I'd encountered at the airport and on the plane.

"Do you still believe these are the Lords of Karma, Linden?" the lama asked, sitting back with his arms crossed.

I sighed and answered, "They sure look like them. . . . Where did you get these?"

The High Lama broke into a victorious smile. "These images have been hanging on the wall of the hallway outside my study for over twenty-five years," he replied smugly. "The same hallway you walked through to meet me the night you first arrived here."

I tried to recall that night. I remembered passing through that hall and noticing some pictures. But it had been quite dark, lit by candles, and I'd barely been able to make out the images. If you'd have asked me what they depicted, I wouldn't have been able to tell you.

"So you think I saw these pictures, registered them in my sub-conscious, and then extracted them in the cave to conjure the Lords of Karma in my mind?"

Lama Sungdare nodded. "The mind is powerful, Linden. Bud-dha taught that we create our entire lives with our minds, and that is why we must meditate to purify our thoughts and intentions."

The students all turned their heads back to me, as if watching to see if I could return a hard serve at Wimbledon.

"If that's the case, Lama Sungdare, how do you explain the fact that before and during an airplane flight that almost crashed, I saw three unusual people who looked remarkably like these individu-als?"

He thought for a little while, bobbing his head slightly. "As I said, Linden, the mind is powerful. Because you held these images in your subconscious mind, you interpreted people you saw through the filter of your selective perception."

Confused and angry, I shut up. I didn't feel like volleying with the old man, who could obviously defeat me in an intellectual duel.

When Lama Sungdare recognized that I had nothing more to say and he was satisfied he'd overcome me, he began to chant: *Om mani padme hum. . . . Om mani padme hum. . . . Om mani padme hum.* Soon all the monks followed.

The lesson was over.

61

First thing the next morning, I threw my stuff together to go home. Lama Sungdare was right—I'd probably made it all up. It wasn't worth risking my life to go back to the cave when Alex was worried and waiting; to make matters worse, her anxiety would emotionally poison the baby. Yes, I could find the cave and see the Lords again. But after the lama's crucifying cross-examination, I would always wonder if they were real or simply players on the stage of my imagination. Disheartened, angry, and confused, I just wanted to get back to my wife and child.

On my way out I stopped by Sonam's room. His door was slightly ajar, and through the crack I could see that he was meditating. As quietly as possible, I tiptoed into the room and sat on the floor, my back against the wall, waiting for him to finish. He heard me and opened his eyes.

"I'm sorry to bother you, Sonam," I told him. "I just came to say good-bye."

"Where are you going?" he asked, unlocking his legs.

"I'm heading back. I just want to get home to Alex."

He seemed surprised. "You mean you're not going on to the cave?"

"Why should I?" I replied. "Lama Sungdare torpedoed my theory quite stunningly."

Sonam rose from his cushion and moved to sit next to me, leaning his back against the wall beside me.

"Linden, there is something you must know," he told me in a flat voice.

"What's that?"

A shade of sobriety settled over the monk's face. "I'm sorry to say this, but Lama Sungdare has deceived you again."

"What?!" I could feel my chest getting hot.

The monk squirmed. "The lama has talked about the Lords of Karma several times over the years. He said that because they are spirits, they do not have a human form. But they have the ability to reveal themselves in human form so they can communicate with people."

I sat up straight and felt a tingling, as I had at the stone circle at the foot of Mount Lasya. "So the people I saw in the cave and at the airport could have been the Lords of Karma, taking on an appearance I would recognize?"

Sonam nodded. "Exactly. Others who have met the Lords have seen them as Guru Rinpoche, Jesus, and even Moses. They were just as real to those who met them."

Goose bumps erupted on my forearms. I *knew* I hadn't been hallucinating.

"Then why didn't the High Lama tell me?"

Sonam let out a heavy sigh and shook his head. "I'm afraid this happens in most religions. Some members of the clergy get old and set in their ways, and they end up working to protect the institution rather than impart the truth the religion was intended to reveal. It's unfortunate, but not unusual."

In some dark way, this made sense. "You mean like in some Christian sects, when a common person has a healing or a miracle and the church is the first to try to disprove it?"

"Exactly."

"Jeez, you'd think Lama Sungdare would want to help someone get liberated if he could," I pondered aloud.

Sonam leaned his head back against the wall and stared at the ceiling. "Let's just say that despite Lama Sungdare's many years of practice, a vein of jealousy still abides in him."

"Why do you say that?"

"Because . . ." Sonam hesitated as if he was trying to decide how much to tell me. Finally he took a deep breath and forced himself to finish his sentence. ". . . years ago the lama visited the cave himself."

My jaw dropped. "Lama Sungdare went to the cave?!"

"He told a few of his close disciples."

I grabbed Sonam's arm as if to keep him from escaping. "And what happened to him?"

"I don't know exactly. He refuses to talk about it in public. But just before Lama Rinzen died last year, he told me that Lama Sungdare had confided in him about the experience."

A soft breeze parted the window curtain and wafted through the room, as if the departed lama was visiting.

"And . . . ?"

"Apparently Lama Sungdare went to the Cave of Khadroma for exactly the same reason you did. He asked the Lords of Karma to help him end all of his lifetimes."

My chest felt as if it was about to explode. "And what did they tell him?"

"They told him he had too much karma to pay off, and he would have to keep being reborn for many more lives until he graduated."

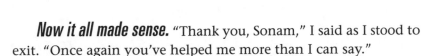

62

Now it all made sense. "Thank you, Sonam," I said as I stood to exit. "Once again you've helped me more than I can say."

Sonam still looked rattled, but relieved. "I must thank you, too, Linden," my friend told me as he rose with me. He faced me and looked me firmly in the eyes. "You've helped me more than you know."

"I have?"

Sonam's monk presentation dissipated, and his countenance became tender. "In a way, Linden, I envy you."

I was shocked. "How's that?"

The fellow looked burdened. "Sometimes I wonder if the monastic life is really for me," he finally said. "When you told me you had found a wonderful woman, I realized that a part of me yearns for that, too. This is very painful for me to admit to you—and myself—since I have taken a vow of celibacy. Yet, if I were to be honest, I would tell you that I crave a loving partner."

Ah, the sweet aroma of truth. I took a moment to absorb Sonam's confession, appreciating the risk he was taking in divulging his secret. "Then may the blessings of Buddha be with you, Sonam," I told him. "May you find what your heart yearns for."

The image of Sonam standing in his doorway as I left is one I'll never forget. He still looked a bit anxious, but I beheld a peaceful glow illuminating his face that even years of meditation hadn't yielded. It was the look of a man who yearned for the permission to love and had just given it to himself.

63

When I arrived at Eyla's house, she was standing in the yard placing an offering of herbs into the fire of an outdoor prayer urn. Her back to me, she didn't see me coming.

"Can you add one more prayer for a return traveler?" I called out as soon as she had finished.

Startled, Eyla turned and saw me, her face awash with surprise and delight. "Linden!" she cried out as she ran to me. "It's so good to see you!"

"You, too, Eyla."

She looked radiant as always, her eyes sparkling in the sun. I opened my arms to hug her, and she accepted my embrace. Suddenly a slew of visceral memories flooded me. For a moment I grew frightened, remembering how much I'd wanted her.

"Let me have a look at you," she said, stepping back, her hands on my shoulders. "You look strong and healthy!"

"Maybe my meditation is finally paying off," I joked.

Eyla moved to fan the flame of the prayer fire one last time and turned to me again. "What are you doing back here?"

"Well, it's sort of a long story." *You have no idea how long.*

"Come inside; I want to hear all about it," she offered, taking my hand and guiding me toward the house.

As I followed her, the inevitable question escaped my lips: "Is your dad home?"

"He took Jangmu to the village to visit my brother," she answered over her shoulder.

All the better.

While Eyla prepared tea, I settled in among the living-room cushions and scanned the place. Everything looked the same. I didn't imagine that much ever changed there.

Eyla returned with a steaming teapot and some homemade pastries. The glimmer in her eye told me that she hoped I'd come back to be with her. "So, let's hear," she said as she sat close to me.

"I'm going back to the cave," I told her right up front. "I need to speak to the Lords of Karma one more time."

Surprise rolled over her face. "I thought they gave you the answer you sought."

Ah, this again. "They did. But things have changed. I need to ask them something else."

Does she think I came back to ask the Lords of Karma about her? I wasn't sure how or what or when to tell her about Alex. But she saved me the trouble of deciding. "Where is Alex?" Eyla asked.

Okay, just go with it.

"Alex is in Melghat," I answered matter-of-factly, purposely avoiding a gender-specific pronoun.

"Why didn't she come with you?"

She?

"Why do you say 'she'?" I retorted, so flabbergasted that I nearly dropped my teacup.

"That's usually what you call a woman, isn't it?" Eyla's eyes bored right through me.

Busted.

I felt embarrassed at first and then relieved. I wouldn't have to play games or dance around the truth. "How did you know?"

"When you live in nature, you sense things," Eyla explained. "Besides, women know women. I suspected it from the minute you arrived. When Alex got so upset after seeing us together, I was sure."

Is there no place to hide? "Why didn't you say something?"

"Because you didn't know," she replied

"How did you know I didn't know?"

"You talked to her like a guy. You were on a mission. You were distracted. You had feelings for me. . . . Do you still?"

Why do women have to be so direct? I started to squirm.

"Yes, I did have feelings for you when I was here," I began awkwardly, searching for the right words, "but I knew I couldn't get involved with you—as much for your sake as mine. Maybe I still would, except—"

"Do you still want to die and not be reborn?" she interrupted. *Couldn't she be at least a little subtle?*

"Well," I practically stammered, "that's one of the things that has changed. I'm not the same person I was when you last saw me."

"And who are you now?"

I could feel my palms getting clammy. I was less scared facing the Chinese border patrol. *Spit it out.* "I've fallen in love with Alex. We're having a baby. I want to live."

Eyla looked even more shocked than she had the night I revealed my mission to her. Then disappointed, like a little girl who'd dropped her ice-cream cone on the sidewalk. I braced myself for her to slam me with a Tibetan rolling pin and boot me out. But she didn't. Instead, she forced a small smile and nodded, "I see." Then she sat quietly for a while, letting the news sink in. After a few moments, her smile became more genuine. "That's good," she said. "I am happy for you, Linden. You have found a reason to live."

Eyla meant it. Or wanted to. Yet a tiny sniffle betrayed her deeper feelings.

"Please forgive me," she said, reaching for a handkerchief. She was embarrassed—a first for me to see. "It's just that it's quite lonely out here. My life is very harsh, and every night I pray for a good husband. The men in this part of the country are coarse and bullheaded—hunters and goatherds who believe a wife is just a sex object and a servant. I vowed that I would never marry a man like that. I yearn for someone who thinks deeply and has a good heart. When you came, I thought for sure that you were the answer to my prayers."

Now I really felt like shit. *What would have happened if I'd hooked up with Eyla during my first visit?* But then there would be no Alex, no baby, no new life. *No, Eyla and I couldn't have happened. It wasn't meant to be.* There was another path for me and for her. She was kind and wise. She deserved someone better than the locals she described.

I put my arm around her shoulders, and she leaned her head against me, trying to be strong. She *was* strong, but I guess we all have our fragile moments. I stroked her hair like I would have a little child's. We would see each other more clearly now.

64

The stone Buddha stood at the top of the hill, more deeply weathered from the heavy spring rains. It was almost one year to the day since I'd made my last pilgrimage, and today's return was all the more eerie for Alex's absence. As I peered down the trail, my legs felt shaky and my solar plexus tightened. Part of me didn't want to do this at all. Another part knew I had to.

A hundred yards down the trail I reached the spot where the chopper had cornered us and I'd told my mom and Bill to piss off. Now they seemed not just oceans, but lifetimes, away. I wasn't angry at them anymore; I just had nothing to say to them. I felt closer to Alex than anyone in my blood family; Eyla and Sonam as well. My true family was one of spirit, I'd come to realize. I cast a final look toward the spot and kept moving. The white-painted stone markers rested timelessly in place. *Who has walked this path since I last did? What twists and turns have their lives taken? Is the Cave of Khadroma a place that changes lives not in the ways people pray for, but in the ways they need?*

When I finally reached the river, it was swollen from the recent snow runoff—not as viciously as the first time I'd faced it, but enough to prevent me from navigating it by myself. Without a crossing partner, I would just have to wait for the water level to drop. I set up my tent a dozen yards from the bank, rolled out a small tarpaulin, and just sat. As I watched the river, it seemed hypnotic, and I grew rapt, lulled into a spontaneous meditation. The river became alive, and the low roar morphed into an entrancing "Om" chant that drew me into its center.

I sat there for a long time and grew very still. When I'd meditated at the dharma center, my mind had ricocheted all over the place. But something about this place, or this moment, was different. Until then I'd always been doing something or going somewhere, or my thoughts were rushing to this place or that. But that day I simply sat and let everything be exactly as it was. I watched the water hurtle by, muddy brown, angry, and determined. I observed an endless procession of branches and leaves streaming by. I beheld the power of nature going where it would, when it would, how it would. I laughed to think of the folly of humanity's vainglorious attempt to control nature. We overrun pieces of it, strutting and crowing over our technological achievements, and crown ourselves king for our egoistic victories. But ultimately nature will have her way.

Sometime during my second day at the riverside, my mind disappeared. I was just . . . there. No thoughts, no past, no future, no agenda, no pain, no birth, no death—nothing. Just there. *Is this the liberation Buddha discovered?*

At one point the river began to speak to me, imparting wisdom without words, insight without intellect. I understood what people meant when they said that God spoke to them. It wasn't a booming, James Earl Jones voice piercing the clouds; that felt cheap compared to what I was hearing. The voice of God that reached me was compelling without volume, moving without drama, illuminating without being blinding. It said plainly: *Just be, Linden. Just be.*

On the third day, the torrent had quelled. Funny, by the time the river was ready for my crossing, I wondered if I still needed to make it. Like a rock in the river's bed, the water had smoothed the jagged edges of my soul. *Maybe my quest for the cave is just my search for myself.* I'd found pieces of myself long buried and dismembered. I felt *re*-membered. Remembered.

65

I arrived at the border-crossing bridge just before nightfall. I could have camped overnight, but that would have further delayed my passage, and after three days' setback, I needed to make up the time. I would have to pass at night.

I tried to see through the forest, in the hopes of crossing the road as we'd done before, but the moon was void and I couldn't negotiate the terrain without either getting lost or calling attention to myself by stepping on branches or disturbing critters. Passing under the bridge was my only option.

From a vantage point fifty yards downstream, I monitored the guards' activity. It was minimal. When it finally appeared that they were holed up in the nearby shack for the night, I made my move. As quietly as possible, I sneaked to the bridge and held my position underneath it to be sure no soldiers were out. I could hear them in the guardhouse, their voices raised, arguing. Good.

I tiptoed onto the ribbon-thin bank between the retaining wall and the water, my face to the wall. When I reached the halfway point, a car approached from the India side, casting its high beams directly over my head as it ascended the ramp. As soon as I heard the car clanking across the rickety beams above me, I scurried to the other side, camouflaging my passage in its din. I hid at the far side of the bridge while the guards checked the car through. When I heard it move on and the station door close, I figured it was safe to continue.

Once out of the guards' earshot, I took more liberties in order to move faster. Now my journey was impeded by an ugly blanket of debris the river had deposited during its latest surge. To make matters worse, the mud at the riverside was soft and deep. When I found a place to step that was free of branches, dead leaves, and rocks, my foot sank rapidly, as if in quicksand. I was tempted to make my way through the brush instead, but Eyla's snake warning was enough to keep me at the riverside. It was the slowest and the most difficult leg of my trek.

❀

By early morning I reached the rope bridge. The wind, rain, and sun had taken another year's toll on the frail suspension; the vine ropes were more ragged, with more broken and missing slats. Surveying what I had to cross, I grew fearful, selfishly wishing that Alex could be there with me for moral support. *But then again, how much moral support had I given* her *by leaving?* I prayed hard at the bridge portal and began to cross, chanting all the way. When I reached the center point, a nasty gust blew up, exactly like the one that had caused me to freeze the last time. *Some spirit guardian must surely test all those who seek to pass here.* Yet the memory of one successful crossing buoyed me and kept me going. Careful not to look down, I trained my eyes on the destination post and didn't let it out of my sight until my foot touched solid ground.

By evening, I reached the bend in the river that afforded me a view of the twin peaks that had lasered the solstice ray onto the cave's location. The vision jogged my memory, reminding me of my last visit to the cave. It had been an empowering moment at the time, but now it haunted me. *One night to go. I'll camp here and ascend in the morning. I'll get what I came for and return to my family.*

I hardly slept that night. Images of meeting the Lords of Karma flitted through my brain, interposed with Alex's face. I even saw the baby's eyes. Then back to the Lords. In one dream they were holding me to my promise, in another exonerating me. Was I really contacting them, or was I concocting it all in my mixed-up subconscious?

Within twelve hours I would know.

❦

I was up before sunrise. This time there were no clouds, and the sun would clearly mark the cave. I wondered if the Lords had taken compassion on me and were making it easy.

I found my way to the stone circle, which had remained remarkably intact. I stepped into its center and gazed up toward the cave's signal rock. But for some reason I couldn't see it, or even another like it. *Is this the proper angle? Have I wandered into a different valley? Was my last visit a hallucination?* I looked again, and the valley was as I remembered it. I strained again to try to pick out the key boulder, but it wasn't there. *Could someone have moved it?* No, it was too huge and heavy to move, even for many men.

I figured that maybe the predawn murkiness was playing tricks on my eyes, so I decided to wait for the sun to clear up my confusion. I took a few impatient breaths, and minutes later the sun rose over the mountains behind me and shone its precious ray between those two crucial peaks. As it did, I focused intently on the spot where the ray landed. But there was no boulder there. I scanned above and below that point, to its left and right, and there was no rock. All I could see was brown. Nothing growing. Just brown.

As the sun rose and illuminated the entire mountainside, I realized the whole area was covered with mud. *There was a mud slide.* Fairly recently. *No, no, it can't be.* I kept searching the mountainside for any sign of where the cave might be. *Nada.*

Maybe if I just get closer. I began to claw my way up the slope, but the climb was nearly impossible: thick, almost impassable mud and small rocks everywhere. I forced myself to keep going another fifty yards, but soon realized the entire ascent would be just as arduous. I stood on a boulder to see if I could get a better view and maybe spot the rock or the cave. *Nothing.*

Then I looked down at the boulder I'd mounted to gain a better view. There I glimpsed an "Om" sign—the very one that had been etched into the entry boulder of the cave. But now it was a quarter mile below its original sentry position. Mount Lasya had swallowed the sacred Cave of Khadroma. There was no way I—or anyone—would ever enter that place again.

❈

I stood on the huge rock for a while, dumbstruck. Surprise gave way to anger, anger to rage, rage to depression. *I've come all this way to find a mountain of mud.* No cave. No Lords of Karma. No spirits. No guidance. No answers. No resolution. *Just mud.* I'd left my partner and child and risked my life for a wild-goose chase.

Suddenly I heard someone laughing. *Out here?* The voice was quiet at first, then louder and more raucous. *Are the Lords of Karma mocking me? Is the last laugh theirs?* But then I realized—it was coming from *me.* From some ancient well deep within, maniacal laughter burst forth, not unlike the release I'd felt when our flight from hell had landed. This time a larger, older dam had cracked, releasing years of pent-up fear, loneliness, sadness, and hostility.

Let it rip, Linden, let it rip. No one will hear you, and no one will judge you. No one will laugh at you. Perhaps the Lords of Karma—if they exist—will laugh with *you. Or take pity. You have climbed literally to the ends of the earth seeking advice from a council of spooks, and you ended up with a mud bath. Laugh, Linden, laugh. . . .*

66

The return journey was far harder—not for the mud, but for the exasperation. How could I have been so stupid? *Try to forgive yourself, Linden. You were just trying to make sense of your life,* an inner voice attempted to comfort me. *Okay, I'll try. I'll go home to Alex and tell her, "My tryst with the Lords of Karma is history. I'm all yours now."*

As I forged along the bank, heading downstream, the sound of a motor broke the silence. It came first as a low hum, and then grew louder to become a dominant drone. *But there are no roads here.* I scanned the sky for an airplane; except for some scattered clouds, it was clear. *Not the chopper again.* I winced. But this noise was different, more like a lawn mower, punctuated by occasional sputters. It was coming from up the river. *A boat. Maybe it's a fisherman and I can hitch a ride.*

I climbed to the top of a large rock and shaded my eyes to scan upstream. Sure enough, a tiny fishing boat came into view a few hundred yards away. *What a miracle! Boats can move on this river when it's high enough, and calm.* "Hey!" I shouted as loudly as I could, jumping and waving my arms. As the vessel came closer, I leaped and yelled again, even louder. Finally the man at the helm noticed me, and the boat turned in my direction. *A huge stroke of luck—the answer to my prayers to get home sooner.*

Soon I could discern three fishermen sitting one behind the other. *Thank you, Buddha.* I jumped down from the rock and readied my gear to board the vessel as soon as it reached shore. *My return journey has just been cut by a day.* A minute later the weathered motorboat and its passengers were in plain view, and I could make out their features: two Tibetan fisherman in the front and a man in a khaki uniform in the back. *Khaki . . . no, no. . . .* But it was. *A Chinese soldier.* When he saw my white face and foreigner's garb, he drew a pistol from his holster, pointed it toward me, and yelled to me in guttural Chinese, his voice booming through the valley like thunder.

Quickly I looked around, seeking a way to escape. But the mud was impassable and the bush behind me thick. He could have easily shot me—and would have—if I'd made a sudden move. With no avenue to get away, I stood and waited for the motorboat and its menacing captain to reach me.

A minute later the boat slid onto shore, the soldier's face contorted in anger as he rattled off more Chinese. The Tibetans passively listened and obeyed his orders, their grave expressions telling me they were acting under duress and felt sorry for me. The gruff soldier—short, stiff, wearing a small cap—motioned for me to get in the boat, pointing to the middle seat. He positioned himself behind me, training the gun at me, and sent the Tibetan who had been occupying the middle seat forward to sit with his compadre. Then he ordered them to get going. We pushed off and were soon motoring downstream, the weapon fixed on me the entire time.

After a tense half hour, we arrived at the border station. As soon as we docked, the soldier pushed me up the hill and yelled something to the guards inside the building. Quickly they ran out, rifles in hand. *This is definitely not working out as I expected.*

At the hilltop I was shoved into the guard station and escorted to a little room off to the side of the main one. It was furnished with only a flimsy wooden table and chair, and reeked of cigarette smoke and liquor fumes. The soldier pointed with his gun to the chair, indicating for me to sit. I obeyed. He left the room and locked the door behind him.

Minutes later the door opened. There stood the station commander, an old man with a square face and prominent jaw. His thick gray hair seemed long for a soldier, and a small chunk of his left earlobe was missing. His uniform bore a load of insignias and decorations, indicating he was a honcho of some kind. *What did this guy do to get stationed here?* This was no prize post. Maybe he'd screwed up somehow and he was being punished, or he was some kind of renegade.

The commander was followed by a younger soldier, in his late twenties. He was tall, thin, and good-looking, with fine black hair combed very neatly. Unlike the other soldiers, he looked like he still had some spirit in his eyes. The two bowed their heads slightly as if they respected me. They didn't.

The old man spoke in Chinese, and the younger soldier translated:

"You have violated Chinese territory," he began, leaving a pause for me to let my sin sink in. "Are you American?"

"That's right."

The soldiers shot each other a quick glance, as if to acknowledge that the stakes were high.

"Do you have a passport?"

"Not with me."

The commander shook his head.

"Do you realize this is a serious crime? You have illegally entered China." He lit a cigarette.

"I'm sorry," I offered. "I didn't mean to bother anyone."

The older man simply glared, revealing no sign of compassion.

"What are you doing here?"

How many times have I asked myself that question?

"I'm on . . . a spiritual quest." The young soldier had a hard time translating that phrase.

"Are you a Buddhist?"

I realized my answer could be incriminating. "I'm not anything . . . I'm just searching."

The old man kept a stone face. The young soldier searched his eyes as if to ask, *What are you going to do?*

The commander took a long drag on his cigarette and slowly blew the smoke toward the ceiling. "We will have to detain you until we receive orders on what to do with you."

I took out the (canceled) credit card I'd held on to for a moment just like this. "I have some money," I pleaded, showing him the card. "I can help you if you can help me."

The commander shook his head. His final words didn't need translation: "I don't make deals. . . . Take him to the cell."

67

Minutes later I found myself imprisoned in a mildewed shack, maybe fifteen feet square, at the edge of the woods twenty yards from the station. One small rectangular window barred with wooden slats allowed in just enough light to tell roughly what time of day it was. The roof was so rotted that rain had leaked through at several points, leaving stains. The "bed" was a thin straw mat on the floor.

The real killer was the stench from the latrine—a small hole cut into the floor at a corner. The waste went nowhere but the ground below, and it appeared that no one had ever bothered to clean it. The smell was so nauseating that I had to shield my nose and mouth to keep from vomiting. I took off my T-shirt and covered the hole, which helped a little. Then I scurried to the opposite side of the room and huddled against the wall there. I leaned my head back and closed my eyes.

❀

Later that afternoon I heard someone fumbling with the thick steel bar that bolted the door from the outside. Soon it opened, revealing the young soldier who had translated for the commander. He held a tarnished metal tray with a couple of dirty, cracked wooden bowls, one containing rice and the other some dreadful-looking pork and vegetables. Nauseated, I took the tray and pushed it to the far corner, near the latrine. The soldier seemed not to care in the least. Expressionless, he silently turned and exited, careful to secure the lock behind him. I looked at the "meal" again and, terribly hungry though I was, could not bring myself to touch it. *How long can I survive without eating?*

Exhausted, I fell asleep soon after sundown and slept through the night, interrupted only by a couple of rats trying to scavenge the food in my bowls; I threw a shoe at them, and they scampered away with a squeal. As I drifted off again, I prayed that when I awoke, I would discover that this was just a bad dream.

But when morning came, the nightmare was as real and horrid as it had been the previous night. I waited anxiously for word of my disposition, but none arrived that day. Nor the next. I could only guess that this outpost was some kind of derelict brigade under the rule of a commander who couldn't care less about inter-national diplomacy. Bottom line, I was trapped in that hellhole.

After a few days of not eating, I began to feel very weak, and my thinking turned fuzzy and circular. I started to get very jumpy, overreacting to every little sound. I grew depressed and had ter-rible headaches. Life was exiting my body by the hour, and I real-ized I would die if I continued on this course. Part of me wanted to; I wondered if a slow, torturous demise was the Lords' answer to my vow.

But when I thought about Alex and the baby, I couldn't bear the thought of leaving them. If I had any reason to live, they were it. So the next morning when the soldier delivered my breakfast, I decided to eat it. I had to hold my nose and close my eyes to con-sume the disgusting slop, but the goal now was pure survival.

My beard grew and I stank. If I didn't perish from starvation, I would die of some unsanitary disease. My skin itched everywhere, and I had terrible diarrhea. To keep my muscles from atrophying, every morning I forced myself to do push-ups and sit-ups. I tried every mental trick imaginable to keep from going over the edge.

Fantasizing helped a little. But when I opened my eyes, I was still in hell.

❀

Maybe a week after I'd been taken prisoner, the guard, who told me his name was Ren Tse, escorted me to the river to bathe. After being cooped up in my dungeon, the simple act of standing in sunlight felt like a weekend at the Four Seasons. Never again would I overlook the luxury of a hot shower and a toilet with a drain away from the building.

The week turned into two, and the two to four. Each week felt like a month, and I couldn't understand why they were keeping me so long. Every day I asked Ren Tse for permission to speak to the commander. Every day he replied that the older man had gone to Beijing on military business, and no one knew when he would return. At first I didn't believe Ren Tse, but as I got to know him, I felt he was sincere. I guessed that the commander was bargaining for his return to civilization.

I tried to bribe Ren Tse and the other guards. Some of them seemed tempted, and others turned their noses up at the offer, but no one took me up on it. The senior officer, I learned, was a hard-ass and everyone toed the line even in his absence. If anyone let me go, the commander would find out who and how, and they would be punished severely.

As I crouched in my dark corner trying to discern even faint sunlight, my heart sank. I knew Alex would be worried sick about me. By now she was entering her ninth month of pregnancy. Every night I prayed to God to take care of my wife and baby, and to forgive me for leaving them. Then one night as the wind and rain pounded on the roof, I had a terrible realization: *I had done to Alex and our child exactly what my father had done to me.* I'd left at a crucial time, perhaps never to return. I had become the man I despised and done the thing I hated most. Just as my father was a prisoner of the fear or addiction that had dragged him to oblivion, I was a prisoner of my spiritual quest. Wrap it in a holy or romantic ribbon if you will . . . it was a selfish delusion nonetheless. Now I was paying dearly for it, along with Alex. I could handle my punishment, but my family didn't deserve to suffer for my stupidity. In my haste to end my karma, I had created lifetimes of karma.

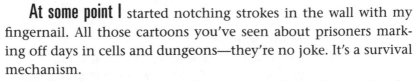

68

At some point I started notching strokes in the wall with my fingernail. All those cartoons you've seen about prisoners marking off days in cells and dungeons—they're no joke. It's a survival mechanism.

Forty-one days of abysmal light, minimal ventilation, slop for food, and stench. No company, little exercise, and no stimulation. It was a wonder I survived that long. My only human contact was with Ren Tse, who engaged me a little bit more each day when he came to deliver my food and occasionally escorted me to bathe.

"What is this spiritual quest you are on?" he asked one day as he led me to the river.

"I went to a cave on Mount Lasya to meditate." I didn't bother going into the Lords of Karma and all that.

"You were willing to risk death to meditate?"

"Yeah, I guess so."

Behind Ren Tse's stone face I couldn't tell if he was thinking, *I respect you* or *You're a damn fool.*

"Who taught you how to meditate?"

"Buddhists in San Francisco."

"Tibetan Buddhists?"

"That's right," I answered without thinking. Suddenly I remembered who I was talking to. I stiffened in dread that he might punish me for my connection to the Tibetans. But his face still displayed no reaction. Yet as he stared at the river while I bathed, I could see wheels turning in his head.

❁

To stay sane, I traveled to places in my mind. I went back to my high-school-football days and replayed the glorious moment when I recovered a fumble and made a game-winning touchdown. I savored the day I drove my first car, a green Pontiac Sunbird, off the used-car lot. I reread the note my English teacher scribbled on my term paper: *I see greatness in you.* Most of all, I went back to Alex. I relived falling for her at Arunima, our cosmic discussions in bed, laughing until my sides hurt, and our sparkling mornings in the garden. I imagined cradling her head on my chest and stroking her hair as she loved me to do. *If I ever get out of this wretched place, there's no way I will leave her again.*

I dispatched my thoughts like homing pigeons, trying to tell Alex: *I am alive. I love you. I will be home. Our baby will have a father.* Sometimes I felt that she was catching my messages; other times I felt like a foolish dreamer.

I prayed.

❁

One evening Ren Tse arrived to deliver dinner as usual. But instead of leaving the tray and returning to the guard station, he closed the door behind him. He set the tray on the floor, stood up straight, and stared me in the eye. *Is he going to interrogate me? Beat me for my association with the Buddhists? Rape me?* Instead, he motioned for me to pick up my rice bowl. When I complied, underneath I found a small metal chisel-like tool. I returned his stare, befuddled.

"Tonight is a holiday, and several of the guards are going to the city," he whispered. "There will be only two on duty, and they will drink Jiugui and play the radio. Use this to wedge open some floorboards; the wood is weak and will give way easily. There is just enough space under the building for you to slip through. If you're careful, no one will hear you. Take the tool with you when you go so no one will suspect I gave it to you."

Ren Tse turned and moved deliberately toward the door.

"Why are you doing this?"

The soldier turned back for a moment with a sober look on his face. "My father was in the Chinese army that invaded Tibet. I don't want the same blood on my hands. I want to use my life to correct my father's errors and restore honor to our family."

69

Later that evening, just as Ren Tse had predicted, music blared from the guard station. I sat and waited. As the evening wore on, slurred laughter spilled from the unit.

When I was satisfied that the guards were sufficiently distracted, I located the most worn-looking floorboard and wedged the chisel in the crack between it and the board beside it. It was stubborn at first, but soon began to give way. When it started to creak, I stopped and pressed it down in case a guard had heard and came to investigate.

No one did.

I resumed my work on the board and it loosened some more. Moving slowly so as not to create any more creaks, I worked my way around until it was completely loose. Carefully I removed it and set it on the floor nearby, in the event someone came by and I had to replace it quickly.

The opening let in a waft of fumes from the latrine. I pulled my undershirt up over my nose to filter the awful smell.

I loosened the edges of the next plank and pulled it from underneath, reaching through the opening from the first board. It came up easily and I laid it aside. If a guard came by now, I wouldn't be able to replace both boards quickly enough to disguise my caper. I would have to move quickly.

Ten minutes later I had four boards removed, allowing just enough space for me to squeeze through. I extended one foot, then the other, through the hole and probed the ground underneath—it was soggy and gross from the runoff from the latrine. I wanted to throw up, but I couldn't stop there. I tried to lower my torso through the opening, but I got stuck—it was just barely too small. I pulled myself back up to the floor and attacked one more board.

Suddenly I heard the guard station door open and then slam. *They've heard me!* Furiously I tried to replace the boards and fill the space, but it was futile. There was no way I could cover the opening in the time it would take for a guard to reach my cell. I froze. It would be just moments until the door opened and I would be shot on sight. *What a horrible way for my death prayer to be answered.*

I became still as a deer in the night forest and heard the sound of water running. No—the guard was taking a piss. He was yards away in the brush behind the guard station. He hadn't heard me. A minute later the guardhouse door slammed again. He was back on duty.

A reprieve.

I returned to my efforts until the last board yielded and I was able to slip through the opening. I had to crawl on my belly to work my way out from the undercroft. The entire area was flooded with feces and urine, absolutely nauseating. But my freedom was worth it—and welcome. As fast as possible (but slowly enough to avoid detection), I crawled out from under the cabin. A minute later I was free.

70

Moving quickly yet stealthily, I found my way to the river, the half moon affording me just enough light to navigate. At the riverside I splashed water on my clothes to purge the sewage that had collected on me during my escape. Then I tossed the chisel into the rushing water to avoid implicating Ren Tse. As the tool was gobbled up, I reflected on his act of mercy. Although I would never see him again, I would be indebted to him forever.

I started toward the underside of the bridge, but soon a fact became obvious: when the guards discovered my absence in the morning, they would proceed downstream to search for me. (Ren Tse had told me the soldiers knew of the secret path from the Indian side of the border.) They would have a boat, and I would be on foot. If I didn't reach the trail before they did, they would find me.

There was only one way to outwit the guards: head back upstream and wait until they stopped searching. They would never look for me there. It would mean a further delay in getting back to Alex, but it might save my life. As I started to work my way up the river, I could hear birds warning each other of my presence, as well as larger animals rustling. The last thing I needed now was to cross paths with a wild boar or another cobra. *Come on, Lords of Karma, cut me a break now.* How odd, I considered, that now I was praying to live as fervently as I had been praying to die not long ago.

In the moonlight I could make out a small crevice formed by several overlapping boulders not far upriver. I was able to crawl into the tiny cavern, out of sight, should anyone look for me upstream. I figured the guards would search for me for a day, if that, before they gave up. They would conclude that I'd continued downstream and found my way back to Indian sanctuary. If I could just take refuge here until the next nightfall, my chances of eluding them were good.

Wet, cold, and mud-soaked, I huddled in my dank nook. Soon I began to shiver, cough, and sneeze. My nose ran, tiny lizards darted over my feet, and I picked a half dozen leeches off my calves. The raw elements were far more brutal than my primitive dungeon had been, and for a fleeting moment I considered returning to the guard station simply for survival. But my need to get back to Alex was far greater, and I decided to tough it out.

I tried to sleep but couldn't in those conditions. I half-dozed and saw Alex in a fleeting vision. She was worried about me and praying for me. I flashed on the scene in *The Wizard of Oz* where Dorothy gazes into a crystal ball and sees Auntie Em back home fretting over her. Yet I had no ruby slippers, and I wouldn't wake up to a warm bed surrounded by loved ones. My route home, if I made it, would be through vicious struggle.

After several hours I could make out faint gray light outside my hiding place. I pulled my collar up and tried to sit on a craggy ledge. Before long, rain began to pound on the rocks. I would do my best to hold out for the remainder of day, and as soon as it was dark, I would make my move.

71

By nightfall I was severely weak. My coughing had given way to an awful-sounding hack, and my shivering had escalated to almost violent shaking. I couldn't expect to survive more than another day under these conditions, and if I did, I would lose so much strength that the rest of the trip would surely do me in.

It was now or never.

I stepped out of my shelter and surveyed the bank of the river. It was *gone*. The water level had risen to the foot of my little cave. I tried to scan downriver, but the clouds had shut out the moon and there was no way I could navigate. The raging waters dashed debris against rocks, the roar eclipsing all other sounds. If hell consisted of water rather than flames, this was it.

I knew that if I hesitated, I wouldn't jump. Any time to think would work against me. So I prayed quickly and fervently: *Dear God or whoever is out there, please help me. If I die, please take care of my family.* Then I threw myself in the river. The water was so cold that I thought I would faint, the current so fierce that I fully expected it would tear me to shreds. Immediately I wished I hadn't leaped. But it was too late.

I hurtled downstream, colliding brutally with rocks and branches. I tried to buffer myself from the big rocks by extending my arms and legs in front of me; I was able to resist some, but it was impossible to avoid others. One collision turned me around so my head was pointed downstream; moments later I was upended again. I felt trapped in a huge liquid cyclone. A few times my entire body got sucked under for almost longer than I could hold my breath, and then the river spat me up, leaving me desperately gasping for air, coughing water out of my lungs. When I got jammed between two boulders, I tried to grasp hold of one for some respite. But the torrent dislodged me as quickly as it had trapped me, and suddenly I was plunging downriver again.

When my leg crashed against a rock, I felt an awful pain in my shin and imagined I saw signs of blood on the river surface. But I couldn't afford to feel pain or even think about it. Even if I broke or lost a limb, that would be insignificant if I could somehow stay alive.

I had no idea how long the river dragged me. Ten minutes? Twenty? At one point I thought I saw the border bridge go by above me, but by that time I was only half-conscious. I noticed a large tree limb moving beside me, and I grasped it in order to stabilize myself. I succeeded for a few moments, and for the first time felt some sense that I might not drown. Yet that, too, quickly gave way. I strained to see the forest rushing by, shadowed by the looming mountains. Everything was dark and blurry. When I caught a brief glimpse of the river ahead of me, I saw that I was speeding toward a huge boulder. Then everything went black.

72

This time the voices were all speaking Tibetan. All men. *The Lords of Karma are welcoming me to the afterlife.*

Then, through slitted eyes, behind a foggy veil, I made out a face. Old. Thin. Gray whiskers. Not Akar . . . or Chuang-Tsu . . . definitely not Teresa. I started to gag.

I felt two arms, then four, reach under me and lift my chest, arching my torso and forcing my head to hang back. Gagging intensely, I resisted, begging without words to be set back down. But the arms kept me in position until I felt my chest begin to clear and the coughing subsided.

"Try to breathe more deeply," a voice instructed in English with a thick Tibetan accent.

I strained to see the speaker, but could make out just a fedora. Below it, Lingpa's face. Blue sky behind him. Daylight.

Two faces hovered beside him: one that looked to be Lingpa's age; and a younger man, fortyish. The older guy wore a maroon bandana around his forehead, above penetrating eyes. His skin spoke of years of merciless sandblasting by relentless Himalayan winds. The younger man's face was round and his eyebrows wide; he wore a small mustache and seemed to smile slightly—or the sun was blinding him and he was wincing. All were peering into my eyes, searching for signs of life.

"You were crazy to go back there," Lingpa told me.

Rub it in, why don't you?

"Maybe he will survive," one of the other guys added with frightening detachment.

Please, let Eyla be with them. She will be gentle. I tried to lift my head to see her, but it hurt; quickly I let it fall back. Best I could tell, we were at the bottom of the hill where the path from Eyla's house met the river.

I let my gaze run down my leg to the place where it had crashed into the rock. The men had tied a makeshift bandage and tourniquet around my calf. Dried blood formed a halo around the fabric's edges. My shin was throbbing like hell. I could see other bruises and swelling around my wrists, forearms, and ankles. My body felt like one big bash, my head pounding and my lower back horribly stiff.

After some shuffling about, the other two men approached with a crude stretcher they'd fashioned of thick branches tied together with vines, strips of cloth, and their belts.

"I don't think I can move," I told Lingpa.

"You do not have a choice," he replied. "Another storm is coming—see for yourself." I lifted my head to view the sky over the mountains; threatening clouds were converging.

Silently the dogged mountain men lifted me onto the stretcher. *"Arrrrhhhh!"* I grunted as my leg twisted, feeling like someone had driven a chisel into my shin. "Hey, could you take it easy there?" I begged. They paid no attention to my plea. They knew what they had to do.

Lingpa commanded the men to lift, and I felt my broken body rise from the hard ground. When they had me steady in the stretcher, the march began. The older guy in front wasn't as tall or as strong as the younger one behind me, so they carried me unevenly, my feet closer to the ground than my head. I was tempted to complain, until I reminded myself that these men had saved my life and they were doing the best they could.

We forged our way up the steep hill at a crawl; every twenty minutes the guys took a break and rotated positions. The brewing storm seemed to stay to the south and sent us only light rains for a few brief periods, as if some unseen hand was keeping it at bay.

"How did you know I was there?" I asked Lingpa when the ground finally leveled out.

"When you did not return after a week, we knew something was wrong," he explained. "We have been coming down to the river every few days to see if there was any sign of you."

Thunder rumbled in the distance.

"Didn't you give me up for dead or lost?"

"*I* did," Lingpa answered, "but Eyla insisted we keep looking. She said your spirit came to her in a dream, and you were calling for help."

Eyla.

"Did you return to the Cave of Khadroma?" Lingpa asked. The other men seemed to perk their ears for my response. They set me down; I wasn't sure whether because it was a convenient resting point or they wanted to hear my story.

"The cave was destroyed by a mud slide," I answered. Their eyes all widened; apparently they knew about the cave. "On my way back I was captured by a border guard. I was put in an awful cell, until one of the soldiers helped me escape."

"I don't understand why they didn't just shoot you," the younger fellow commented, lighting half a cigarette. "My uncle was killed trying to sneak back to Tibet to see his family." He took a few drags of the cigarette and passed it to his friend.

"Maybe because this man is an American," the older man replied, accepting the butt. "They don't want any international problems."

"They wouldn't stop because of that," the young one retorted. "They would have simply buried you, and you would be just another missing Himalayan mountain climber."

Lingpa shook his head. "It's none of that."

"Then what?" the men asked almost simultaneously.

I thought I saw a flash of lightning in the distance. Another clap of thunder rumbled, louder and closer this time.

"The Lords of Karma were protecting you," Lingpa answered. "The cave was destroyed, but not the Lords."

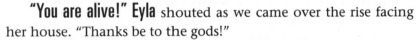

"You are alive!" Eyla shouted as we came over the rise facing her house. "Thanks be to the gods!"

Somebody say, "Amen, sister."

"Where did you find him?" Eyla asked her father as she reached us, trying to catch her breath.

"At the end of the path," the old man answered. "He looked like a dead fish. We were about to toss him back, but I saw he was still breathing." *My lord, does Lingpa have a sense of humor?*

I tried to lean forward to grasp Eyla's arm, but it hurt too much.

"Don't try to move," she insisted as the men began to carry me down the hill. When we reached the house, she turned to the stretcher bearers and commanded, "Take him to my father's bedroom—and be gentle, you clumsy yaks."

Ah, the tenderness of a woman melded with the tenacity of an ox herder.

Eyla followed the "yaks" into the bedroom and supervised them while they transferred me to Lingpa's bed. I doubt she'd discussed this with him, but it appeared he would have to live with her decision.

When I was settled, Eyla turned to my leg and unbandaged the wound. When she saw it, she made an ugly face.

"Not pretty, huh?"

"You are lucky. The broken bone didn't pierce the skin, although it tried."

Eyla went to the kitchen to boil some water. Ten minutes later she returned with a hot, damp cloth and began to wipe down my wound. The warmth felt good. She continued to wash my legs, arms, and face, but before I could thank her, I was asleep.

❈

When I awoke, I could think clearly for the first time since I'd been thrown in the hellhole. From the position of the sun, I figured I'd slept at least fourteen hours. My leg was killing me, and the swelling from my multiple bruises had blown me up like the Michelin Man. But at least I was alive and safe. As soon as possible, I would make my way back to Alex and our baby.

When Eyla peeked around the doorjamb to see if I was awake, she seemed pleased to see my eyes open. She entered with a handful of fresh bandages, sat on the bed beside me, and placed her hand on my forehead to check my temperature. "How are you feeling, Linden?"

I forced a small smile and answered, "Just great." Eyla knew I was kidding, and we both laughed.

"I made some soup. Are you hungry?"

"Any yaks, oxen, lizards, cobras, boars, or odd things in it I should know about?"

"Just vegetables. We'll keep it light until you are on your feet again." She rose to head for the kitchen.

Until you are on your feet again. That could be a month; I couldn't afford to stay that long. "I need to get back, Eyla," I told her almost desperately. "Alex is due to deliver—maybe she already has."

Eyla thought for a moment and nodded. "This afternoon I will go into the village and see if I can find someone to help you."

"Someone with a car? A telephone?"

"A healer."

He appeared early the next morning. An ancient Tibetan with a bulbous nose and long ears resembling paintings of Buddha, Trulpe entered the room with quiet dignity. Dressed in a red and gold ceremonial robe and pointed hat, he carried a sacred *dorje* in his left hand and a handheld skull drum in his right. The dorje, I'd learned at the dharma center, was a ceremonial tool representing a diamond that can cut but cannot itself be cut. The drum had two little strings attached to it with stones on the ends that beat the drum when rotated. The healer bowed to Lingpa and Eyla and then to me. Quickly my hosts bestowed their guest with a white prayer shawl, a symbol of welcome and respect.

Since Trulpe spoke no English, Eyla translated: "I understand you hurt your leg on a quest to find the Lords of Karma." Trulpe, whom I guessed was about seventy-five years old, had an impish glow in his eyes and no teeth.

"That's right."

The shaman gave me a serious look. "You are lucky this is all that happened to you."

"So I hear."

"Eyla tells me you want to leave quickly," he noted as he began to unpack some items from a small red cloth bag.

"I have a baby coming in Arunima."

Trulpe's eyes looked off to the side as if he was listening to another voice.

"Your wife is very worried about you. She believes she has lost you. She has been sick, and her pregnancy has been difficult."

My worst fears.

"But the baby is strong-willed. An old soul."

"Who's telling you this?"

"The ancestors in spirit," he explained. "They are telling me to pray to heal you. Your desire to leave soon is right."

Trulpe walked to a small table, set out three butter lamps, and lit them reverently. Then he placed a small mirror against the wall, facing me. "This is the mirror of spirit doors," he told me. "The gods will walk through it to meet you."

The shaman returned to the bed, lifted the dorje, and began to beat the skull drum. He closed his eyes and muttered some prayers in Tibetan. He went on for quite a long time, circling the bed as if going into a trance. It appeared that some invisible entity was starting to possess him, infusing his frail body with an otherworldly power. Trulpe chanted louder and louder, beat the drum harder, and danced more wildly until he crescendoed into a fervor. His breath quickened, becoming so rapid that I feared he'd have a heart attack. Writhing as if he was having some kind of seizure, he started to wobble and fall, and Lingpa and Eyla rushed to catch him.

This is getting weird.

Finally the healer calmed down, and glassy-eyed, moved to my leg. He placed his hands over the injured area, crossing them so both palms were lined up one behind the other, facing the wound. He closed his eyes, stopped chanting, and began to direct his attention to the affected area.

Something inside me told me to close my eyes, too. Soon I could feel a warm energy bathing the wound. *Maybe it's just his body heat.* But the sensation grew stronger, as if he was holding an electric light right over my leg. I opened my eyes to see if he had taken hold of some hot stone or other object. But it was only his hands. *Okay, we are having an experience.* I closed my eyes again and tried to be receptive.

Then something really bizarre happened: My father's face flashed before me—just a quick blip, but strong and clear. Dad was smiling and seemed peaceful . . . no words or drama—simply a rapid, compelling image. After he disappeared, a wave of peace ensued, flowing through me like a balm. Startled, I opened my eyes.

Suddenly Trulpe went limp. The spirit that possessed him had departed. Slowly the little man opened his eyes and appeared disoriented, even stunned. He gazed around the room and then at me. The glazed-over look in his eyes disappeared. He was back.

"I saw my father," I told the healer, Eyla translating again.

Trulpe nodded. "Those in spirit are with you."

"Does that mean my father is dead?"

"Probably," he answered dryly.

A multitude of feelings ran through me. Sadness that my father had passed before I'd had a chance to see him again. Anger at him for leaving my mother and me. Appreciation that he'd come to me in my vision. Compassion for the mess he'd gotten himself into. Yearning to simply embrace him and tell him I loved him.

Trulpe rose and told me, "Your father says you are headstrong like him, but unlike him, you have chosen the path of honor. He is proud of you."

I could feel tears starting to fill the back of my throat. *Maybe it was all for this.*

"Your leg will heal faster than you expect," Trulpe added. "You must return to your wife as soon as you can."

"I know. But how?"

Trulpe's eyes peered off to the side again, as if he was trying to access information, but none seemed to come.

Eyla interrupted, "There is a man who comes to the village to buy goji berries and ship them to America. He flies into Dharamsala in a small private plane. He was here a few days ago."

"Then he is gone now," Lingpa interjected. "And he will not be back for a month."

Well, thanks, Lingpa. We can always count on you for encouragement.

"I will go into the village and ask if anyone knows how to contact him," Eyla offered.

Trulpe blew out the candles and addressed me: "I have done all I can for you. I will continue to pray to the gods to heal you." Then he turned to pack the mirror of spirit doors.

Minutes later Lingpa walked Trulpe to the door and out into the yard, where he picked up a goose and proffered it to the healer, a gift on my behalf. Perhaps I had been too quick to judge Eyla's father. And mine.

74

Eyla threw on her jacket and dashed out the door to catch a ride into the village with Trulpe's driver. I was still reeling from my spirit encounter with my father. *How did Trulpe know so much about him and my relationship with him? Was his guidance about Alex and the baby correct?* If invisible spirits were real, my visit with the Lords of Karma was no fantasy. I sat up and prayed to them, Buddha, Jesus, or whoever was out there for help. I asked my dad if he could pull some strings from the other side.

I dozed on and off for most of the day, but whenever I started to relax, my mind went to Alex and our baby. At one point I sat up and tested my injured leg, pressing it very lightly against the floor. It hurt, but not nearly as badly as it had yesterday. Maybe Trulpe's treatment and prayers had had some effect. I felt light-headed in the aftermath of his ceremony, as if I'd taken a mild drug. Eventually I drifted off and slept well through the night.

✸

"Linden, you must get ready to go now." Eyla shook me. It was morning.

"What's up?" I sat up with a start.

"The man with the plane is still here," she informed me. "I found Vijay at the market loading his berries. He was delayed by the rain. He is driving back to Dharamsala now and flying to Mumbai this afternoon. He will fly you to Arunima; all he asks is that you give him some money for fuel."

Someone out there heard me.

I bolted out of bed. *Yeeeeooooowww!* As I applied my weight to my leg, it nearly collapsed. "You must take it easy," Eyla warned, rushing to steady me. My hostess brought me a change of clothes and helped me prepare to go. Lingpa marched through the door carrying a makeshift crutch he'd hammered together—a long branch nailed to a shorter piece to fit under my arm. Crude, but it would do. Eyla fashioned a simple splint to help keep my leg straight. Not quite state-of-the-art either, but functional.

Father and daughter helped me hobble into the yard, where Eyla mounted a saddled horse and Lingpa helped me up to sit behind her. He followed on his own steed, toting another goose under his arm.

After a thirty-minute bumpy haul, we reached the main road and stationed ourselves in the hopes of a vehicle passing. Eyla kept peering down the road, straining to see a car. She explained that in this region everyone stopped for hitchhikers; it was considered unkind to pass one by. Our problem wasn't a lack of friendly drivers; it was a lack of drivers, period.

After another half hour, Eyla was pacing back and forth, worried that my pilot would take off without me. "I will ride into the village," she announced, and started to mount her horse. Just then we heard the faint sound of a distant motor, followed by the sight of a truck sputtering out of a mountain pass. Eyla dashed into the middle of the road to flag the vehicle down—no, make that block it entirely. A minute later a lorry ground to a noisy halt a few yards in front of us. It was a Frankenstein of disparate ancient parts, held together by caked mud, Bondo, and prayers. The cab was painted bright rainbow colors, dotted with a score of little meditating Buddhas. In the rear bed lay a dozen large concrete pipes, tied together with old rubber straps, which would have made me nervous to drive behind. The driver was elated to see a ravishing woman hitchhiking, and disappointed in equal measure when she pointed to me as the passenger. But it was too late now, and he motioned for me to jump in. I hobbled toward the cab.

As Lingpa offered the goose to the driver, Eyla walked me to the door. "I wish I could go with you," she told me with sadness in her eyes.

I took one last look at this extraordinary woman, the wind sweeping her hair as the sun artistically highlighted the contour of her cheekbones. God, Eyla was beautiful—nothing less than a goddess. I knew I would never be back there and I'd never see her again. I have a hard time with good-byes; *forever* good-byes are especially excruciating.

"I wish you could come with me," I told her.

Eyla simply nodded. She understood.

We shared one last poignant glance before I turned and opened the door. Then it hit me. Hard. *How could I have missed it?*

I turned back and said to Eyla, "Come with me."

Her face contorted with confusion. "You want me to come with you?"

"Yes, Eyla, I do. Please just get in the truck with me."

"I don't understand, Linden," she pleaded, befuddled. "Now you want me to be with you? . . . What about Alex . . . and your baby?"

"Just trust me, Eyla. I may have the answer to your prayer."

Eyla looked over at Lingpa, now taking back the goose from the driver, who had politely declined it. "What shall I tell my father?"

"Whatever you want . . . just come."

I worked my way up onto the seat and wedged my crutch behind it. Through the dirty, cracked windshield I could see Eyla telling her father she was going with me. Soon their conversation became heated. When Lingpa began to raise his voice, Eyla cut off the debate. She climbed the running board and slipped into the seat beside me, slamming the bulky door behind her. Then she ordered the driver to vamoose, leaving Lingpa, horses, and the goose in the dust, and her father scratching his head.

75

The bumpy road amplified the pain in my leg tenfold, making the three-hour drive feel like ten. The swarthy thirtysomething driver wore an Arnold Schwarzenegger "The Governator" T-shirt and a small, pointy native cap disturbingly reminiscent of Beldar Conehead. He kept eyeing Eyla, talking past me as if I was invisible. Several times I tried to slice into the conversation without success. In between the driver bragging in broken English about his James Bond DVDs and his embarrassing ABBA imitations, I gleaned that he was delivering drainage piping for a road project in the lower city.

When we reached Dharamsala, I told Eyla I needed to stop by the monastery to bid farewell to my friends there. She protested, worrying that we'd miss the plane, but when I convinced her I owed it to them, she acceded. Luckily she knew the area and guided the driver to the monastery on the north ridge.

When we arrived, a monk cleaning the walkway recognized me and called inside to announce my arrival. Soon Sonam emerged from the prayer hall with his signature smile and un-Buddhist embrace. His hair had grown in quite a bit, now considerably longer than the other monks'.

"What happened to your leg?" he asked when he saw me hobbling.

"A little karmic residue," I explained.

Wasting no time, I directed my attention to Eyla. "Sonam, I would like you to meet Eyla, a true angel . . . Eyla, this is my good friend and spiritual brother Sonam."

The two exchanged polite greetings in English, respecting my presence. "What village are you from?" Sonam asked her.

"Near Shailesh."

"Eyla is Lingpa's daughter," I told Sonam, knowing he would recognize her father as the underground railroader he'd directed me to.

"I see," Sonam replied with a nod. "I didn't know Lingpa had a daughter." Read between the lines: *And a lovely one, at that.*

"I stay at home mostly," Eyla said. "I do not socialize much with the local people."

"Neither do I," Sonam replied. "I prefer to be in nature."

That sparked Eyla's interest. "I would rather read than gossip with the village women. I like stories, especially of the ancient yogi Milarepa."

"Milarepa?" Sonam's eyes lit up. "He is my favorite. Have you read Tenzin's biography of him?"

Eyla looked intrigued. "No, I haven't been able to find it. I have been looking for that for years."

"I have a copy in my library. I'd be happy to lend it to you, if you'd like."

"That would be wonderful! Thank you . . . Sonam, is it?"

I practically had to step between the two to break into their conversation. "If you'll both excuse me, I need to go fetch a few items I left here. I'll be back in a minute."

Frankly, I didn't think they noticed.

76

When I returned, the two were still engaged in animated conversation. "Sonam, can I impose on you to drive me to the airport?" I asked him. "A man is waiting there to fly me to Arunima."

Sonam pulled it together enough to answer, "Sure, no problem. Give me a minute and I'll bring the van around."

As soon as Eyla and I were alone, I asked her, "So what do you think of Sonam?"

"He is very easy to talk to," she answered, showing more enthusiasm than she would likely have admitted to, yet still cautious. "And he seems kind."

"He is as good a man as I have ever known," I told her.

A minute later the van pulled up in front of the temple, and Eyla and I slipped into it. I sat in the backseat to let vibes mingle in the front. This time they spoke in Tibetan, and continued to have an endless array of things to talk about. Eyla laughed and seemed more bubbly than at any time since I'd told her I was on my way off the planet. Sonam had to force himself to keep his eyes on the road; he looked like a teenager on his first big date. I sat back, arms crossed, one might even say smugly. This time my invisibility was welcome.

At the airport we sped to the private-plane area, hoping Vijay was still there. Off to the side of the runway we saw a white-with-red-trim four-seater Cessna, propeller revving. A nicely dressed fifty-ish fellow in a leather jacket paced along the fuselage, looking at his watch. When he saw us, he waved us to hurry. Sonam practically drove the van into the side of the plane, jumping out to help me to my feet. Then he hustled to the rear of the van to remove my pack, which he delivered to Vijay to load.

Eyla met me at the door and steadied me. "Well, are you coming with me?" I asked in a mock tone.

"I think you know the answer to that," she answered with a sly smile.

"Sonam is a rare soul, Eyla. I think you would do well to get to know him."

Eyla nodded.

"And women do not come any better than you," I told her.

She simply lowered her head, characteristically humble.

"Who knows?" I mused. "At another time, another place, maybe destiny would have brought us together as soul mates."

"Destiny did bring us together," Eyla noted, looking straight at me now, "obviously for a reason."

"Obviously." I took a final moment to look at Eyla and bask in my thanks for all she'd done for me. No, it was more than that—it was gratitude for who she *was*.

"Be well, Eyla."

She gave me a small kiss on the cheek. "Be well, Linden. You'll be a great dad."

I turned to Sonam, gave him a final hug, and whispered in his ear, "She is gold."

My heart satisfied, I turned toward the plane. Vijay helped me into the rear seat, where I could elevate my throbbing leg. He handed me a headset and plugged it into the console in case we wanted to talk. He pulled the pilot's door shut, the engine roared, and a minute later my head fell back as we hurtled down the runway. Soon we were in the air, and I gawked out the window, watching Eyla and Sonam fade to invisibility. Minutes later Dharamsala became just an idea. As the aircraft gained altitude, I strained to see if I could make out the valley of the cave. I thought I could see it, but then I wasn't sure. Sort of symbolic, I figured.

77

I scanned the cockpit like a kid in a candy shop of dials, meters, and blinking lights. Then I noticed an emblem centered above the dashboard: *Cessna 172 Skyhawk.*

Skyhawk? Aw, shit, here we go again.

"How far is it to Arunima from here?" I asked Vijay over the intercom.

"Roughly 1,200 kilometers," he answered. "That's about 700 miles."

That now-familiar shudder pulsed through me. *Is this meant to be the end? Have all my adventures, my striving, my pains and prayers, led to* this *hawk devouring my efforts?* I started to slip into the same tailspin I'd succumbed to on the flight from Mumbai, in my cell, and on a half dozen other occasions. But this time it felt old. I was tired of wrestling with fear. *The hell with it,* I thought. *If this is it, this is it. I refuse to waste any more energy wondering and worrying.* As much as I wanted to live, if life was about living in fear, I didn't want any part of it.

"Your wife is having a baby?" Vijay asked over the intercom. Eyla must have told him.

"Any moment. Maybe already."

He opened the throttle a bit.

"Do you have children?" I asked him.

Vijay shook his head. "I wanted children, but my wife was unable. We tried treatments, but she died before we could succeed."

"I'm sorry to hear that."

I recalled a story I'd heard about a young woman who came to Buddha after her father had died. When she asked him to bring her father back to life, he handed her a cup and told her, "Take this cup to the houses in your village and fill it with honey from the home of someone who has not felt the sting of a loved one's death. When you return with the honey, I will resurrect your father." The woman set out to have the cup filled, but, alas, she couldn't find anyone who hadn't felt the pain of such a loss.

"And you never remarried?"

Vijay shook his head. "I married my plane," he quipped with a stoic tinge of sadness, affectionately stroking the dashboard.

I just sat quietly, remembering the advice a lama once told me: *Be gentle with everyone, for everyone is fighting an inner battle.* I closed my eyes and leaned my head against the window.

❀

As the Skyhawk rocked and swayed in the mountain gusts, I strained to see out the window, wondering if we would make it to Arunima, and anticipating seeing Alex if we did. *Within a few hours I might be holding my child in my arms.*

"Hang on—it's going to be choppy. Monsoon season has arrived," the pilot called back to me, adjusting the flaps. I tightened my seat belt a bit, as if the extra inch would make a difference.

"Say, Vijay, do you believe in karma?" I asked him.

He seemed surprised by my question, but he took it in stride. After a moment he answered, "Sure, but not in the way most people do."

"What do you mean?"

"I think that how we think about things affects our destiny more than what we do."

I decided to tell him my story—what the hell. We were suspended in the air, and maybe he could help me make some sense of the cosmic questions that had shredded my peace and thrown my family into turmoil. If we didn't survive the flight, nothing mattered anyway. So I told him about that fateful night at the bridge, meeting Tashi, connecting with Alex, trekking to the cave of the Lords of Karma, and all of it—all of it . . . right up to that very moment. Vijay listened intently—a feat considering he was maneuvering a flimsy aircraft through a thunderstorm. "So what do you think?" I asked him when I was done.

Vijay smiled. "I don't think you need to worry about not being reborn."

"How's that?"

He spoke plainly into the headset. "That lonely, angry, fearful man with a broken heart standing on the rail of the bridge is no more. The fellow I am talking to has been born in his place. This man is a passionate lover of life and his family. He has a good, strong heart; and he is doing everything he can to stay in life and be with his beloved."

I never thought of it like that.

"If the Lords of Karma have done anything, they have pushed you out of a miserable existence and helped you find a life with meaning," he added.

That sure feels better than worrying if I'll be struck down when I least expect it.

"That leaves one question I've been wrestling with ever since I met Tashi," I told him.

"What's that?"

"Why would God create a world the purpose of which is to escape?"

Vijay thought for a long moment and turned to face me. "I can't say I know the answer to that, Linden," he replied. "But I do know that pain has a way of pushing people to grow in ways they would have missed if their lives were easier."

His idea set my brain afire. "So my going to the bridge was my first step toward ending a bad life and beginning a new one? It actually led me to my destiny?"

The pilot adjusted a dial on the dashboard and answered, "Draw your own conclusions, my friend. Draw your own conclusions."

❋

By then we'd begun our descent and we were gazing up at the underside of the swollen gray-black clouds that dominated the sky. The Skyhawk, in spite of a blustery welcome, found its way (almost) gracefully to the earth coordinate known as Arunima. As the tiny craft touched down—with bumps and rattles, but safely, nevertheless—our landing put to rest once and for all my terror of the hawk. *Another demon fallen.* We taxied for a while, and Vijay pulled the craft to a halt in line with some other private planes.

"We made good time." He smiled as he removed his headset. "I'll have a chance to grab some dinner before I go on to Mumbai."

The pilot exited and made his way around the Cessna's nose to open my door and help me out. When he was satisfied that I was steady on my crutch, he let go and dusted off my shoulders in a fatherly way.

"Vijay, I can't thank you enough," I told him.

"I'm glad to help," he replied with a kindly smile.

Now to deal with the awkward subject of money. "About the fuel cost . . . how much do I owe you?"

He did some mental calculations. "About 4,000 rupees." Roughly a hundred bucks. Fair enough—but I didn't have a penny, in any currency. "Is there, uh, any way I can mail that to you?" I asked sheepishly, feeling a bit guilty that I'd taken him up on his offer knowing I didn't have the cash on hand.

Vijay didn't seem surprised. He nodded and answered, "That would be fine." (It appeared he'd figured this was a charity run from the beginning.)

"I'll take your address," I replied quickly, eager to demonstrate my intention to pay. Vijay found a pen and scrawled his address on the back of an aeronautics magazine he had stashed under the front seat of the Skyhawk. As he tore off the swatch and handed it to me, I noticed a ring on his finger bearing a symbol that looked familiar—*the circular sign I saw in the Cave of Khadroma and again in Ramesh's photo!*

"That symbol on your ring—what does it mean?" I asked breathlessly.

Vijay looked down at the ring as if he'd forgotten he was wearing it. "A Tibetan monk gave this to me many years ago when I did him some favors," he answered, polishing it fondly with the thumb and forefinger of his other hand. "He said it would bring me good luck."

"Please, Vijay, what does it mean?"

He stared at the ring. "The circle in the center is the source of all life, shooting out in rays beyond the limits of form. It means you are in your right place and, no matter what appearances say to the contrary, the gods are watching over you."

78

As the taxi driver carved our way through crooked back roads, I went over in my mind how I would greet Alex and maybe even hold my child in my arms. Part of me ached to see my baby, and part of me hoped the birth hadn't yet taken place so I could be with Alex for that extraordinary moment.

I kept urging the driver to go faster. At first he did and then, after giving me a few choice Hindi words, ignored my demands. He was right—what a bummer it would have been to survive all those horrible trials and then get killed during the last kilometer home.

When we reached the resort, we sped past the security gate, leaving the guard leaning out of his booth, ranting. I ordered the cabbie to drive across the lawn to our bungalow. We probably tore up the grass, but I didn't care. I didn't care about anything except reconnecting with my family.

Before the vehicle came to a full stop, I leaped out and hobbled to the door, yelling, "Alex, I'm back! It's me, Linden!" I grabbed the door handle, but it refused to turn. *Must be jammed.* I tried again, harder, but it was still stuck. *What's the matter with this stupid door? Why can't they keep things fixed here?* Then I realized the door was locked. I scurried to the window and peeked through a crack between the drapes, hoping to find Alex taking a nap. But the bed was empty and neatly made. None of her possessions, or mine, were present. The room was vacant.

As fast as my leg would allow, I dashed across the courtyard to Dr. Reddy's office, the taxi driver in pursuit, shouting, "Hey, you owe me 1,000 rupees!"

The light in the doctor's office was on. *Maybe she's in there with Alex.* I burst into the waiting room; no sign of doctor or patient. I reached to open the door to the examining room, but something told me I'd better knock. So I did. Loud. Fast. Hard. I might as well have pulled the door open.

Seconds later Dr. Reddy appeared, flustered and angry. When she saw that it was me, her eyes bulged as if she'd seen a ghost. "Linden!" she burst out. "My god, Linden, you're alive! We all thought you were dead!"

"Yes, I'm very much alive," I answered. "Where is Alex? Is she all right? Did she have the baby?"

Dr. Reddy's countenance dropped. "Alex went back to America."

"What?!" My stomach sank horribly.

As the doctor closed the door behind her, I noticed an older white woman sitting on the examining table, pulling a sheet up over her bosom, looking quite rattled.

"We were having some complications with the pregnancy," Dr. Reddy told me. "Nothing serious, but we didn't want to take any chances. Alex will get better medical care having the baby in the U.S. She said something about her father's insurance."

No, no, no. This can't be happening. "Why didn't she wait for me?"

"She did, Linden," the doctor answered sternly. "She waited for almost two months. That's a very long time for a pregnant woman. Her spirit grew weaker every day you were gone. Finally she gave up hope. We all did. We thought something terrible had happened to you. Maybe you were injured or killed or captured, or you deserted her. Or your 'Lords' commanded you to stay. We had no idea. Alex wanted to be with her family. I think she made a wise choice, considering the circumstances."

I felt myself losing my balance as if I might fall headlong onto the floor.

"But you still might catch her," the doctor added with a tinge of optimism in her voice.

"Catch her?"

"She left yesterday. She was going to stay with some friends in Mumbai last night and fly out tonight." The doctor shot a quick glance at the clock: *8:15*. She shook her head. "You'll never make it by car."

I kissed Dr. Reddy on the cheek and started to bolt out the door. But the taxi driver was blocking my way, his arm extended, palm open. I turned back to the physician.

"Say, doctor," I asked, "can you help me out here? I need 1,000 rupees for this guy—wait . . . make that 2,000 for both ways."

The cabbie looked happy to have the business back to the airport, yet dismayed to have me as the passenger. I'm sure he would have preferred to just take the money and run.

The good doctor reached into her purse under the desk and pulled out a handful of bills. She counted them and handed the dough to the cabbie, telling him something in Hindi, which I imagined was: "Take care of this guy, and if you dillydally, I'll cut off your Viagra prescription." Whatever she said, the cabbie nodded like a frightened boy.

"Thanks again, doc," I said. "I'll put in a good word for you with the Lords of Karma."

"That's nice of you, Linden," she replied. "Just find your family and stay home for a while, would you?"

79

The rain had intensified and nearly doubled our time back to the airport. When we finally arrived, the cabbie returned me to the spot where Vijay had parked—but the plane was gone. I hobbled into the little dispatcher's office, where I found a short, stout Indian guy wearing a maroon U2 sweatshirt. His feet were up on the desk, and his face was hidden behind an Indian version of the *National Enquirer* boasting a photo of a Hindu baby with an alien's head. "Where is Vijay's plane?" I demanded.

"You mean that one there?" he answered, lowering the rag sheet and pointing to several blinking red lights ascending into the night sky.

"He took off already?"

"Five minutes ago."

Damn. I pounded my fist against the wall. "You've got to get him back!"

"Too late," he answered coldly.

"Can't you radio him or something?" I shouted. "This is really important!"

"When you're gone, you're gone," the young dispatcher added, proud of his snotty English.

I had no patience at that moment for a cocky air-traffic controller. I picked up my crutch and poked it at his throat. "Listen, you arrogant dweeb . . . I say that when it looks like you're gone, you may not be. Now get your ass on the radio and get him back here or I'll make your face so ugly that the only chick you'll be able to marry is that alien on the front of that newspaper!"

"Okay, okay," he said, and picked up the radio microphone. He flicked the switch and mumbled a bunch of call letters, echoed by annoying static, squeaks, and squawks. Finally I heard a garbled voice—Vijay's.

"What do you want?" the controller asked me.

"Tell him that Linden needs a ride to Mumbai. My wife is there, and she's leaving for America tonight."

The guy had a brief high-pitched Hindi interchange with the pilot and switched off the radio. He nodded and pointed again to the sky, where the plane was circling back to the runway.

Apparently, reality in that little corner of the world was flexible.

80

As the Skyhawk rocked us in the wind, Vijay radioed for the Air India flight schedule and found that the next flight connecting to San Francisco, via London, was scheduled to depart at 10:30 P.M. We had less than an hour to cover 200 kilometers. "What airspeed can we do?" I asked.

"In daylight and good weather, 260 kilometers an hour. In this rain and wind at night, 190 if we're lucky."

Not good. Vijay felt my anxiety. "I'll do my best," he told me.

"Can we radio ahead to get someone to tell Alex I'm coming?"

"We're out of range. When we get closer to Mumbai, I can try."

I tried to relax and be patient, but it was no use. All of my meditation and Buddhist training went out the window. I wished I could just reach into the clock dial, grab the hands, and keep them from moving. But they had a life of their own; the more I set myself against time, the more it defeated me.

❀

Half an hour later I could resist no longer. "How far to go?" I asked Vijay.

"Over a hundred kilometers." He shook his head. "It doesn't look good."

I leaned forward as far as possible, trying to psychically pull Mumbai closer to us. I'd read about yogis manipulating time and space; failing that, another idea hit me: Maybe Alex's plane would be delayed. Maybe the same rains that had slowed us down would keep her flight from departing. That was the miracle I would pray for. I kept going over that petition in my mind, hoping it would reach God's ears.

A few minutes later the sprawling Mumbai lights came into view on the horizon. *Maybe . . . maybe. . . .* I grabbed Vijay's shoulder with my left hand and pointed with my right. He reached to the console and pressed a few buttons. A few moments later I could hear him conversing with a manager at the terminal. "What's Alex's last name?" he asked me over the intercom.

"Leister," I yelled back. *"L-E-I-S-T-E-R."*

Vijay carefully spelled the letters into his microphone and fell silent. I could hear a short, perfunctory response from ground control. "They will check and radio me back," Vijay reported.

I sat back and attempted to be patient, but by that time it was impossible.

Five minutes later the manager came through again over the radio. Then Vijay turned to me. "They checked that flight, and there is no one with that name on it."

"But the doctor told me she was on that plane."

"Sorry, Linden . . . maybe she changed her plans."

Now what? I leaned back and tried to think. I was exhausted, and my thoughts all ran together.

A few minutes later I heard the voice come over the radio again. This conversation was shorter. When the manager had signed off, Vijay reported, "They found her."

"They found Alex?!" I practically jumped out of my seat. "Can they get her off the flight before it takes off?"

Vijay shook his head. "She's not on the London flight. She's on the flight to Singapore. Maybe she couldn't get a seat on the London one, so they routed her through Singapore."

My miracle. "When does that flight leave? Maybe we can make it!"

Vijay shook his head and told me somberly, "It left an hour ago."

My gut caved. *So close—and yet so far.*

81

We finally landed around 10:45, after all the flights connecting to the U.S. had departed. Vijay, keenly aware of my disappointment, offered to accompany me to the Air India terminal, where the ticket agent confirmed that Alex was indeed on the Singapore flight—wheels up at 9:08.

"Can you radio and get the plane to turn around?" I begged the agent.

"I'm sorry, sir, that's impossible."

No, it can't end here. "Then can you get me out on the next flight to San Francisco?"

The agent punched some keys, studied the computer screen, and told me, "There are two or three legs to your routing, and the next time we have availability for all the legs is a week from Tuesday."

No, no, that won't do. "Nothing sooner?"

"Sorry, sir. All the flights are full. This is the high-travel season."

I searched Vijay's eyes. Like me, he was at a loss. I'm sure that if he could have flown me to America, he would have. "Maybe you can go standby," he suggested.

"Yeah, how about if I go standby?" I turned back to the agent.

"You can if you wish, sir . . . tomorrow night?"

"If that's the earliest," I came back, leaning over the counter and trying to get a glimpse of the computer screen, more forward than politeness would dictate. I reached into my bag and pulled out my tattered ticket, which the agent stapled to a paper indicating I was on the wait list. I stuffed the papers in my pack and started toward the gate.

"Where are you going?" Vijay asked.

"I'll just camp out in the airport until they put me on some flight . . . like that guy in the movie who lived in the terminal."

Vijay shrugged his shoulders. "Maybe I'll come with you and have a drink before I head out."

"Fine, it's on me," I joked. We both knew my pockets were empty.

As we made our way toward the bar, Vijay turned to me and asked, "If you get on tomorrow's flight, when will you see Alex?"

Suddenly I realized I had no idea where Alex was going. Her father lived in New York, but she was emotionally closer to her brother in Houston. Her sister had a family in Atlanta, and Alex might go there for advice from a fellow mother. Or she might forgo her family and stay with a friend. She could be anywhere in the country. I didn't even know her e-mail address. I could phone her father, but he would hang up on me, if not trace my call and have me arrested.

"I don't know, Vijay," I replied, dejected. "I don't know if I will ever see her again." Then another depressing thought accosted me: when the immigration agent saw my long-expired visa, they would kick me out of the country, maybe for good. "And I don't even know if I'll ever be able to come back to see you or anyone else here again."

But Vijay wasn't listening. He was distracted by a commotion down the hall. I looked in the direction he was staring, where some police officers were scurrying around a door marked AIR INDIA CUSTOMER ASSISTANCE CENTER. Several emergency medical technicians were hurrying into the room. "Some poor bloke's probably having a heart attack," Vijay guessed. I silently said a little prayer for whoever was in trouble.

As we passed the door, Vijay asked one of the cops what was going on. "Some lady's having a baby in there," he answered in English.

I smiled to think it was a blessed event rather than a life-threatening emergency. Thinking of Alex on the plane and how pregnant she must be, I quipped to Vijay, "Everyone is having babies these days."

We walked a few more paces, stopped simultaneously, and exchanged a stunned look: *Could it be?*

We hustled back to the officer and Vijay asked him, "An Indian woman?"

The man shook his head. "Some American. They pulled her off a flight just as it was about to leave. She lied about how pregnant she was and went into labor before the plane took off."

"Alex?!" I yelled.

82

The scene inside the room was controlled chaos—emergency personnel milling around, bright portable lights, and two-way-radio voices droning. Some of the staff appeared authoritative, others confused.

The focus of the commotion was a couch in the far corner of the room, where the mother-to-be was stretched out, surrounded by a handful of paramedics. I strained to see her face, but too many people were blocking my view. Agonized shrieks pierced the hall.

I pushed my way through the small crowd, jostling several people; I'd come too far and gone through too much to be polite. *This will either be Alex or it won't. Either way, the game will be over.* Finally I forced two medics aside and poked my head into the maternity scene to get a look at her face.

"Alex!" I yelled.

Peering up in the midst of the throes of labor, her face blanched and sweat dripping off her brow, Alex met my eyes. It took her a moment to recognize that it was me. "My God . . . Linden! You're here! You're alive! I can't believe you're here!" Then she burst into tears. I pushed my way through to the couch, wrapped my arms around her, and began kissing her face profusely. I've never been as happy in my entire life as I was to see Alex lying there having our baby. The fact that her legs were spread apart, with a half dozen strangers peering into her birth canal didn't bother me at all. All I cared about was that we were together again.

"Let me look at you, sweetheart. Let me touch you," she exclaimed, fingering my face with her hands. "It's you! It's really you! You came back!"

"Yes, Alex, I'm here. I'm so sorry I left you. I was an idiot. I promise I'll never leave you again. I'm in it for the distance. I swear I am."

"You have one hell of a knack for timing, buddy," Alex remarked as she shook my shoulders in mock rebuke. Then she pulled me to her chest and held me tight.

I reached down to touch her tummy and felt the baby in her belly moving like crazy. "You're so pregnant!"

"Not for long, Papa," a technician called from behind me, moving me aside. "Push, madam!" he instructed in a thick Indian accent. "Breathe deeply and push!"

Alex made the most awful-looking grimace, scarier than the faces of sour-looking Hindu gods. But at that point it was obvious she didn't care what she looked like—no one did. Everyone in that room had one thing on their mind: *get the baby out.*

"That's good!" the paramedic told Alex. "Keep pushing and breathing, pushing and breathing. The baby wants to come!"

I moved my attention from Alex's face to her legs under the canopy of sheets, then to her vagina, now hugely dilated. For a moment I thought I would faint, but I forced myself to stay upright. I felt a hand on my shoulder and turned to see Vijay. I can't tell you how glad I was that he'd stayed. I needed a friend now, a man.

Then the most amazing thing happened: I saw the crown of my baby's head emerging. Amid this frenzied scene a little hairy head was poking forth. *How in God's name did a real, live little person get in there? How will it get out?* I started to feel woozy; every cell in my body was on triple overload, along with my mind and emotions. It took everything I could muster to hold it together.

Then, in one big swoosh, the baby slid—make that *popped*—out. How it actually happened, I can't describe. It just did.

Alex let forth one final long, deep groan and went limp; her head fell back, and her eyes rolled up. She started to laugh—first a giggle, then a belly laugh, and then boisterous peals. "Is it over?" she asked, almost delirious. "Am I done?"

Almost. A minute later the afterbirth followed, a mass of blood and gook.

When Alex heard the baby cry, a huge smile spilled over her face.

"Now, honey, you're done," I told her. "And you did a great job."

With that, a round of applause rose from everyone in the room. And I collapsed.

83

I awoke to a disgusting smell invading my nostrils. For all the movies I'd seen where someone was revived with smelling salts, I never realized how vile they are. Maybe that was a metaphor for my journey: *If you're deeply asleep and you need to wake up, something has to really stink to get your attention.*

Alex was half sitting up on the couch, propped by a bunch of cushions, holding our baby in her arms, gazing at the child with an expression in her eyes I'd never seen before. It was the look of a mother. *Holy Stromboli, I'm a father! I never thought I would see this day.* I flashed back to the night I perched myself on the rail of the Golden Gate Bridge, when I thought I would never see another day, period. Life has a strange way of changing your plans.

It was a boy—a ruddy mini-me with dimples and pudgy arms flailing about. *How will I ever teach him? Protect him? Give him the confidence to choose life at the crossroads where I chose death?* But there was no way I would answer these questions in the Air India Customer Assistance Center. *Maybe over time. Maybe life will reveal everything on a need-to-know basis.* I grew up a lot in those few moments, thinking about what my son's life would be and how I could make it the best possible.

I made my way to the couch and squeezed behind Alex, enfolding her in my arms. A nurse had wrapped "mini-me" in a thin blue

Air India blanket and topped him with a miniature round knit hat. His face was all scrunched together like a little jack-in-the-box waiting to pop, and his eyes were closed. Weird looking, but beautiful.

Alex leaned into me, and I received her. Now that we were together again, I realized how empty my world had been without her. Not just during the past two months, but also for all the years I'd wandered lost, alone, and confused. I kissed her on the forehead and told her, "It's good to be back, sweetheart. Very good."

"Would you like to go the hospital, madam?" the chief technician asked.

Alex just shook her head. "We'll be staying with a friend in Mumbai. If anything comes up, I'll go in."

One by one the paramedics and technicians cleared out, and a porter entered with a wheelchair. Vijay helped Alex into the chair and placed the baby in her arms. It warmed me to see my new friend having a moment of vicarious fatherhood. As I glimpsed Alex's face, there was that look again in her eyes. *I'm going to like this.*

84

As we emerged into the lobby, a small group of Air India staff had gathered; news had gotten around about the birth, and people were curious. They all smiled and went gaga over the baby. We returned their smiles as politely as possible, but kept moving, intent on getting out of the airport.

Just as we found an opening in the crowd, I noticed a small cluster of flight attendants standing at the edge of the gathering. One of them looked familiar. It didn't take me long to identify him: it was the Tibetan who'd taken our tickets for the flight that had malfunctioned—the man who resembled Akar, Lord of Karma. I glanced to his right and recognized his companion as the Chinese flight attendant from the plane—or Chuang-Tsu. *Aren't they done with me yet?* Even more astounding, next to him stood the nun-looking woman who had sat opposite me on that bizarre flight. She had no business being there; the flight personnel, maybe, but she'd been a passenger.

We pushed our way through the crowd, I on my crutch and Vijay directing Alex's wheelchair. I faced the three and asked them outright, "What are you all doing here?"

They exchanged glances, as if deciding who was going to speak. Finally the Tibetan answered, "We heard about the birth."

"And you?" I confronted the nunlike passenger.

"I was evicted from where I was staying, and I had to come back here on business."

I squared my stance. "You were all there the day that flight almost went down."

"Yes, that was quite a ride," the Chinese man commented, raising an eyebrow. "Thank goodness that 'almost' is not a sure thing."

I shot a glance at Alex. She recognized them, too.

"Will you be leaving?" the Tibetan asked me.

"No, I will be staying," I answered, gesturing to Alex and the baby. "Now I have a good reason to stay."

"Did you change your ticket?" the nun asked.

"Yeah, I changed my ticket."

The Tibetan smiled. "Yes, customer service is good about that. Tickets can be changed if a passenger changes his plans. Sometimes people headed to one place find a good reason to choose another."

I scanned their eyes for a long moment. There was love.

"Well, we have to get going now," I told them, placing my hands on Alex's shoulders. "We have a life to live."

EPILOGUE

We named him Alexander Sonam Vijay Kozlowski, covering all the bases: Alexander for Alex's dad, who financed his parents' getting together without knowing it; Sonam for my spiritual brother who kept my vision alive; Vijay for his godfather; and Kozlowski for the long Polish tradition that bestowed the perseverance to turn a fool's journey into a lifetime blessing. We were quite certain that no child had ever been born with this ethnic combination of namesakes, and for that we are very proud.

Vijay was equally proud to attend the naming ceremony a month later at Chateau Ramesh in Melghat, where he was unashamed to shed a public tear at finally being a father. (He did waive the fuel bill in light of the honor afforded him.)

Beside Vijay stood my dear friends Sonam and Eyla, who had traveled all the way from Shailesh, where Sonam had moved to help Eyla with some chores around the farm (or so he said). Next to the couple stood Lingpa, who didn't look nearly as suspiciously upon Sonam as he had upon me. The good Lingpa held a goose under his arm, little Alex's first pet.

Ramesh supplied the fresh vegetables for the feast, cooked to curried perfection by his wife, a favor he called in after making the final payment on the Pepto-Bismol palace. Ramesh's daughter, Aahna, did Alex's makeup, confessing what a pleasure it finally was to make someone up who was fully dressed.

Also present was Dr. Amrita Reddy, proud to have walked two naïve gringos through a highly unexpected pregnancy, and to be designated Alexander Sonam Vijay Kozlowski's official pediatrician. We did note a certain spark between her and Vijay as they stood next to each other, but I'm unable to speculate about its outcome at the present time. Let's just say that in helping save my butt, he may have saved his own.

❀

"So now what do we do?" Alex asked as she nursed little Alexander on the porch the morning after the ceremony. The sun was just coming up over the mountains, casting a golden glow on her cheeks. "Should we just stay here and disappear into the Melghat countryside, worlds away from the life we left behind?"

I scanned the lush mountain vista, but my mind was elsewhere. "I need to tell someone about this, Alex. What happened to us is nothing short of a miracle."

"That's for sure."

"Maybe we could send our story to the *San Francisco Chronicle*," I pondered aloud.

Alex laughed. "Are you kidding? They've been getting near-death enlightenment stories since the '60s. Half the people who work there are acid survivors. A lot of them have seen God more times than *Star Trek* reruns."

"You're probably right," I concurred. "I just don't think I can sit on this for the rest of my life without doing something about it."

"Then why don't you write it down?"

I shrugged my shoulders. "For who?"

"It doesn't matter, Linden. Just express yourself. Your story will find its way to the right people." Little Alexander looked up and cooed as if to affirm his mother's idea.

"And who do you think are the right people?"

"Anyone who's ever wondered if their life is worth living, or believed that there is someone or something out there who decides their destiny more than they do."

I scratched my head. "Come on, Alex, I wouldn't even know where to start."

Cradling the baby, Alex opened the screen door and motioned me to follow her into the kitchen. She opened a spiral notebook and set it on the kitchen table before me. Then she pulled a pen from a cup on the counter and placed it in my hand. "Just tell your truth, Linden," she said in a firm voice. Then she headed back toward the porch.

"Where are you going?"

"This is between you and you," she told me. "And . . . who knows who else." Alex blew me a kiss and closed the door behind her.

I sat for the longest time just staring at the paper, hoping some invisible muse would dictate what to say. But nothing came. *This is crazy.* I tossed the pen down and started to stand up. Then I noticed the leaf from the Bodhi tree that we'd framed on the kitchen wall. Sonam's words echoed in my head like a bell ringing through a deep Himalayan valley: *A man's story is worth telling if the truth he discovers is greater than the pain that led him to seek it.*

I sat down again, grabbed the pen, and reached for the most honest words I could find:

> *"For as many times as I wondered how I would die,*
> *I never imagined it would be at my own hand."*

It was a start.

ACKNOWLEDGMENTS

Linden's adventure has been shared and empowered by many. I am deeply grateful to the family, friends, and colleagues who have helped bring this book to life.

Most of all I appreciate my beloved Dee, who has stood by my side and believed in me and this book. Dee scrutinized the manuscript, dove with me into broad metaphysics and minute detail, traced Linden's Bay Area footsteps, and supported this work at every turn. I feel blessed to be with such a rare and precious partner who has traveled this journey with me and brought her unique wisdom, vision, and joy to my life and this story.

Dear friends Kathy McDuff and Rich Lucas have given valuable input from their expertise and their hearts, inviting the characters to come to life to deliver their gifts to you.

The team at Hay House has demonstrated that excellence, care, and service are the foundation of their business and relationships. I thank and honor Louise L. Hay for the immense contributions she has made to uplifting me and millions of others; Reid Tracy for his intuitive confidence to get behind *Linden;* Jill Kramer for her longtime editorial support; Alex Freemon, whose direct editorial input and gracious spirit have tuned the manuscript in important ways; Amy Rose Grigoriou for her outstanding cover design; and

Tricia Breidenthal for her perfectly appropriate interior design.

The thoughtful and skilled input of story consultants Pat McEnulty and Christopher Vogler has bolstered the novel and imbued it with integrity, color, and depth. Thank you, skilled colleagues and mentors.

I am grateful to Dr. Toby Weiss and Teresa Weiss of Power Places Tours, longtime friends who offered their vast world-travel expertise to make Linden's adventures in India and Tibet as accurate as possible. Mary Manin Morrissey's experience about Dharamsala brought that segment to life.

Linden's story has been further enhanced by input from friends whose comments on the manuscript and cover design were extremely helpful: Kristelle Bach Sim, Leslye Love, Catherine Fenske, Maureen Coleman, Teresa Albers, Heather Westing, Steve Croce, Valerie Johnson, and Meg Lauerman.

I honor all of my teachers, mentors, and guides over many years who have shown me vistas beyond those I once recognized, and illuminated why a soul is empowered by love to choose life.

And thank you, the reader, for sharing the journey. Together we are opening doors.

ABOUT THE AUTHOR

Alan Cohen is the author of 22 popular thought-provoking books, including the bestseller *The Dragon Doesn't Live Here Anymore* and the award-winning *A Deep Breath of Life*. He is a contributing writer for the *New York Times* #1 best-selling series *Chicken Soup for the Soul,* and his work has been featured on **Oprah.com** and in *101 Top Experts*. Alan's books have been translated into 23 foreign languages, and his column "From the Heart" appears in magazines internationally. He keynotes and presents seminars in the field of life mastery and vision psychology. He resides in Maui, Hawaii, with his family, who keeps him inspired and entertained.

For information on Alan Cohen's books, CDs, videos, seminars, and online courses, contact:

Website: **www.alancohen.com**
E-mail: info@alancohen.com
Phone: (800) 568-3079
(808) 572-0001 (outside U.S.)
(808) 572-1023 (fax)

Or write to:

Alan Cohen Programs and Publications
P.O. Box 835
Haiku, HI 96708
U.S.A.

HAY HOUSE TITLES OF RELATED INTEREST

YOU CAN HEAL YOUR LIFE, the movie,
starring Louise L. Hay & Friends
(available as a 1-DVD program and an expanded 2-DVD set)
Watch the trailer at: **www.LouiseHayMovie.com**

THE SHIFT, the movie, starring Dr. Wayne W. Dyer
(available as a 1-DVD program and an expanded 2-DVD set)
Watch the trailer at: **www.DyerMovie.com**

❁

*THE COMPASSIONATE SAMURAI: Being Extraordinary
in an Ordinary World,* by Brian Klemmer

THE DOLPHIN: Story of a Dreamer, by Sergio Bambaren

THE GURU OF JOY: Sri Sri Ravi Shankar & the Art of Living,
by François Gautier

THE JOURNEY HOME: A Kryon Parable, by Lee Carroll

SOLOMON'S ANGELS, by Doreen Virtue

WAITING FOR AUTUMN, by Scott Blum

All of the above are available at your local bookstore,
or may be ordered by contacting Hay House (see next page).

❁

We hope you enjoyed this Hay House book.
If you'd like to receive our online catalog featuring additional information on
Hay House books and products, or if you'd like to find out more about the
Hay Foundation, please contact:

Hay House, Inc.
P.O. Box 5100
Carlsbad, CA 92018-5100

(760) 431-7695 or **(800) 654-5126**
(760) 431-6948 (fax) or **(800) 650-5115 (fax)**
www.hayhouse.com® • **www.hayfoundation.org**

Published and distributed in Australia by: Hay House Australia Pty. Ltd.,
18/36 Ralph St., Alexandria NSW 2015 • *Phone:* 612-9669-4299
Fax: 612-9669-4144 • www.hayhouse.com.au

Published and distributed in the United Kingdom by: Hay House UK, Ltd.,
292B Kensal Rd., London W10 5BE • *Phone:* 44-20-8962-1230
Fax: 44-20-8962-1239 • www.hayhouse.co.uk

Published and distributed in the Republic of South Africa by: Hay House SA
(Pty), Ltd., P.O. Box 990, Witkoppen 2068 • *Phone/Fax:* 27-11-467-8904
info@hayhouse.co.za • www.hayhouse.co.za

Published in India by: Hay House Publishers India, Muskaan Complex, Plot No.
3, B-2, Vasant Kunj, New Delhi 110 070 • *Phone:* 91-11-4176-1620
Fax: 91-11-4176-1630 • www.hayhouse.co.in

Distributed in Canada by: Raincoast, 9050 Shaughnessy St., Vancouver, B.C.
V6P 6E5 • *Phone:* (604) 323-7100 • *Fax:* (604) 323-2600 • www.raincoast.com

---

<u>Take Your Soul on a Vacation</u>

Visit **www.HealYourLife.com®** to regroup,
recharge, and reconnect with your own magnificence.
Featuring blogs, mind-body-spirit news, and
life-changing wisdom from Louise Hay and friends.

Visit **www.HealYourLife.com** today!

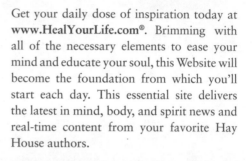